Rails-to-Trails

California

"There's no better guide for these multipurpose trails. Like the Rails-to-Trails system, this series is a service that's long overdue."

—Sarah Parsons, Associate Editor, *Sports Afield*

"Recreation trails are one of America's great outdoor secrets, but probably won't be for much longer thanks to the Rails-to-Trails Conservancy Guidebook Series. Now adventurers of all abilities have an excellent guide to help them enjoy all that the paths have to offer."

—Stephen Madden, Editor-in-Chief, *Outdoor Explorer*

D1510249

Help Us Keep This Guide Up to Date

Every effort has been made by the author and editors to make this guide as accurate and useful as possible. However, many things can change after a guide is published—hiking trails are rerouted, establishments close, phone numbers change, facilities come under new management, and so on.

We would love to hear from you concerning your experiences with this guide and how you feel it could be improved and kept up to date. While we may not be able to respond to all comments and suggestions, we'll take them to heart and we'll also make certain to share them with the author. Please send your comments and suggestions to the following address:

The Globe Pequot Press
Reader Response/Editorial Department
P.O. Box 480
Guilford, CT 06437

Or you may e-mail us at:

editorial@globe-pequot.com

Thanks for your input, and happy trails!

Great Rail-Trails Series

THE OFFICIAL
Rails-to-Trails
CONSERVANCY GUIDEBOOK

California

by
Tracy Salcedo-Chourré

The
Globe
Pequot
Press

Guilford, Connecticut

Cover illustration: Neal Aspinall
Cover design: Nancy Freeborn
Text design: Lesley Weissman-Cook
Maps: Tim Kissel/Trailhead Graphics, Inc.; © The Globe Pequot Press.
The map on page 101 was adapted from a map in *Explore the Forest of Nisene Marks,* written by Jeff Thomson and published by Walkabout Publications.

Photo credits: All photos are by Tracy Salcedo-Chourré. The photo on page 1 depicts the Hammond Coastal Trail; page 41, the Sir Francis Drake Bike Path; page 119, the Truckee River Trail; page 153, the Ojai Valley Trail; and page 175, the Hermosa Valley Greenbelt.

Library of Congress Cataloging-in-Publication Data
Salcedo-Chourré, Tracy.
   Rails-to-Trails: California / by Tracy Salcedo-Chourré.—1st ed.
    p. cm. — (Great rail-trails series)
   ISBN 0-7627-0448-9
   1. Rail-trails—California—Guidebooks. 2. Outdoor recreation—California—Guidebooks. 3. California—Guidebooks. I. Title. II. Series.

GV191.42.C2 C46 2000
917.9404'54—dc21   00-033575

Manufactured in the United States of America
First Edition/First Printing

For my parents

CONTENTS

ABOUT THE AUTHOR

Tracy Salcedo-Chourré has been passionate about outdoor recreation for most of her life, enjoying hiking, mountain biking, skiing, and other recreational pursuits. In addition to authoring several magazine articles and serving as an outdoors columnist for a weekly Colorado newspaper, she has written more than ten hiking guides to destinations in both Colorado and California. She lives with her husband and three young sons in the Wine Country of Northern California.

ACKNOWLEDGMENTS

As you peruse this book, you will see that a trail manager is mentioned for each hike. These managers, and their staffs, as well as the historians and other experts to whom they referred me, were critical to the compilation of this guidebook. They are too numerous to name here, but my heartfelt thanks go out to each and every one of them.

Likewise, I would like to thank the staff members of the Rails-to-Trails Conservancy, in both San Francisco and Washington, who took time to help me with my research.

Thanks also to Jeff Serena and the editors at The Globe Pequot Press for their infinite patience and for thinking of me when this project was proposed. Finally, I would like to acknowledge my debt to my husband, Martin, and my sons, Jesse, Cruz, and Penn, who were real troupers as we crisscrossed California hiking and cycling these trails. Without their love and support, this book would not have been possible.

INTRODUCTION

I n a state as large and diverse as California, it should come as no surprise that its rail-trails run the gamut. Trails in the mountains, trails along the beach. Trails in the boondocks, trails in the city. Trails that stretch for miles and miles, trails little more than a block in length. Trails steeped in the history of the railroads that once ran on the grades, trails that run alongside active railroad lines. They all are here, and they all are intriguing.

The Merced River Trail is one of the most challenging and beautiful rail-trails in California.

California can be divided into distinct regions which vary greatly not only in topography but also culturally. The rail-trails in each region mirror the landscape and the temperaments of the people who live there.

In northern California, the land is rugged and densely forested, from the high country surrounding Paradise and Lassen Volcanic National Park all the way west to the beaches at Fort Bragg and Eureka. The railroads punched through these woodlands were primarily used for logging, so the trails that now run along them thread through thick stands of timber and snake through spectacular river canyons.

In the San Francisco Bay Area, city and country struggle to find balance. The beauty of the landscape—oak woodlands amid rolling hills, and redwood forests that stretch toward the ocean—is integral to the draw of the region, and Bay Area residents grapple daily with the issue of preservation versus development. Their dedication to preserving quality of life shows in the number and quality of the rail-trails that have been established here. From the relative seclusion of the Sir Francis Drake Bikeway and the Loma Prieta Grade to the more urban but equally appealing Ohlone Greenway and Tiburon Linear Park, the trails in the area are superlative.

Eastward, in the Sierra Nevada, the terrain again grows rugged, folding sharply upward from the flats of the Central Valley toward high snowy peaks. Most of the rail-trails in this region lie in the foothills—Gold Country—again following the grades of railroads that served either logging or mining interests. These are perhaps the most challenging of all California's rail-trails, for they have been shaped by the steepness of the mountains through which they run. Some, like the Truckee River Bike Trail, are extremely popular and often crowded; others, like the West Side Rails from Hull Creek to Clavey River, venture into remote areas, where you will be lucky to find another soul on the trail.

The trails of Central California, a nebulous region that, for the purposes of this guide, stretches from Monterey south to Ventura and east to Fresno, are an eclectic bunch. The Monterey Peninsula Recreational Trail, for example, is a well-established regional attraction, while the Ventura River Trail and two new trails in the Fresno area are still defining themselves, the subjects of vigorous—and justified—promotional efforts by their proponents.

Southern California, in spite of its notorious love affair with the automobile, has established an intriguing system of rail-trails. Often the focal point of linear parks, like the charming Electric Avenue Median Park, these trails are urban or suburban in nature, and serve primarily as commuter or neighborhood paths. There are two stunning exceptions to this general rule: the Mount Lowe Railway Trail, which climbs into the steep San Gabriel Mountains, offering unsurpassed views of the Los Angeles basin, and the Silver Strand Bikeway, a breathtaking stretch of trail that traces the narrow strip of land separating San Diego Bay from the Pacific Ocean.

A Slice of California's Railroad History

California fostered a love affair with the railways that blossomed around the turn of the twentieth century and lasted until the automobile began its ascendance in the 1930s. The Golden State's railroads served a number of industries in California, but those that have been converted to rail-trails came primarily from two classes: railroads that moved timber, and railroads that moved people.

The gold that drew men by the thousands to California may have played out relatively quickly, but the forests held another, seemingly

The Depot Historical Museum on the Sonoma Bike Path preserves our railroading past.

limitless source of wealth: trees. Vast forests carpeted the Sierra Nevada, the Coast Ranges, and much of Northern California, and the American philosophy of manifest destiny that drove settlers westward demanded, for better or worse, that these resources be utilized. A number of railroads in the state were established to serve logging industries, including the Hammond/Little River Railroad in Eureka, the Fernley and Lassen Branch of the Southern Pacific, and the Loma Prieta Lumber Company Railroad, all of which are now spectacular rail-trails.

Transporting passengers from city to city, and from place to place within large urban areas, also proved a lucrative endeavor. Some of the rail lines established for this purpose blossomed into mini empires, like the Pacific Electric Railway system, which ran its famous Red Cars throughout the Los Angeles area during the early 1900s. Many of the rail-trails now in place in the Los Angeles basin have been built on former Pacific Electric grades.

The lines of smaller interurban railroads, many of which were electric, also have made significant contributions to California's rail-trail system. Two of these systems—the Sacramento Northern Railway system, which ran north from Sacramento to Chico and east into the San Francisco Bay Area, and the Northwestern Pacific Railroad complex, which served the North Bay—enjoyed great success and popularity in the early part of the twentieth century. They also both suffered increasing losses beginning in the 1930s that were attributed to the Great Depression and the increasing popularity of the automobile. The systems were gradually abandoned, and some of their tracks scrapped during World War II, but their legacy lives on in wonderful trails like the Sonoma Bike Path and the Lafayette–Moraga Trail in the Bay Area, and the Sacramento Northern Bike Trail in Sacramento.

The History of the Rails-to-Trails Conservancy

As road construction and increased reliance on cars forced railroads to the sidelines, the question arose: What to do with all the abandoned tracks that crisscrossed the state?

Enter the Rails-to-Trails Conservancy, an environmental group that since 1986 has campaigned to convert the railroad tracks to nature paths.

The beauty of the Rails-to-Trails Conservancy (RTC) is that by converting the railroad rights-of-way to public use, it has not only

preserved a part of our nation's history, but allows a variety of outdoor enthusiasts to enjoy the paths and trails.

Bicyclists, in-line skaters, nature lovers, hikers, equestrians, and cross-country skiers can enjoy rail-trails, as can railroad history buffs. There is truly something for everyone on these trails, many of which are also wheelchair accessible.

In California, there are more than fifty-five rail-trails in place, and more are slated to come on line each year. Some are so secluded you can imagine yourself a pioneer arriving with the first iron horses, others are meshed completely in the urban landscape, and many combine aspects of both, offering users a diverse experience.

The concept of preserving these valuable corridors and converting them into multiuse public trails began in the Midwest, where railroad abandonments were most widespread. Once the tracks came out, people started using the corridors for walking and hiking while exploring the railroad relics that were left along the rail beds, including train stations, mills, trestles, bridges, and tunnels.

Although it was easy to convince people that the rails-to-trails concept was worthwhile, the reality of actually converting abandoned railroad corridors into public trails proved a great challenge. From the late 1960s until the early 1980s, many rail-trail efforts failed as corridors were lost to development, sold to the highest bidder, or broken into many pieces.

A family enjoys the Larkspur-Corte Madera Path.

In 1983, Congress enacted an amendment to the National Trails System Act directing the Interstate Commerce Commission to allow about-to-be abandoned railroad lines to be "railbanked," or set aside for future transportation use while being used as trails in the interim. In essence, this law preempts rail corridor abandonment, keeping the corridors intact as trails or for other transportation uses into the future.

This powerful new piece of legislation made it easier for public and private agencies and organizations to acquire rail corridors for trails, but many projects still failed because of short deadlines, lack of information, and local opposition.

In 1986, the Rails-to-Trails Conservancy was formed to provide a national voice for the creation of rail-trails. The RTC quickly developed a strategy that was designed to preserve the largest amount of rail corridor in the shortest period of time. A national advocacy program was formed to defend the new railbanking law in the courts and in Congress; this was coupled with a direct project-assistance program to help public agencies and local rail-trail groups overcome the challenges of converting a rail into a trail.

The strategy is working. In 1986, the Rails-to-Trails Conservancy knew of only seventy-five rail-trails in the United States, and ninety projects in the works. Today there are more than a thousand rail-trails on the ground and many more projects are underway. The RTC vision of creating an interconnected network of trails across the country is becoming a reality.

The thriving rails-to-trails movement has created more than 7,700 miles of public trails for a wide range of users. People across the country are now realizing the incredible benefits of the rail-trails.

Benefits of Rail-Trails

Rail-trails are flat or have gentle grades, making them perfect for multiple users, ranging from walkers and bicyclists to in-line skaters and people with disabilities. In snowy climates, people enjoy cross-country skiing, snowmobiling, and other snow activities on the trails.

In urban areas, rail-trails act as linear greenways through developed areas, efficiently providing much-needed recreation space while serving as utilitarian transportation corridors. They link neighborhoods and workplaces and connect congested areas to open spaces. In many cities and suburbs, rail-trails are used for commuting to work, school, and shopping.

In rural areas, rail-trails can provide a significant stimulus to local businesses. People who use trails often spend money on food, beverages, camping, hotels, bed-and-breakfasts, bicycle rentals, souvenirs, and other local products and services. Studies have shown that trail users have generated as much as $1.25 million annually for a town through which a trail passes.

Rail-trails allow for the preservation of historic structures, such as train stations, bridges, tunnels, mills, factories, and canals. These structures shelter an important piece of history and enhance the trail experience.

Wildlife enthusiasts also enjoy the benefits of rail-trails, which can provide habitats for birds, plants, wetland species, and a variety of small and large mammals. Many rail-trails serve as plant and animal conservation corridors; in some cases, endangered species can be found in habitats located along the route.

Recreation, transportation, historic preservation, economic revitalization, open space conservation, and wildlife preservation—these are just some of the many benefits of rail-trails and the reasons people love them.

The strongest argument for the rails-to-trails movement, however, is ultimately about the human spirit. It's about the dedication of individuals who have a dream and follow that vision so that other people can enjoy the fruits of their labor.

Cyclists stop to check out the sights along the Tiburon Linear rail-trail.

How to Get Involved

If you really enjoy rail-trails, there are opportunities to join the move-ment to save abandoned rail corridors and to create more trails. Donating even a small amount of your time can help get more trails up and going. Here are some ways you can help the effort:

- Write a letter to your city, county, or state elected official in favor of pro-trail legislation. You can also write a letter to the editor of your local newspaper highlighting a trail or trail project.
- Attend a public hearing to voice support for a local trail.
- Volunteer to plant flowers or trees along an existing trail or to spend several hours helping a cleanup crew on a nearby rail-trail project.
- Lead a hike along an abandoned corridor with your friends or a community group.
- Become an active member of a trail effort in your area. Many groups host trail events, undertake fund-raising campaigns, pub-lish brochures and newsletters, and carry out other activities to promote a trail or project. Virtually all of these efforts are orga-nized and staffed by volunteers and there is always room for an-other helping hand.

California is fortunate to have an RTC office within the state. The office is located at 26 O'Farrell Street, Suite 400, San Francisco, CA 94108. The telephone number is (415) 397–2220; the e-mail address is rtcofca@aol.com.

Whatever your time allows, get involved. The success of a com-munity's rail-trail depends on the level of citizen participation. The Rail-to-Trails Conservancy enjoys both local and national support. By joining the RTC you will get discounts on all of its publications and merchandise while supporting the largest national trails orga-nization in the United States. To become a member, use the order form at the back of the book.

How to Use Rail-Trails

By design, rail-trails accommodate a variety of trail users. While this is generally one of the many benefits of rail-trails, it also can lead to occasional conflicts among trail users. Everyone should take respon-sibility to ensure trail safety by following a few simple trail etiquette guidelines.

One of the most basic etiquette rules is "Wheels yield to heels." The figure below indicates the correct protocol for yielding right-of-way. Bicyclists (and in-line skaters) yield to other users; pedestrians yield to equestrians.

Generally, this means that you need to warn the users to whom you are yielding of your presence. If, as a bicyclist, you fail to warn a walker that you are about to pass, the walker could step in front of you, causing an accident that easily could have been prevented. Similarly, it is best to slow down and warn an equestrian of your presence. A horse can be startled by a bicycle, so make verbal contact with the rider and be sure it is safe to pass.

Here are some other guidelines your should follow to promote trail safety:

- Obey all trail rules posted at trailheads.
- Stay to the right except when passing.
- Pass slower traffic on the left; yield to oncoming traffic when passing.
- Give a clear warning signal when passing.
- Always look ahead and behind when passing.
- Travel at a responsible speed.
- Keep pets on a leash.
- Do not trespass on private property.
- Move off the trail surface when stopped to allow other users to pass.
- Yield to other trail users when entering and crossing the trail.
- Do not disturb the wildlife.
- Do not swim in areas not designated for swimming.
- Watch out for traffic when crossing the street.
- Obey all traffic signals.

How to Use This Book

At the beginning of each chapter, you will find a map showing the location of the rail-trails within that region. The main rail-trails featured in this book include basic maps for your convenience. It is recommended, however, that street maps, topographic maps such as USGS quads, or a state atlas be used to supplement the maps in this book. The text description of every trail begins with the following information:

Trail name: The official name of the rail-trail.

Activities: A list of icons tells you what kinds of activities are appropriate for each trail.

Location: The areas through which the trail passes.

Length: The length of the trail, including how many miles are currently open and, for those trails that are built on partially abandoned corridors, the number of miles actually on the rail line.

Surface: The materials that make up the rail-trail vary from trail to trail. This section describes each trail's surface. Materials range from asphalt and crushed stone to the significantly more rugged original railroad ballast.

Wheelchair access: Some of the rail-trails are wheelchair accessible. This allows physically challenged individuals the opportunity to explore the rail-trails with family and friends.

Difficulty: The rail-trails range from very easy to hard, depending on the grade of the trail and the general condition of the trail.

Food: The book will indicate the names of the towns near the rail-trails in which restaurants and fast-food shops are located.

Rest rooms: If a rest room is available near the trail, the book will provide you with its location.

Seasons: Most of these trails are open year-round, but special circumstances, such as severe winter rains or localized flooding, may preclude the use of certain routes during some seasons.

Access and parking: The book will provide you with directions to the rail-trails and describe parking availability.

Rentals: Some of the rail-trails have bicycle shops and skating stores nearby. This will help you locate bike or skate rentals, or a shop in which you can have repairs made if you have problems with your equipment.

Contact: The name and contact information for each trail manager is listed here. The selected contacts are generally responsible for managing the trail and can provide additional information about the trail and its condition.

Description: The major rail-trails include an overview of the trail and its history, followed by a mile-by-mile description, allowing you the chance to anticipate the experience of the trail.

Key to Activities Icons

Backpacking

Bird-watching

Camping

Cross-country Skiing

Fishing

Historic Sites

Horseback Riding

In-line Skating

Mountain Biking

Paddlesports

Road Bicycling

Running

Swimming

Walking/Day Hiking

Wildlife Viewing

Key to Map Icons

P Parking

I Information

Rest Rooms

R Rentals

Δ Camping

Note: All map scales are approximate.

Rails-to-Trails

NORTHERN CALIFORNIA

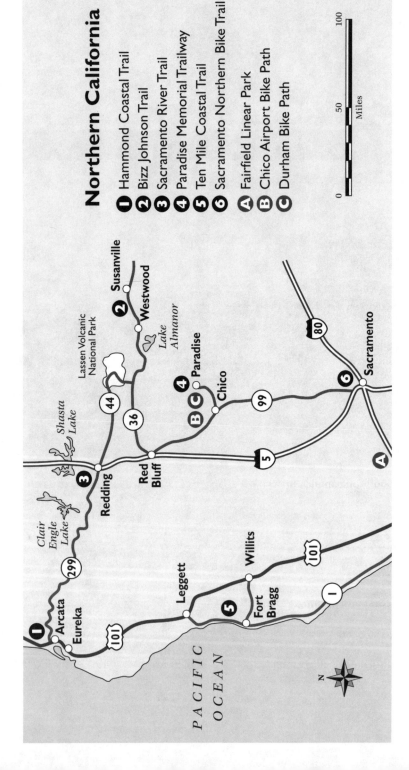

Northern California

1. Hammond Coastal Trail
2. Bizz Johnson Trail
3. Sacramento River Trail
4. Paradise Memorial Trailway
5. Ten Mile Coastal Trail
6. Sacramento Northern Bike Trail

A. Fairfield Linear Park
B. Chico Airport Bike Path
C. Durham Bike Path

Northern California's

TOP RAIL-TRAILS

1 Hammond Coastal Trail

Although the north coast of California usually brings to mind towering old-growth forests (and the controversy that surrounds logging those forests), the Hammond Coastal Trail showcases the spectacular beaches that stretch along the coastline.

Activities:

Location: McKinleyville, Humboldt County

Length: 3 miles of the trail are currently in place, but once links are completed at Widow White Creek and around the vista point south of Clam Beach County Park, the trail will be 5 miles long.

Surface: Asphalt and crushed stone

Wheelchair access: The 3 miles of trail that are in place are suitable for wheelchair users.

Difficulty: Moderate. The path is exposed, and the southernmost portion includes some short but steep hills.

Food: You can pick up a snack at Roger's Market, which is near the southern end of the trail at the intersection of Fischer Avenue and School Road. This is also the only place along the route where you will find water, so bring what you need.

Rest rooms: There are public rest rooms at Hiller Park, which is at about the halfway point of the paved portion of the trail.

Seasons: The trail can be traveled year-round.

Access and parking: To reach the southern end point at Mad River Bridge from U.S. Highway 101 in McKinleyville, take the Janes Road/Giuntoli Lane exit. Go west on Janes Road for 1.4 miles to Upper Bay Road, and turn right (west). Follow Upper Bay Road for 0.7 mile to Mad River Road, and turn right (north). The trailhead is at the bridge 2.4 miles north on Mad River Road. There is limited but adequate parking at this trailhead.

To reach the end of the 3-mile section of trail in place as of spring 2000, take the Murray Road exit off U.S. Highway 101 and go 0.3 mile west to where Murray Road ends; the trailhead is west of the end of the road. There is ample streetside parking here.

To reach the northern end point of the trail at Clam Beach County Park, continue north on U.S. Highway 101 to the Clam Beach County Park exit. The trailhead is adjacent to the west side of the freeway, tucked in the dunes. There is a large parking lot at the park.

Transportation: There is no public transportation serving the trail.

Rentals: There are no rentals along the trail.

Contact: Bob Walsh, Parks Department Supervisor, Humboldt County Department of Public Works, 1106 Second Street, Eureka, CA 95501-0531; (707) 839–2086. The Friends of Hammond Trail, part of the Redwood Community Action Agency, has been very active in development of the trail. Contact Jennifer Rice, Planner/Interpreter with the Natural Resources Services division of the RCAA, at (707) 269–2060.

• •

The Mad River Bridge is a dramatic beginning to the evolving Hammond Coastal Trail. The old railroad trestle launches the rail-trail through several separate coastal environments, including the pastoral expanses of the Arcata Bottoms, the pleasant neighborhoods on the west side of McKinleyville, shady arbors formed by gnarled shore pines, and the spectacular estuary at the mouth of the Mad River. A tangled riparian zone hugs the shores of Widow White Creek at the end of the contiguous paved section of the route. Beyond the breach in the trail, a short distance north of Widow White Creek, the trail arcs west around a vista point to skirt the beach fronting the Pacific Ocean, passing through rolling dunes to Clam Beach County Park.

Beginning at the turn of the twentieth century, the Hammond/Little River Railroad used the oceanside route to link logging operations in Crannell, east of Clam Beach County Park, with the Hammond Lumber Mill of Eureka. The railroad system was badly damaged in a forest fire in 1945, and, rather than rebuilding the tracks, many of the grades were converted to roadways. The line was abandoned in the late 1950s, and development of the trail, which has been built in segments, began in 1979.

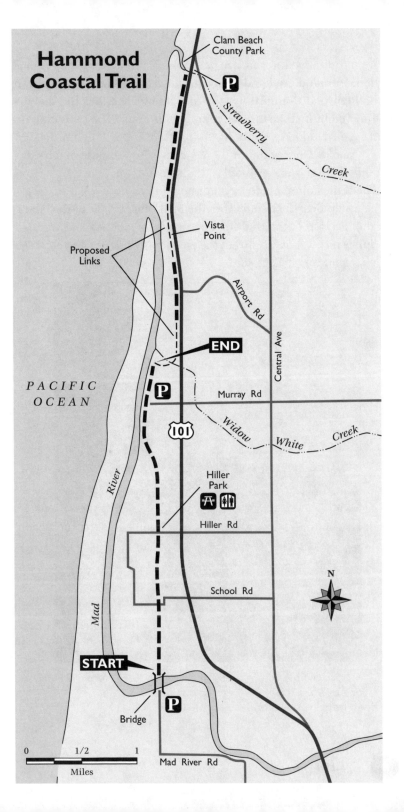

An informative interpretive pamphlet distributed by the Friends of the Hammond Trail and the Natural Resources Services division of the Redwood Community Action Agency describes the diverse natural and human history surrounding the trail. The pamphlet includes a discussion of the indigenous Wiyot tribe, which thrived in the Humboldt Bay region until the 1850s, when disease and battles with invading settlers resulted in their near extinction.

The trail is interrupted by a missing link at Widow White Creek, so the trail is described here from the Mad River trestle to the creek. Another section of the trail has been paved heading south through the dunes near Clam Beach, but the pavement ends before you reach the vista point near Letz Road.

A picnic bench overlooks the Pacific Ocean on the Hammond Coastal Trail.

Climb a relatively steep hill from the signed trailhead onto the Mad River Bridge, which affords a wonderful overlook of the tidal river and the verdant bottomlands that surround it. Beyond the bridge, the trail merges with a narrow county road and traverses pastureland to a steep hill at 0.5 mile. Once atop the hill, the trail, which is basically a country lane, runs north through a small community to the intersection of the lane (Fischer Avenue) with School Road at 0.8 mile. Roger's Market sits on the northwest corner of the intersection.

Continue north on Fischer Avenue to the end of the road at 1.1 miles, where the Hammond Trail, which is part of the Coastal Trail, enters a tree- and blackberry-lined greenbelt that runs between homes. At 1.4 miles you will cross Hiller Road and enter Hiller Park, which boasts a playground, ball fields, and rest rooms. The trail skirts the east side of the park, then passes a gate and again is contained within a lush greenbelt lined with ferns and overhung with evergreens.

At about the 2.4-mile mark, the rail-trail crosses Kelly Street amid a cluster of elaborate homes that resemble castles. Pass a picnic bench that offers wonderful views of the Pacific Ocean and the narrow line of dunes that separate it from the placid Mad River. The paved path is etched into the bluff overlooking the ocean until it arcs sharply east at 2.7 miles and ends on Murray Road.

You can follow the obvious railroad grade, however, for another third of a mile to the north, where it ends at a gate near the mouth of Widow White Creek. This section of the route is dirt, and a few rails peeking out of the sand and scrub attest to its origins. A narrow switchback path leads onto the bluff and into the forest overlooking the creek drainage, but you can go no further north without doing some serious bushwhacking and trespassing.

2 Bizz Johnson Trail

The Bizz Johnson Trail is the longest, and arguably the most scenic, rail-trail in California. The wonderful route leads through the dense woodlands of the high country into the spectacular Susan River canyon, and incorporates numerous historic sites, including trestles and tunnels.

Activities:

Location: From Westwood to Susanville in Lassen County

Length: 25 miles one-way

Surface: Gravel and original ballast

Wheelchair access: There is limited wheelchair access at the Susanville end point.

Difficulty: Hard

Food: There is no food or water available along the trail, so be sure to pack what you need. Restaurants and grocery stores can be found in Susanville.

Rest rooms: There are rest rooms at the Susanville Depot, at Devils Corral, and in Goumaz.

Seasons: This trail can be used year-round, although it can be difficult to utilize when it is muddy. The Westwood end of the trail generally has snow on it from December to March.

Access and parking: There is abundant parking available at both Mason Station Depot in Westwood and the Susanville Depot in Susanville, and at the trailheads at Goumaz and Devils Corral. All trailheads can be reached from California 36, which runs between Chester and Susanville.

To reach the Mason Station trailhead, turn north off of California 36 onto Lassen County Road A–21. Follow County Road A–21 north for 3 miles to the intersection with Lassen County Road 101, which breaks off to the right (northeast) and is signed for the Bizz Johnson Trail. Follow County Road 101 for about a quarter of a mile to the trailhead, which is on the left (northwest) side of the dirt road.

To reach the Goumaz trailhead, continue east on California 36 from Westwood to the summit of Fredonyer Pass, and turn left (north) onto Lassen Forest Road 30N29. Follow this road north for 6 miles to the Goumaz trailhead. The Devils Corral trailhead, which is well signed, is on the south side of California 36 just east of where the highway crosses the Susan River at the base of the pass.

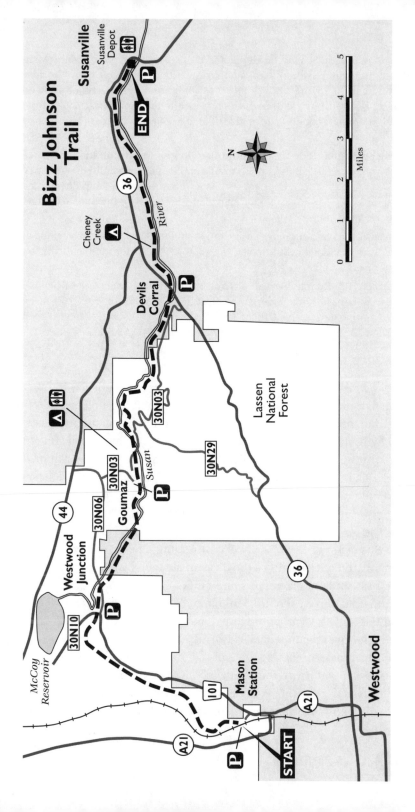

To reach the Susanville Depot and the eastern end point, follow Main Street to its intersection with Weatherlow Street. Turn south on Weatherlow Street, following until it becomes Richmond Road. Richmond Road continues south to the depot, which is on the left (southeast) side of the road; more parking and a formal trailhead are located across the street by the caboose.

Transportation: The Lassen Rural Bus provides transportation for those who want to shuttle between Susanville and Devils Corral, Fredonyer Pass, or Westwood. Bus schedules are available from the Lassen Rural Bus service (530–252–7433), the Susanville Depot (530–257–3252), or the Bureau of Land Management (530–257–0456).

Rentals: You can rent bicycles at the Susanville Depot, which is located at 601 Richmond Road in Susanville. Call (530) 257–3252 for more information or to reserve a bike.

Contact: Bill Koontz, Bureau of Land Management, Eagle Lake Resource Area Office, 2950 Riverside Drive, Susanville, CA 96130; (530) 257–0456; Mike Zunino, Recreation Officer, Eagle Lake Ranger District, 477–050 County Road A1 (Eagle Lake Road), Susanville, CA 96130; (530) 257–4188.

• •

Of all the jewels in the rail-trail system of California, the Bizz Johnson Trail is among the brightest and most beautiful.

Like any quality gem, the Bizz Johnson Trail has many facets. Up high, near Westwood, it is a meditative track that cuts a straight line through the thick woodlands east of Lassen Volcanic National Park. The route passes stations that once bustled with the loggers and millers who supplied the business of the railroad; these stations are now lonely outposts marked by white signs.

The trail picks up speed, much as the trains used to, after it meets the Susan River near Westwood Junction. The river dives into a canyon and out of sight as the descent steepens, and the trail whistles past spills of black talus and cliffs of orange rock. Beyond the Goumaz station, at about the midpoint of the trail, the pitch mellows and the trail slips out of the forest into a broad valley, then down to meet the river again at Devils Corral.

On its easternmost leg, the rail-trail runs alongside the Susan River, a broad waterway that has sliced a lovely canyon through the foothills of the mountains. The railroad carved a separate but parallel path, plunging through rock outcrops that barred its passage, necessitating the construction of long, dark tunnels, which add mystery and history to the journey.

The trail rides atop the former Fernley and Lassen branch of the Southern Pacific Railroad. This line, and a number of spurs in the high country, served the thriving lumbering community that worked the dense forests of Lassen County in the early part of the twentieth century. Established in 1914, the railroad operated for more than forty years, transporting logs, milled lumber, and people from Westwood to Fernley, Nevada, and to points in between.

The last trail ran on the line in 1956, and Southern Pacific abandoned the line in 1978. That was when the Rails-to-Trails Conservancy, along with Congressman Harold "Bizz" Johnson (for whom

A sign announces Westwood Junction on the Bizz Johnson Trail.

THE SUSANVILLE DEPOT

Located at the eastern end point of the Bizz Johnson Trail, the Susanville Depot is a great place to learn more about the history of the rail line that served the area. Built in 1913, the depot was destroyed by fire in 1989, but an addition built in 1927 survived the blaze, and now serves as both depot and visitor center. Inside, you'll find educational displays and an abundance of information about the area, as well as souvenirs and a friendly and knowledgeable staff. The depot is open during the summer season, from May 1 to mid-October, and can be reached by calling (530) 257–3252.

The Lassen Land and Trails Trust (LLTT), a nonprofit organization that helps preserve land and restore historic sites throughout Lassen County, owns the depot. The LLTT and the city of Susanville, along with the Bureau of Land Management and the U.S. Forest Service, have invested a lot of energy in the development and promotion of the Bizz Johnson Trail, and celebrate annually with a Rails-to-Trails Festival. This popular autumn event features great food, railroad handcar racing, arts and crafts, and, of course, hiking and cycling activities on the rail-trail. The festival is a fund-raiser for the land trust. Call the Susanville Depot at (530) 257–3252 for information.

the trail is named), the Bureau of Land Management, the U.S. Forest Service, and a number of community groups, set to work converting the old line into a trail. Their hard work paid off in a big way, resulting in one of the best long-distance trails in the state.

The entire trail can be ridden one-way via mountain bike or horseback comfortably in a single day. If you are on a bike, you can take advantage of the Lassen Rural Bus or you can make other arrangements for a shuttle back to the original trailhead. You can also enjoy the trail in segments, on foot, wheels, or hooves. The most popular short route heads west out of Susanville into the Susan River canyon, where you will find the railroad tunnels, as well as a number of swimming holes that are especially inviting in late summer when the weather is warm and the river is placid.

The trail is described here in its entirety as a downhill run from

Mason Station in Westwood to the Susanville Depot. A short connector trail leads from the parking area and informational billboard to the trail proper, which lies adjacent to the existing tracks of the Burlington Northern and Santa Fe Railroad. This is Mason Station, as is noted on the interpretive sign. Indeed, you will find that this section of the Bizz Johnson Trail is very well signed and interpreted, with posts at regular intervals as well as mile markers designating the distance of the remote stations from Southern Pacific's base station in San Francisco.

Head east along the open swath through the forest, passing Facht Station and Lasco Station, and crossing a couple of forest service roads. The trail climbs almost imperceptibly as it follows long straightaways and sweeping turns through the forest, arriving at Westwood Junction at the 7.3-mile mark. Southern Pacific had a maintenance station at this junction from 1923 to 1930. Not quite a half mile beyond this marking, you will pass the Westwood Junction Trailhead. A broad meadow stretches to the north, in the direction of McCoy Reservoir.

Pass Blair Station at about the 8-mile mark. A large red sign that directs snowmobilers playing on the maze of roads in winter points left (north) down a forest service road at this point. The Bizz Johnson Trail continues straight (east) on the flat, fairly obvious railroad grade.

The rail-trail continues into the seemingly endless forest, blazing a straight and marginally monotonous line until it reaches a bridge over the fledgling Susan River at about the 10-mile mark. Cross the bridge and pass through the gate. This is a turning point; the trail's aspect goes from predictable to enlivening beyond.

The river is placid in its willow-lined bed on the right (south) side of the trail, then dives into a canyon. The route is bordered by cliffs and black talus, dropping to pass an old shack, "Frank's House," at 11 miles. Pass another gate, then arrive at the Goumaz station at 12.3 miles.

At Goumaz, you will find rest rooms, a parking area, and a billboard upon which is posted trail information and a description of the history of the Goumaz station. Lying about halfway between Westwood and Susanville, this is a great place to rest and picnic.

On the east side of Goumaz, you will pass another gate and cross a bridge, then begin a steep downhill run that is cut into a mountainside, exposing the crumbly orange rock underlying the forest. Another gate, at 17 miles, marks the trail's passage through private property, where you must remain on the railroad grade to avoid trespassing. The broad river valley opens to the left (north) as you descend, and the ranch buildings of the lucky souls that work this high-country paradise are visible across the grassy valley floor.

The forest and its undergrowth pick up a more desertlike quality as you pass through the ranch, exiting through another gate at 18.1 miles. Continue to descend to a spectacular and thrilling bridge at 18.7 miles; the Susan River lies far below. An old bridge spans the river on the north side; the highway, on a sturdy and modern bridge, lies to the south.

Beyond the span, the trail veers sharply down to the right (south), and plunges under the highway bridge, then climbs just as steeply to the gate at the Devils Corral at 19.3 miles. Remember to close the gate behind you.

Devils Corral, like Goumaz, is host to parking, an information kiosk, and rest rooms. The trail skirts the corral on its south side, slips through another gate, and proceeds eastward into the Susan River canyon, with the river a tempting companion.

The Cheney Creek Camping Area lies riverside at about the 21-mile mark; beyond it you will encounter the first tunnel. It's dark and creepy inside, and reflective posts keep you safely away from the tunnel walls. A bridge lies on the east side of the tunnel. Another bridge and tunnel follow, the tunnel again a cool and intriguing addition to the experience. As you continue down the canyon, you will also pass a waterfall that runs into late summer, and several swimming holes.

You near the end of the trail at the signs for Hobo Camp. A gate admits you onto a fire lane, then the rail-trail continues for about 0.3 mile to a last informational billboard, which indicates that the Susanville Depot lies a quarter mile to the east.

To reach the depot, drop down paved Miller Road to Lassen Street, and turn right (south). Cross the bridge to the trail sign, and climb up alongside the railroad tracks, where you again pick up the rail-trail. Follow the tracks east past the caboose; cross Richmond Road to the quaint depot.

3 Sacramento River Trail

This has to be the best-kept secret of California's rail-trail system. The trail follows the broad Sacramento River up a beautiful canyon to a striking "stress ribbon" bridge, then arcs back along the river's opposite bank to the trailhead. It also links to a 5-mile loop through the stunning Redding Arboretum.

Activities:

Location: Redding, Shasta County

Length: 5.5 miles round-trip, plus an optional 5-mile lollipop loop through the arboretum

Surface: Asphalt and concrete

Wheelchair access: The entire trail is wheelchair accessible.

Difficulty: Hard. Although the portion of the trail that is on the railroad grade is easy, the portion that isn't features several steep hills. The length of the route also precludes an easier rating.

Food: There is no food available along the trail, but there are many restaurants and markets nearby in Redding. Water fountains are few and far between on the path, and Redding is notorious for its summertime heat, so bring plenty to drink with you.

Rest rooms: There are no rest rooms on the upper part of the trail, but several are located downstream from the trailhead, in Lake Redding Park and at the entrance to the arboretum.

Seasons: The trail can be used year-round, but when the Sacramento River is high, portions may be flooded.

Access and parking: To reach the trailhead from Interstate 5 in Redding, take the exit for California 299/California 44. Head left (west) on California 299 toward Eureka. The highway leads into downtown Redding, where the freeway ends. Signs mark the passage of California 299 as it winds through town, first heading west on Shasta Street, then right (north) on Pine Street, then left (west) on Eureka Way. Follow Eureka Way/California 299 to Court Street. Turn right (north) on Court Street and follow it for a half mile to the parking lot on Middle Creek. The lot is on the left (west) side of Court Street just before it crosses the bridge over the Sacramento River.

Transportation: There is no public transportation serving the trail.

Rentals: There are no rentals near the trail.

Contact: Terry Hanson, Manager of Community Projects, City of Redding, 777 Cypress Avenue, Redding, CA 96001; (530) 225–4009.

• • • • • • • • • • • • • • • • • • • •

The broad Sacramento River and the incredible "stress ribbon" bridge that spans it just below Keswick Dam are the centerpieces of this wonderful rail-trail.

The river, milky green and swift, has carved a gentle canyon that curls through the center of Redding. It waters a strip of riparian habitat on either shore, through which the riverside path meanders. The Sacramento River Trail Bridge, a simple, graceful arc of concrete more than 400 feet long, links the sections of trail that run down the opposite banks at the western edge of the route. At the eastern end, the historic and more traditional Diestelhorst Bridge ties the trails into a pleasing, 5.5-mile loop. The Diestelhorst is mirrored by the Court Street bridge, which runs alongside and is overshadowed by the high trestle that supports an active Southern Pacific line. Watching a train pass over this trestle will thrill more than railroad buffs.

Interpretive signs placed along the route describe the natural and man-made history of the area, and add to the trail's charm. Views westward are of the Trinity Mountains; if you head eastward on the north side of the river, you will be treated to vistas of Lassen Peak,

The Diestelhorst Bridge is at the east end of the Sacramento River Trail loop.

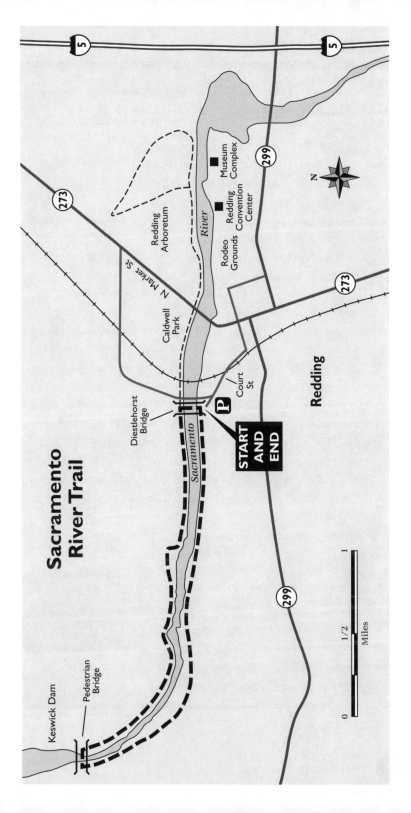

Sacramento
River Trail

Keswick Dam

Pedestrian
Bridge

Diestelhorst
Bridge

Sacramento

Sacramento

River

Caldwell
Park

N Market St

Redding
Arboretum

Museum
Complex

Redding
Convention
Center

Rodeo
Grounds

Court
St

P

**START
AND
END**

Redding

N

5

5

299

273

273

299

0   1/2   1
         Miles

THE REDDING
ARBORETUM LOOP

It is clear, given the number of people who run, hike, or ride bicycles on the path, and the incredible investment made in the route over the years, that the city of Redding takes great pride in the Sacramento River Trail.

That pride will find new expression when the Turtle Bay Pedestrian Bridge, a spectacular structure that will span the river between the Redding Arboretum and the city's convention center complex, is completed. The structure is scheduled to be in place by autumn of 2001, adding yet another facet to this gem of a trail.

Although the railroad portion of the trail doesn't extend into this neck of the woods, it's worth exploring. From the Diestelhorst Bridge, you can continue south on the concrete path, which leads first through Lake Redding Park, with its playground, rest rooms and picnic facilities. Beyond, you will pass the Redding Museum of Art and History, then the rolling lawns and picnic grounds of Caldwell Park.

The path drops under the Market Street bridge, and the surface of the trail changes from concrete to asphalt. About a mile east of the Diestelhorst Bridge, you will arrive in the parking area for the 200-acre Redding Arboretum. Within the arboretum are rich archaeological sites left by the Wintu tribe, as well as a fantastic oak savanna. The Turtle Bay Pedestrian Bridge, only a construction site as of early 2000, will rise in this area, its sail-like pylon soaring 220 feet into the air. The bridge will link the arboretum to cultural exhibits in the convention center complex on the south side of the river, including a Wintu interpretive exhibit, a butterfly exhibit, an otter exhibit, and Paul Bunyan's Forest Camp, which showcases the area's rich forestry and logging history.

A paved loop winds through the arboretum, which is currently tied to the Sacramento River Trail via a temporary steel bridge spanning Sulphur Creek. The savanna rings with birdsong, an enclave of wildness that dances with shadows at sunset. The loop leads back to the Sacramento River Trail, which returns you to the Court Street trailhead.

one of two Cascade volcanoes that dominate Redding's northern and eastern skylines. The other, Mount Shasta, can't be seen from the river valley.

But that's not all. Follow the river east of the Diestelhorst Bridge, and you will reach the Redding Arboretum, which is home to an oak savanna of unrivaled beauty and is rich with artifacts left by the Wintu tribe that lived in the area prior to the arrival of Europeans.

Only a mile of the trail is on a former railroad grade, with the rest of the route on historic roads that served mining operations along the river. That mile of former railway, which was installed with the rest of a line in the 1880s as part of the Southern Pacific system in the area, was incorporated into the portion of the trail on the south side of the river when it was built in 1986.

The trail begins at the western end of the parking area. Pass the water fountain and the initial trail sign; rest rooms lie 0.2 mile up the route.

The path overlooks the turquoise river and is overhung with trees and bushes that bloom pink and white in spring and are alive with darting hummingbirds and butterflies. Benches and mile markers line the route. At 1.2 miles, pass a riverside bench dedicated to the memory of Christine Munro, whose memorial is colorful with artificial—eternal—flowers.

At 1.5 miles, the trail breaks out from under the cover of the trees, and views open to the western mountains. Climb a short hill onto the railroad grade, which runs above the exposed and rocky shoreline. Here an interpretive sign explains how the area was damaged by hydraulic mining in the early 1900s.

Cross a bridge over a small creek, beyond which the railroad grade is elevated, running alongside the trail on its south side. Pass a private home, then cross the bridge spanning Middle Creek, which also has an interpretive marker.

At 2.5 miles the gray ramparts of Keswick Dam and the silver strand of the Sacramento River Trail Bridge come into view. The formal trail bears right (north) across the bridge, but a proposed trail extension, which has some funding, would continue on the railroad grade past the Keswick Dam for approximately 10 miles to the Shasta Dam.

On the north shore of the river, the trail bends east and mimics a roller coaster as it undulates past trail signs, a rest room, and an interpretive marker that identifies the Copley Greenstone/Quartz Mine at the 3-mile mark.

Lassen Peak, often snow-covered into late spring or early summer, dominates the eastern horizon as you continue downstream. Climb a rather steep hill, arcing through a drainage in the midst of a cluster of madrone and oak. At 4 miles, the trail loops past a couple more interpretive markers and over a small bridge to a quiet residential street. Go about 400 yards down the street to the continuation of the trail, which heads for the river through a small meadow on the right (south) side of the road.

The trail is now more suburban, passing the yards of lovely riverfront homes. At 5.4 miles, you will enter the elaborate memorial to Leisha Montel Graves, with its stone bench and green arches. The train trestle and Diestelhorst Bridge are 0.1 mile south of the memorial. To return to the trailhead, head left (north), away from the concrete riverside path, onto the bridge approach, and turn right (south) to cross the bridge.

For a longer excursion, stay on the riverside path, which continues downstream, passing under the triad of bridges, to Lake Redding Park and beyond.

4 Paradise Memorial Trailway

The thick woodlands that insulate and decorate the charming town of Paradise are the setting for this delightful rail-trail.

Activities:

Location: Paradise, Butte County

Length: 5.2 miles one-way

Surface: Asphalt, with a short section of dirt that can be avoided by using on-street bike lanes

Wheelchair access: The trail is wheelchair accessible.

Difficulty: Hard, due to the trail's length and relatively steep incline. The difficulty can be whittled down if the trail is taken in sections, or if you plan a shuttle.

Food: There is no food available along the route, other than quick access from the trail to a fast-food joint at about the midway point. You are never far from the commercial strip that lines Skyway through Paradise, however, where you will find restaurants and markets. There is no water available along the route, so bring what you need.

Rest rooms: There are no public facilities along the rail-trail or at either end point.

Seasons: The trail is passable year-round.

Access and parking: To reach the southern trailhead, follow the Skyway, the main route through Paradise, to its intersection with Neal Road, which is at the southernmost end of town. There is a small parking lot at this location. To reach the upper, northernmost trailhead, follow the Skyway through town to its intersection with Pentz Road. The trail heads off to the right (south) from this intersection. There is limited parking off the roadway at this end point, with more on-street parking available on Pentz Road.

Transportation: Butte County Transit provides some bus service to the area, but doesn't run regularly from trailhead to trailhead. Call (530) 342–0221 for schedule information.

Rentals: There are no rentals along the trail in Paradise.

Contact: Craig Baker, Senior Planner, Town of Paradise, 5555 Skyway, Paradise, CA 95969-4931; (530) 872–6291.

• •

W ith a name like Paradise, it had better be good. Fortunately, like the town through which it runs, the Paradise Memorial Trailway lives up to its billing. Climbing into the pine-shrouded foothills that buckle up where California's great Central Valley meets the Sierra Nevada, the trail is gentle and rugged, on the safe side of untamed. It is mostly wooded, with evergreens dominating the landscape higher up, and more diverse oak woodland flourishing down low. Insulated for the most part by the curtain of the forest, the trail offers easy access to the Skyway, Paradise's main drag, and all the amenities of the town.

The Diamond Match Company was the primary user of the Southern Pacific rail line upon which the trail now lies. The company, like many other enterprises in the mountains of California, ran logging and milling operations that required railroads for hauling logs and lumber. The company's logging town was located north of Paradise in Stirling City, and the line ran through Butte Canyon down into Chico. Southern Pacific Railroad eventually abandoned it, and the opportunity to transform the corridor into a rail-trail was opened. Five miles of trail are in place, and there are "tentative" plans to extend the trail both up toward Stirling City and down toward Chico.

The grade of the Paradise Memorial Trailway averages 3 percent, making for an easy downhill run, especially on a bicycle, and a more strenuous uphill trek. The trail is described here heading downhill from the Pentz Road end point, but if you don't plan to shuttle, you might want to reverse the direction so you aren't laboring uphill at the end of your adventure.

The trail is set down a bit below the grade of the Skyway as it heads south from Pentz Road, sheltered from the road by a row of evergreens—you can almost imagine that the hum of the thoroughfare is the wind in the trees. Private homes and cabins are on the left (southeast) side of the paved path. Small mile markers measure the route.

At 0.7 mile, the trail rises to meet the Skyway, then the two are separated again by a thin wedge of trees and broom. Beginning at the 1-mile mark, the trail stretches uninterrupted through the woodlands until it reaches a bench and its intersection with Rocky Lane at 1.7 miles.

Plunge back into the woods beyond Rocky Lane, reemerging to

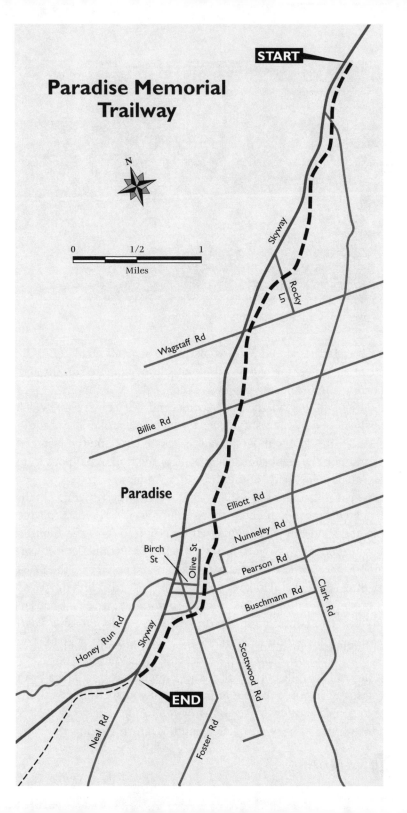

Paradise Memorial Trailway

START

END

Skyway

Rocky
Ln

Wagstaff Rd

Billie Rd

Paradise

Elliott Rd

Nunneley Rd

Birch
St

Olive St

Pearson Rd

Clark Rd

Buschmann Rd

Honey Run Rd

Skyway

Scottwood Rd

Neal Rd

Foster Rd

0   1/2   1
Miles

N

Lovely forests caress the Paradise Memorial Trailway.

cross Wagstaff Road at 2.2 miles. Between Wagstaff Road and Billie Road, at 2.9 miles, the woodlands open, allowing more sun through the canopy and exposing patches of red earth.

South of Billie Road, the trail becomes more of a town path, which is easily shared by hikers, cyclists, dog walkers, strollers, and squirrels. At 3 miles you will pass Paradise's skate park and the fast-food restaurant on the right (northwest) side of the trail. A ballpark is on the left (southeast) side of the route at 3.5 miles.

The paved path makes a sharp right-hand (west) turn and climbs to Black Olive Street at about the 4-mile mark; a memorial plaque marks the spot. But it's obvious that the rail-trail, now dirt, continues south, passing the yard of the Paradise Irrigation District Corporation. Those who wish to stay on pavement should take the Black Olive Street detour, and follow on-street bike paths that link the paved portions of the rail-trail. Those who are on foot, horseback, or fat-tired bikes can continue on the dirt track, carefully crossing Pearson Street, then winding behind quaint homes to Foster Road. The pavement picks up again on the west side of Foster Road.

The final 0.7 mile of the trail passes through oak woodlands, with only a scattering of pines to remind you that you are in the foothills. Birdsong and wildflowers accompany you to the trail's end at Neal Road. Unless you have arranged a shuttle, return as you came.

Magical beaches fronting on the Pacific Ocean lend their enchantment to the Ten Mile Coastal Trail (a.k.a. the Logging or Haul Road), a spectacular rail-trail that runs the length of a relatively remote state park.

Activities: 🚶 🚲 🚲 🛼 ⛺ 🦅 🏊

Location: MacKerricher State Park, Fort Bragg, Mendocino County

Length: 8 miles one-way

Surface: Asphalt, except where the trail is washed out in the Ten Mile Dunes

Wheelchair access: The trail is wheelchair accessible from Pudding Creek through the main part of MacKerricher State Park, but wheelchairs—or any other kind of wheeled machine, for that matter—cannot negotiate the section of trail that has been washed out in the Ten Mile Dunes.

Difficulty: Hard, due to the trail's length and the stretch of beach walking at the Ten Mile Dunes. The difficulty can be cut to easy if the trail is taken in short sections.

Food: There is no food available along the route, but you can find water in the campgrounds within the state park. The park also has areas for picnicking. Restaurants and a market can be found in Fort Bragg to the south of the park.

Rest rooms: There are public rest rooms available in the campgrounds of the state park.

Seasons: The trail is passable year-round, although high tides and inclement weather may render the trail impassable at times.

Access and parking: To reach the southern end point of the trail at Pudding Creek from California 1 in Fort Bragg, head north from town to the bridge that spans Pudding Creek. Access to the Logging Road and Pudding Creek Beach is just north of the bridge, on the left (west) side of the highway.

The Ten Mile Coastal Trail can also be reached via the main entrance of MacKerricher State Park, which is about 3 miles north of Fort Bragg on California 1. Turn left (west) into the park, following Mill Creek Road past the entrance station and the access road to the East and West Pinewood campgrounds. Mill Creek Road arcs south around the west shore of Lake Cleone, and forks. Take the right (west) fork into the parking area for the main beach and Laguna Point. The left fork leads south into the Surfwood campground.

Transportation: There is no public transportation serving the trail.

Rentals: There are no rentals available along the trail.

Contact: Gary Shannon, Landscape Architect, Russian River–Mendocino District, California State Parks, P.O. Box 123, Duncan Mills, CA 95430; (707) 865-3132. California State Parks Department, Mendocino Office, P.O. Box 440, Mendocino, CA 95460; (707) 937-5804.

• •

F rom end to end, the views from the Ten Mile Coastal Trail are mesmerizing. The uncrowded beaches are washed with rhythmic insistence by the waves, which in some locations have created tidal pools that grow warm and inviting under the summer sun, and in others have shaped dunes that offer refuge to seabirds and trail travelers alike.

The trail's local nickname, the Logging Road, reflects the route's previous incarnation as a road used to haul lumber from woodlands in the Ten Mile River watershed to the Union Lumber Company mill in Fort Bragg. The railroad that originally occupied the route was established in 1916 by the lumber company, which operated the line until 1949. The tracks were ripped up in a single day, according to historian Gene Lewis of Fort Bragg, so that the lumber company could build a private "high speed" logging road that could accommodate special logging trucks.

The lumber company used the Logging Road until 1983, when rainwater spilling out of the dunes in MacKerricher State Park washed out nearly 7,000 feet of the trail. The state parks department, which had acquired most of the land surrounding the road, didn't permit the road to be rebuilt. It was subsequently abandoned, and transformed into a lovely rail-trail.

The trail runs through the sensitive habitat of three endangered species, including the snowy plover, a lovely little bird whose numbers have been in decline due to increased use of beaches by people. There is some controversy about access to the trail north of Ward Avenue, where it enters the dunes at the washout. If you venture into this spectacular but sensitive territory, tread with care, and obey all signs.

The trail begins at Pudding Creek, near an old trestle that is

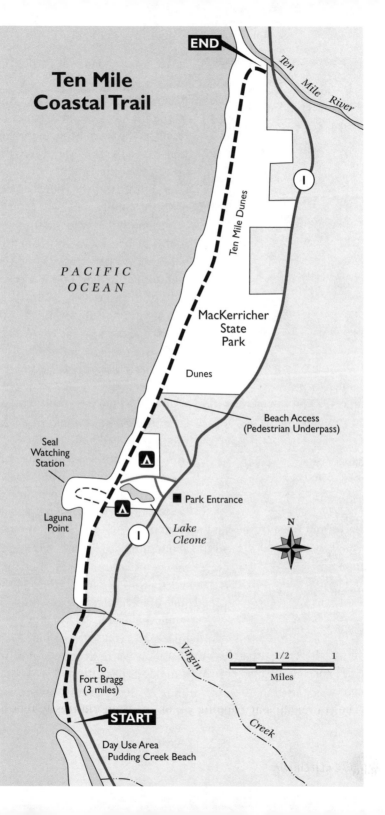

Ten Mile Coastal Trail

END

Ten Mile River

PACIFIC OCEAN

Ten Mile Dunes

MacKerricher State Park

Dunes

Beach Access (Pedestrian Underpass)

Seal Watching Station

■ Park Entrance

Laguna Point

Lake Cleone

N

Virgin

0   1/2   1
Miles

To Fort Bragg (3 miles)

START

Day Use Area
Pudding Creek Beach

Creek

TAKE A RIDE ON THE SKUNK TRAIN

In addition to the Ten Mile Coastal Trail and lovely MacKerricher State Park, Fort Bragg is also the western end point of the famous California Western Railroad Skunk Train. This historic train travels 40 scenic miles through the redwoods and oak woodlands of the Coast Ranges to the town of Willits, climbing to an elevation of 1,700 feet and tracing the path of the Noyo River as it spills to the sea.

Trains depart from the Fort Bragg Depot, located on Laurel Street one block west of California 1. The trip is extremely popular with families and railroad buffs, so it is recommended that you make reservations for your journey. For information and reservations contact the Fort Bragg Depot, P.O. Box 907, Fort Bragg, CA 95437; (800) 77–SKUNK, www.skunktrain.com.

currently closed to trail traffic. The rail-trail heads north, passing between the backyard lawns of motels on the east side and the narrow beach on the west. At about the 1.5-mile mark, the rail-trail crosses the bridge at Virgin Creek, then passes northward into the core of MacKerricher State Park.

At about 2.5 miles, the paved roadway breaks away from the ocean as it skirts the east side of Laguna Point. The point, a highlight of MacKerricher State Park, juts out into the ocean, and boardwalks lead out past the woodlands on the promontory to the open areas surrounding the seal-watching station.

North of the point, the elevated trail passes the main beach at the park, and side trails lead through the driftwood onto the soft sand. The Surfwood campground and Lake Cleone are on the right (east) side of the road.

The path is arrow-straight and abundantly scenic as it continues northward over the pedestrian tunnel that allows folks camping in the Pinewood campgrounds to reach the beach. At about the 3.5-mile mark, you will pass the beach access at Ward Avenue and head into the dunes.

The washout is about a quarter mile north of Ward Avenue. Leave the railroad grade and walk down onto the beach via a small trail, then follow the beach northward. You can hop back onto the paved trail or remain on the beach once you've passed the washout. It's all dune and ocean from this point north about 4 miles to the trail's end at the Ten Mile River, which marks the end of the Ten Mile Coastal Trail. There is no public access at this point, so you will have to re-trace your steps to the trailhead.

Joggers pad along the Ten Mile Coastal Trail in MacKerricher State Park.

6

Sacramento Northern Bike Trail

The Sacramento Northern Railroad slices through a cross-section of Central California, leading from the old neighborhoods of Sacramento through the suburbs to the north of town, then out into scenic farmland.

Activities:

Note: You can picnic in Discovery Park or in one of the gazebos along the route, as well as at Rio Linda.

Location: From Sacramento to Rio Linda in Sacramento County

Length: 8 miles one-way

Surface: Asphalt

Wheelchair access: The entire trail is accessible to wheelchair users.

Difficulty: Hard, given the trail's length. If taken in short enough sections, the rail-trail's difficulty can be reduced to easy.

Food: The trail passes a grocery store in Del Paso Heights, which is the nearest food outlet along the route, and there is a small market across the street from trail's end in Rio Linda. Other restaurants and stores are located in Sacramento and neighborhoods along the route. There are picnic facilities at the Rio Linda–Elverta Community Center at trail's end.

Rest rooms: The only public facilities along the trail are at the Rio Linda–Elverta Community Center at the Rio Linda end point.

Seasons: The trail can be used year-round, but in spring, when the American River runs high, the portion from California 160 to the intersection with the Jedediah Smith National Recreation Trail may be flooded.

Access and parking: To reach the Sacramento end point from the westbound lanes of Interstate 80, take the 15th Street (California 160) exit (the 16th Street exit if you are headed eastbound). Go north on 16th Street, which is a one-way road, to D Street. Go right (east) on D Street to 20th Street, and turn left (north) on 20th Street to reach C Street. The trail, which is obvious, is located between 19th and 20th Streets, on the north side of the road. There is plentiful streetside parking.

To reach the Rio Linda end point from Interstate 5 in Sacramento, head north on I–5 to its junction with California 99. Go right (north) on California 99 to the Elkhorn Boulevard exit. Follow Elkhorn Boulevard east to Rio Linda Boulevard. Turn left (north) on Rio Linda Boulevard and follow it to

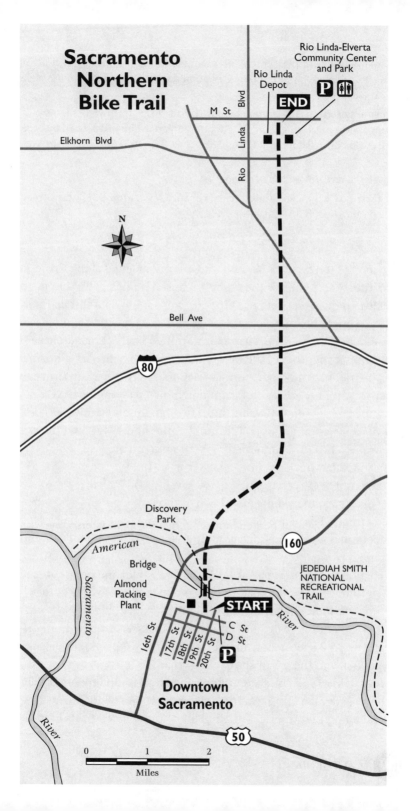

M Street. Turn right (east) on M Street and follow it to Front Street; the entrance to the park, the Rio Linda Depot, and the trailhead are on the right (south) side of M Street.

Transportation: Sacramento Regional Transit District, which operates public transportation throughout the Sacramento area, can be reached by writing P.O. Box 2110, Sacramento, CA 95812-2110. Call (916) 321–BUSS; the Web site is www.sacrt.com.

Rentals: There are no rentals along the trail.

Contact: Ed Cox, Bicycle Coordinator, City of Sacramento, 927 Tenth Street, Sacramento, CA 95814; (916) 264–8434.

• •

Four of the faces of Sacramento are in evidence along this rail-trail. You will pass the grand Victorian homes of the old town area, the industrial complexes that thrive along most railroad lines, the unremarkable but pleasant neighborhoods north of the American River, and the rural farm communities of Rio Linda. These 8 miles take a snapshot of life in the heartland of northern California.

The trail runs along the former Sacramento Northern Interurban Electric Rail line, which ran from downtown Sacramento to Chico, carrying passengers between these two bustling agricultural communities. The trains stopped running in the mid-1940s, and the rail line was eventually abandoned. Construction on the trail, which has been upgraded through the years, began in 1980.

The trail begins on C Street between 19th and 20th Streets, at the edge of a charming old neighborhood of classic homes and sycamore-lined streets. There are no signs, but the trail is obvious, beginning adjacent to the railroad tracks on the east side of the Blue Diamond almond factory.

Head north on the paved trail, passing under the bridge of the active Union Pacific Railroad tracks, and meander through industrial complexes for a half mile to a trail intersection. Stay right (north) on the Sacramento Northern trail, which passes across the American River on a spectacular metal trestle, then drops into the riparian greenery on the north shore of the river.

At 1.0 mile, you will pass under California 160 and merge briefly with the Jedediah Smith National Recreation Trail, which runs east to west along the American River. Follow the merged trails east for

Cyclists check out the Rio Linda Depot on the Sacramento Northern Bike Trail.

0.3 mile to the next trail intersection, and head left (north) across Del Paso Boulevard into Discovery Park. This section of the trail, along with the trails that border the ponds in this area of the park, may be flooded in spring.

The westbound continuation of the Jedediah Smith trail branches off to the left (northwest), circling the shady ponds that ring with birdsong. The Sacramento Northern trail takes the high road, climbing right onto the raised bed, from which you can look down upon the ponds.

At about 1.5 miles, the trail leaves the raised bed and drops down across the railroad tracks, then continues north. Industry gives way to homes as you cross a small bridge, then pass under the arch that marks the border of Noralto. Paths break from the trail to both right and left, giving access to neighborhood streets, and kids from these neighborhoods share the trail with the more serious recreationalists. You will cross a series of residential streets, most of which are quiet, but all of which will require care.

Homes border the trail to about the 3-mile mark, where the trail enters a narrow greenbelt lined with garbage cans. The greenbelt is brief, and after a quarter mile you are once again traveling among backyard fences.

At 3.9 miles, pass over a creek and its twin levees, then leave

Noralto for Del Paso Heights, with the border again marked by a green arch. This is another quiet residential neighborhood, but the trail is broader here, with gazebos that offers shade, benches, trash cans, and a water fountain.

At about the 5-mile mark, just beyond the last gazebo on this stretch of trail, you will reach Harris Avenue. Turn right (east) on Harris Avenue for 25 yards to the crosswalk, and cross busy Rio Linda Boulevard. The trail continues north on the east side of Rio Linda Boulevard. Cross a couple of side streets, then pass under the arch designating the border of Robla, and the Interstate 80 overpass. A second arch for Robla is at 5.2 miles.

Yet another gazebo offers respite and shade in the broad, exposed greenbelt at the intersection of Bell Avenue and Rio Linda Boulevard. Cruise through a section of trail that hints at country, with widely spaced homes on large pieces of property bordered by rustic fences. Then you reenter suburbia, and a dirt footpath borders the paved rail-trail.

Cross Marysville Boulevard at 6.7 miles; a last gazebo marks the spot. The trail now enters country proper, stretching between pastures that are richly green and dotted with wildflowers in spring, and bleached blond after the long, hot summer. Pass under an arch that bears no name, then cross a series of levees and a creek at 7 miles.

The canopies of broad-leaved trees shade the trail and insulate it from the airport that borders the trail on the right (east) side. At 7.6 miles, you will cross a stream and pass the memorial for Jeromy Shinault; beyond, the oaks form a substantial and welcome bower of shade over the lovely path. The waterway runs alongside the trail, adding its coolness to that of the trees.

Pass a ball field on the right (east) side of the path, then cross a rather busy roadway to a series of bridges spanning a braided creek or ditch that has cut ragged channels into raw-looking earth.

Trees again crowd the trail as you head into the park complex surrounding the Rio Linda–Elverta Community Center, which is at the trail's end at the 8-mile mark. The community center grounds include a tot lot, broad lawns, picnic facilities, and the Rio Linda Depot, an open, gazebo-like structure housing picnic tables. You can get cool drinks and snacks at the small market across M Street from the park.

Unless you've arranged a shuttle, return as you came.

MORE RAIL-TRAILS

 Fairfield Linear Park

This is primarily a commuter route that leads from downtown Fairfield to the Solano Community College. A portion of the trail runs through a nicely landscaped greenbelt featuring small playgrounds and benches.

Activities:

Location: Fairfield, Solano County

Length: 4 miles one way

Surface: Asphalt and concrete

Wheelchair access: The route is entirely wheelchair accessible.

Difficulty: Moderate

Food: Fast-food outlets are located in the Solano Mall at the trail's west end. Other restaurants are available throughout Fairfield.

Rest rooms: Portable toilets are available at the ball fields on the Solano Community College campus at the trail's western terminus. Rest rooms also can be found in the Solano Mall.

Seasons: The trail can be used year-round.

Access and parking: To reach the western end point from Interstate 80, take the Abernathy Road exit. Go north on Abernathy Road for 0.5 mile to Rockville Road. Turn left (west) on Rockville Road, and go 1.7 miles to Suisun Valley Road. Turn left (south) on Suisun Valley Road, and go 0.3 mile to Solano Community College. Circle the college to the baseball diamond, which is in the southeast section of the campus. The trail begins across the bridge on the southwest side of the field, behind the backstop and home base. There is ample parking at this location.

To reach the northern end point from Interstate 80 in Fairfield, take the Travis Boulevard exit. Follow Travis Boulevard east to Solano Mall, and park in the mall parking lots fronting on Travis Boulevard. The trail is located opposite the mall, on the south side of Travis Boulevard between Second Street and Pennsylvania Avenue.

Transportation: Fairfield/Suisun Transit System operates in this area. Contact the Public Works Department of the City of Fairfield at 1000 Webster Street, Fairfield, CA 94533-4883; (707) 422–BUSS.

Rentals: There are no rentals available along the trail.

Contact: Fred S. Beiner, Park Planner, Community Services Department, City of Fairfield, 1000 Webster Street, Fairfield, CA 94533-4883; (707) 428-7431, www.ci.fairfield.ca.us.

• •

Built on a railroad right-of-way that once belonged to the Sacramento Northern Railroad system, the rail-trail that runs through the Fairfield Linear Park now serves two distinct communities.

The first is the commuter crowd: The trail provides students of Solano Community College and other residents an ideal alternative for traveling from the school to homes or work in Fairfield without using an automobile.

The second group consists of residents of neighborhoods bordering the section of trail that winds through a verdant greenbelt near

Solano Mall. These folks use the trail to stroll, ride bikes, skate, walk their dogs, and bring their children to play in either of two small tot lots.

Beginning at Solano Community College, the asphalt trail curves to the south around the school's ball fields, then heads east, jogging through farmland until it is separated from the freeway by little more than a hedge of flowering oleander trees. After about 3 miles, you'll cross a bridge and a major intersection at Texas Street; the trail passes

A small bridge connects portions of the Fairfield Linear Park Trail.

under Interstate 80 at this point, and continues on the interstate's south side.

From the interstate to the second end point at the Solano Mall, the rail-trail winds behind the homes of quiet subdivisions, buffered from backyards by fences and well-maintained strips of lawn dotted with benches, young trees, and other pleasant landscaping. Two playgrounds lie along the route, which is transected by four neighborhood streets. The concrete surface is perfect for teaching children how to ride bikes; adjacent grassy areas invite resting and picnicking, and a parcourse allows the exercise-minded to get a workout as they run or walk on the route. The trail reaches busy Travis Boulevard, across from the Solano Mall, at the 4-mile mark.

Ⓑ Chico Airport Bike Path

The grassy expanses surrounding the Chico Airport are surprisingly scenic, hosting a variety of songbirds that raise a pleasant ruckus in spring. This rail-trail runs from the airport into town, where it offers residents an alternative to walking or cycling on the streets.

Activities:

Location: Chico, Butte County

Length: 3.5 miles one way

Surface: Asphalt

Wheelchair access: The trail is entirely wheelchair accessible.

Difficulty: Easy

Food: There are no stores or restaurants at the airport end of the trail, but the path ends on Esplanade, which runs through the heart of town and provides access to a variety of eateries and markets. No water is available along the route, so pack all you will need.

Rest rooms: No rest rooms are available along the trail.

Seasons: The trail can be used year-round.

Access and parking: To reach the Chico Airport trailhead from California 99 in Chico, take the Cohasset Highway/Mangrove Avenue exit. Head north on Cohasset Road for about 3 miles to Boeing Avenue, and turn left (west). Follow Boeing for 0.2 mile to Fortress Street, and turn left (south). Sikorsky Avenue intersects Fortress Street at about 0.1 mile; the rail-trail is on the left (east) side of Fortress Street.

The southern end of the rail-trail is at the intersection of Esplanade and Eleventh Avenue. To reach this from California 99, take the Cohasset Highway/Mangrove Avenue exit and head west on Cohasset Road. Follow Cohasset Road for 0.5 mile to its intersection with Esplanade, and turn left (south). Follow Esplanade for 0.3 mile to Tenth Avenue and turn left. The rail-trail is located just north of this junction. There is no public parking in the convenient lots of the Chico Nut Company; the nearest parking is along the residential streets south and east of the trailhead.

Transportation: For bus route information, contact the Chico Area Transit System at (530) 342–0221.

Rentals: There are no rentals available along the trail, but Chico is a biking town; it was rated the Most Bike Friendly City by *Bicycling* magazine in 1997. It should come as no surprise, then, that the town boasts a number of shops offering bike rentals and repairs. For more information about rental shops, and for brochures about the various trails, contact the Chico Chamber of Commerce, 300 Salem Street, Chico, CA 95928; (800) 852–8570, www.chicochamber.com.

Contact: Mike Parks, Assistant Director of Public Works, Municipal Services Department, City of Chico, P.O. Box 3420, Chico, CA 95927; (530) 895–4800.

• •

It's always a bit startling—and completely wonderful—when what appears to be a strictly urban/commuter rail-trail turns out to have pleasing natural attributes. The Chico Airport Bike Path is one of those trails.

It runs from the center of town to the local airfield, so yes, it does serve a very utilitarian purpose. What is unexpected, however, is the simple beauty of the landscape surrounding the airport—a broad, grassy plain watered to an iridescent green by the rains of winter and spring and burnished gold in summer and autumn. Numerous songbirds reside in the grass, filling the sky in far greater numbers than aircraft.

The trail runs on the former grade of the Sacramento Northern Railroad, which ran an extensive electric railroad system that reached from California's capital city north to Chico and east to San Francisco.

The trail begins beside a hangar at the airport, winding south through its grassy backyard for 0.3 mile before coming to rest parallel to Cohasset Road. From here, it's a straight shot through the grasslands, amid the songs of the birds and the occasional drone of a small plane or jet taking off or landing on a nearby runway. At 0.7 mile the route crosses a small bridge; a second, much larger bridge is crossed at 1.4 miles, just before the rail-trail crosses Eaton.

By the 1.8-mile mark, the trail is passing between the backyards of quiet neighborhoods. The trail continues to plow a straight shot among fences draped with vines, shaded from the sometimes brutal summer sun by the mingling canopies of a variety of trees.

You will cross a number of city streets with the assistance of only your own common sense before you arrive at East Avenue, where a bike signal forces traffic to stop. The trail boasts street lamps for a stretch, then passes beneath an overpass to Rio Lindo Avenue.

The last major street that must be crossed is Cohasset Road. A trestle spans Lindo Channel just before the route ends at Esplanade and Eleventh Avenue.

Ⓒ Durham Bike Path

Orchards, brilliant with pink and white blooms in spring, laden with fruit in summer and autumn, and naked in winter, line this rural bike path, which borders the Midway road in southern Chico.

Activities:

Location: Chico, Butte County

Length: 2.5 miles one-way

Surface: Asphalt

Wheelchair access: The trail is entirely accessible to wheelchair users.

Difficulty: Easy

Food: There is no food or water available along the trail. Eateries and markets abound, however, just a few miles north in central Chico.

Rest rooms: There are no public rest rooms along the trail.

Seasons: The trail can be used year-round.

Access and parking: To reach the northern end point of the Durham Bike Path from California 99 in Chico, take the Paradise/Park Avenue exit. Go east on East Park Avenue to Midway, and turn south. Follow Midway south to Hegan Lane, where you will find limited parking.

To reach the southern end point at Jones Avenue and Midway, continue south on Midway for 2.3 miles to its intersection with Jones Avenue. There is perhaps room for a single car alongside the road at this end point.

Transportation: For bus route information, contact the Chico Area Transit System at (530) 342–0221.

Rentals: There are no rentals available along the trail. As noted in the Chico Airport Bike Trail description, Chico is a biking town, and there are a number of shops that offer bike repairs and rentals. For more information about rental shops, and brochures about the various trails, contact the Chico Chamber of Commerce, 300 Salem Street, Chico, CA 95928; (800) 852–8570, www.chicochamber.com.

Contact: Mike Parks, Assistant Director of Public Works, Municipal Services Department, City of Chico, P.O. Box 3420, Chico, CA 95927; (530) 895–4800.

• • • • • • • • • • • • • • • • • • • •

The trees of the orchards that line the Durham Bike Path present themselves in rows as straight and orderly as military regiments. At times they provide shade for travelers on the path, but, regardless the ripeness of their fruit, no sustenance until that fruit has been harvested by the owner and shipped to market.

The neatly cropped trees are ubiquitous along this easy rail-trail, which runs on the former bed of the Sacramento Northern Railroad, an interurban electric line that ran between Sacramento and Chico. Indeed, the predictability of the paved path has an almost meditative quality, easy and rhythmic, like an old familiar song. It is very popular with cyclists and in-line skaters, and it links with other bike routes that lead south, west and east from the rail-trail's end at Jones Avenue.

The trail begins at Hegan Lane and heads southeast, with the orchards on either side and the Midway to the west. Several streets interrupt the orchards: Entler Avenue at about the 0.7-mile mark, McFadden Lane, and then, at 1.9 miles, the Oro-Chico Highway. The clean, slightly elevated path ends at Jones Avenue, where you will find a memorial dedicated to Brad Keohly.

Rails-to-Trails

SAN FRANCISCO BAY AREA

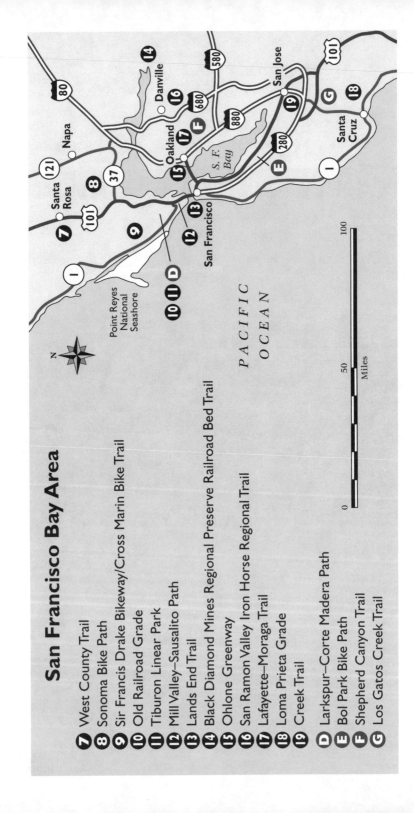

San Francisco Bay Area

7 West County Trail
8 Sonoma Bike Path
9 Sir Francis Drake Bikeway/Cross Marin Bike Trail
10 Old Railroad Grade
11 Tiburon Linear Park
12 Mill Valley–Sausalito Path
13 Lands End Trail
14 Black Diamond Mines Regional Preserve Railroad Bed Trail
15 Ohlone Greenway
16 San Ramon Valley Iron Horse Regional Trail
17 Lafayette–Moraga Trail
18 Loma Prieta Grade
19 Creek Trail

D Larkspur–Corte Madera Path
E Bol Park Bike Path
F Shepherd Canyon Trail
G Los Gatos Creek Trail

San Francisco Bay Area's

• • • • • • • • • • • • • • • • • •

TOP RAIL-TRAILS

7 West County Trail

The springtime green and summertime gold of the oak wood-lands that border the middle of the West County Trail hint at what the landscape of Sonoma County looked like prior to development.

Activities:

Location: Sonoma County

Length: 5.5 miles one way

Surface: Asphalt

Wheelchair access: The entire trail is wheelchair accessible.

Difficulty: Moderate, due to the trail's length

Food: The town of Sebastopol, through which the trail passes, boasts a number of restaurants and grocery stores.

Rest rooms: There are no public rest rooms along the trail.

Seasons: The trail can be used year-round.

Access and parking: A small parking lot is available at the Sebastopol Road trailhead, but parking is limited at other trailheads. To reach the Sebastopol Road trailhead from U.S. Highway 101 in Santa Rosa, take the California 12 exit. Follow California 12 west for 3 miles to the stoplight at Wright Road. Turn left (south) on Wright Road, and go 0.2 mile to Sebastopol Road. Turn right (west) on Sebastopol Road for 0.2 mile to the road's end in the trail's parking area.

In Sebastopol, the only trailhead parking is along the road fronting Analy High School. To reach this trailhead, follow California 12 to its intersection with California 116 in Sebastopol. Turn right (north) on California 116, and follow it to its intersection with North Main Street. Go 0.1 mile north on North Main Street to the trailhead, which is on the left (west) side of the road opposite the high school. There is no parking at either access point on California 116.

Transportation: Sonoma County Transit provides service to the Santa Rosa and Sebastopol areas. Bus schedules can be obtained by calling (707) 576–7433.

Rentals: You can rent a bike at the Bicycle Factory, 195 North Main Street, Sebastopol, CA 95472; (707) 829–1880.

Contact: Ken Tam, Planner, Sonoma County Regional Parks Department, 2300 County Center Drive, Suite 120A, Santa Rosa, CA 95403; (707) 565–2041.

• •

S onoma County has become synonymous with the Wine Country, but this trail passes through a landscape that harkens back to the county's ranching roots. For a couple of miles, the route passes adjacent to expanses of oak woodland and grassland, vistas similar to those that once dominated the landscape. This pastoral terrain, however, is under enormous threat of development by homes and businesses or by the vineyards that have supplanted dairies and apple orchards as the mainstay of Sonoma County agriculture.

The trail follows the bed of the Petaluma and Santa Rosa Railroad, an electric line that carried passengers between Santa Rosa and Forestville. The first part of the trail, from Merced Avenue in Santa Rosa to Petaluma Avenue in Sebastopol, is named for Joe Rodota, the first director of Sonoma County Regional Parks Department. The route as described here can be done as a single trail or separated into two sections. The first section, from Santa Rosa to downtown Sebastopol, is friendlier for in-line skaters and cyclists looking for a workout; the section that heads west out of Sebastopol is more neighborly, lending itself nicely to hiking and walking.

The trail begins amid businesses and homes just south of California 12. It heads west from the Sebastopol Road trailhead parking area, paralleling the highway and shaded by oaks and eucalyptus. Go for 0.4 mile, crossing several residential streets, to the Merced Avenue trailhead, where limited parking is available.

Beyond Merced Avenue, the trail's character changes. Although it still runs adjacent to the highway, separated from the road by oak trees and shoulder-high cow parsnip, the land to the south is open pastureland dotted with the occasional oak. Blackberry brambles

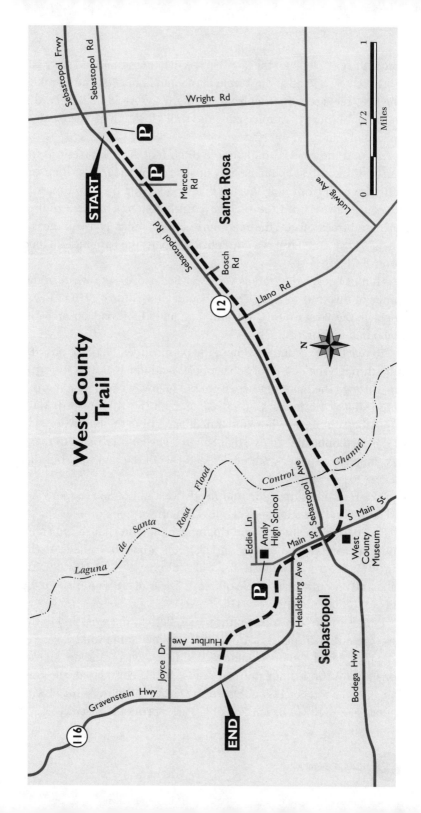

border the path; look for the tasty berries in late summer and early fall.

Cross Bosch Road at the 1-mile mark, and Llano Road at 1.3 miles. The trail veers south, away from the highway. An industrial yard is on the right (north), emphasizing the trail's location on the brink of the urban and rural interface.

Beyond the road, cattails line a ditch that runs adjacent to the trail on the south side. Blackberry bushes climb the fences that separate the path from neighboring businesses. The trail continues to arc south, away from the highway, until distance and a buffer of earth and trees muffle the road noise. At 2.7 miles you will cross a small bridge; at 3.0 miles a larger bridge spans the Santa Rosa Flood Control Channel.

Homes border the trail as you near Sebastopol, the western terminus of this trail section. The trail ends on California 116 in town, opposite the West County Museum and an old railroad car on a disembodied section of track.

To reach the second section of the path, you will have to pass 0.5 mile through the center of Sebastopol. Head north along California 116, through the heart of town, until the highway veers west in front of the United Methodist Church. Go straight (north) on North Main Street for 0.1 mile, to where the trail departs from the left (west) side of the road opposite Analy High School. The county plans to make a connection using city streets located east of the highway, but this has yet to be completed.

The trail picks up again and heads west out of Sebastopol via a tree-shrouded corridor between lovely homes. The summer scents of blackberry, eucalyptus, and ripening apples alternate as you continue, crossing two quiet residential streets. About 0.5 mile from the North Main Street trailhead, the rail-trail crosses East Hurlbut Avenue and enters a small apple orchard. The trail ends after about 0.8 mile on California Highway 116.

Extensions of the West County Trail, both to the west and to the east, are either in place or in the process, but some links have yet to be completed. Others lie along existing roadways, and not all sections are on the former railroad grade. When completed, the trail will extend a total of 12.5 miles, from near U.S. Highway 101 in Santa Rosa to Steelhead Beach Regional Park north of Forestville.

The scenic splendor of the Wine Country surrounds this short rail-trail, which passes several historic sites, including the lovely home of General Mariano Vallejo, as it winds through downtown Sonoma. The trail also passes the Depot Park Museum, where you can peruse exhibits that focus on both railroad and other aspects of local history.

Activities:

Location: City of Sonoma, Sonoma County

Length: 3 miles round-trip

Surface: Asphalt

Wheelchair access: The trail is entirely wheelchair accessible.

Difficulty: Easy

Food: The trail is located only blocks from Sonoma's famous Plaza, where fine dining establishments abound. A grocery store is located within easy walking distance of the trail's end at Maxwell Farms. There are picnic tables at the park.

Rest rooms: There are rest rooms at Depot Park, near the midpoint of the trail, and at the western end point in Maxwell Farms Regional Park.

Seasons: The trail can be used year-round.

Access and parking: To reach the eastern end point from California 12 and Napa Street, which intersect on the south side of the Plaza, go right (east) on Napa Street for less than a half mile to Fourth Street East. Turn left (north), and follow Fourth Street East for about a half mile to Lovall Valley Road. There is limited parking along the street. You also may park in the lot for the Sebastiani Vineyard.

To reach the western end point from California 12 at the Plaza, follow Napa Street/California 12 west to where California 12 veers north near Petaluma Avenue (follow the signs). Follow California 12 north about 1 mile to Verano Avenue, and turn left (west). The entrance to Maxwell Farms Regional Park is on the left (south) side of Verano Avenue. Abundant parking is available at Maxwell Farms.

Transportation: Sonoma County Transit provides service to the Plaza and other points along the trail. Call (707) 576–7433 for more information.

Rentals: There are two local establishments that rent bicycles. Goodtime Bicycle Company is at 18503 California Highway 12 in Sonoma; (707) 938–0453. Sonoma Valley Cyclery is at 20093 Broadway in Sonoma; (707) 935–3377.

Contact: Patricia Wagner, Engineering Assistant, City of Sonoma, No. 1, The Plaza, Sonoma, CA 95476; (707) 938–3794.

• •

Aah, the fabled Wine Country. Bunches of fragrant grapes, both red and bright green, weighing down orderly vines. The smells of gourmet cheeses and other delicacies wafting from restaurants with doors flung open to the warm summer breezes. Hills shaded by stately oaks rolling up to a sky painted a perfect California blue.

The Sonoma Bike Path captures all this in a neat, easy package. The paved path begins adjacent to a vineyard, passes through quaint Depot Park, where the old depot now serves as a historical museum, then rolls through the former estate of Spanish landowner General Mariano Vallejo, now part of the Sonoma State Historic Park. Wander south from the trail down a quiet neighborhood street, and you'll find yourself on the Plaza, where you can shop, eat, take in a bit of California history at the Sonoma Barracks or Mission San Francisco Solano de Sonoma, then relax and unwind in the rose garden.

The Sonoma Valley Railroad Company, organized in 1879, operated the passenger and freight trains that ran on what was initially a narrow-gauge line through the valley. The line ran from Vineburg to the Sonoma Plaza, and was later extended north to Glen Ellen. Later, after the track was changed to standard gauge, the SVRR became part of the Northwestern Pacific Railroad complex, which in turn was purchased by Southern Pacific.

The railroad began its decline in the early 1940s, when passenger service north to Kenwood was discontinued and the tracks torn up. Trains had stopped running on the main line by 1960. Historical information about the Sonoma Valley Railroad, and other railroads in the region, can be explored at the Depot Museum, which lies along the rail.

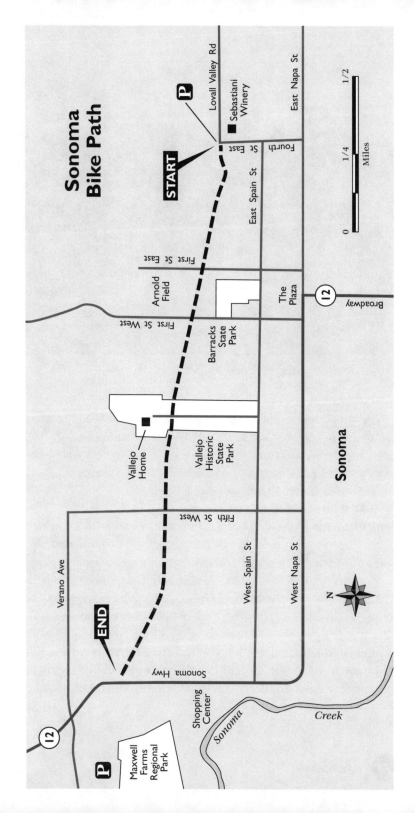

A walker passes by the historic General Vellejo home.

The trail begins opposite the Sebastiani Winery at the intersection of Fourth Street East and Lovall Valley Road. The path rolls through grapevines, then is bordered on either side by well-kept backyard gardens. A series of residential streets intersect the path, and at Second Street East, a parcourse begins.

At First Street East, you will enter Depot Park. Here you'll find picnic sites and ball fields busy with baseball games in spring and soccer games in autumn. The Depot Historical Museum, complete with a Southern Pacific Railroad car on a salvaged strip of track, is the centerpiece of the park. The museum is open Wednesday through Sunday from 1:00 to 4:30 P.M., and can be reached by calling (707) 938–1762. First Street East also offers great access to the Plaza.

At about the half-mile mark, you will cross First Street West, pass the Depot Hotel and more ball fields, then enter the near-pristine meadow serving as a buffer to the Vallejo Home. The home was once known as Lachryma Montis, which is Latin for "mountain tears," although it's difficult to imagine being sad amid all the beauty surrounding the place. After crossing the paved driveway serving the historic site, the trail enters a residential area and appears to split. Stay right on the bike path.

Cross the busiest street intersection at Fifth Street West at about 1 mile; beyond, the trail passes petite Olsen Park and becomes distinctly residential in nature. A series of street intersections follows. Most are quiet neighborhood drives, but cross with care. Beyond the intersection with Robinson Road, the trail splits again. As before, stay right (north) on the bike path.

At the 1.5-mile mark, you will reach California 12. The trail ends here, but Maxwell Farms Regional Park, with a series of paved paths, frontage on Sonoma Creek, a playground, and manicured lawns, as well as a skateboard park and other amenities, lies just across the street. This is a busy crossing: It's best and safest to head south along the sidewalk to the signal and crosswalk at Maxwell Village Shopping Center, then backtrack north to the park. Return as you came.

Sir Francis Drake Bikeway/ Cross Marin Bike Trail

This spectacular rail-trail in western Marin County parallels the course of scenic Lagunitas Creek. Sunny meadows and rolling hills overlook the waterway, and dark, cool redwood groves lie along the path. Samuel P. Taylor State Park is at the midpoint, offering picnic facilities and other amenities.

Activities:

Location: From Tocaloma to Shafter's Bridge in Marin County

Length: 4.5 miles one-way

Surface: Asphalt for 3 miles, to the Irving Group Picnic Area; dirt and ballast for the last 1.5 miles, from the picnic area to Shafter's Bridge

Wheelchair access: Yes, on the paved section of the trail. Hardy wheelchair users may attempt the dirt section to Shafter's Bridge, but this is generally fairly rough, and can be muddy in wet weather.

Difficulty: Moderate, due only to the trail's length

Food: None is available along the trail, so bring a picnic. If you plan to eat before or after visiting the rail-trail, a deli and a restaurant featuring local oysters are available in Olema, which is 2 miles west of Tocaloma at the intersection of Sir Francis Drake Boulevard and California 1. Point Reyes Station, which offers a variety of restaurants as well as a market, is located 2.3 miles north of Olema on California 1.

Rest rooms: Rest rooms, including those accessible to persons with disabilities, are available in Samuel P. Taylor State Park.

Seasons: The trail can be used year-round. The dirt/ballast section of the trail may be muddy in winter and early spring.

Access and parking: There is limited roadside parking at both ends of the Sir Francis Drake Bikeway. To reach either trailhead from U.S. Highway 101 in Larkspur/Corte Madera, take the Sir Francis Drake Boulevard exit and head west on Sir Francis Drake Boulevard through the towns of Kentfield, San Anselmo, and Fairfax, and then through the pastoral San Geronimo Valley. Shafter's Bridge is 15.5 miles from U.S. 101; the Tocaloma parking area at Platform Bridge Road is 20 miles.

The best parking and access can be found at the Tocaloma end point. At the intersection of Sir Francis Drake Boulevard and Platform Bridge Road, turn right (north), and park in the pullout on the left (west) side of Platform

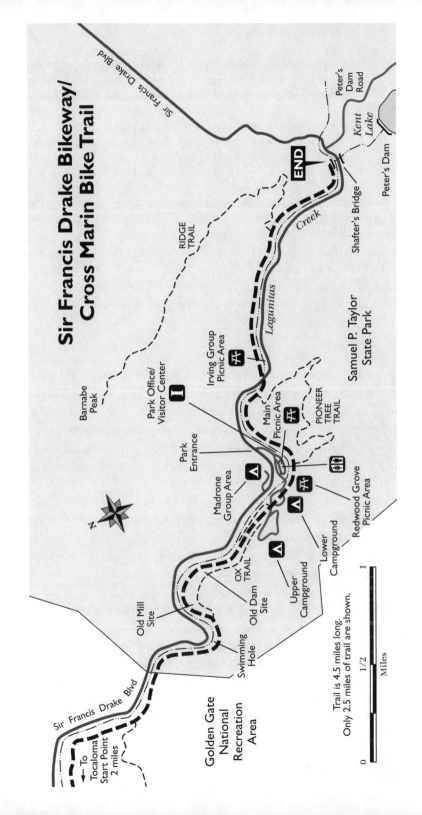

Bridge Road, at the east end of the old bridge (about 100 yards from Sir Francis Drake Boulevard). A few additional spots are available 0.1 mile west of Platform Bridge Road on Sir Francis Drake along the right (north) side of the road.

Parking at Shafter's Bridge is extremely limited and located just beyond the bridge along the north side of the highway. Additional parking is available in the small lot on the south side of Sir Francis Drake Boulevard, which is open for a few months in the winter when the steelhead and salmon make their spawning runs up the creeks.

You may also reach the rail-trail through Samuel P. Taylor State Park. The park entrance is midway between Shafter's Bridge and Tocaloma. Pay the fee and follow the park road to parking adjacent to the trail.

Transportation: Unless you coordinate a car shuttle, this is an out-and-back affair. There is no public transportation from end point to end point.

Rentals: There are no rental facilities available near the trail.

Contact: The ranger's office at Samuel P. Taylor State Park, P.O. Box 251, Lagunitas, CA 94938-0251; (415) 488–9897.

• •

If you simply must have it all now, you can find it along the Sir Francis Drake Bikeway. A gentle, inviting creek with a swimming hole; a sun-drenched meadow with views onto rolling pastureland dotted with black-and white dairy cows; cool, dark redwood groves; a lovely picnic area with all the amenities; a scenic cascade filling rock basins with clear water . . . this easy, mostly paved trail is a Marin County dream come true.

The soul of the trail is Lagunitas Creek, also known as Papermill Creek. This creek played an important role in the history of western Marin County. In the mid–nineteenth century, Samuel Penfield Taylor, for whom the state park is named, used the proceeds of a gold-mining operation to purchase property along the creek. Instead of logging the land, a logical endeavor for entrepreneurs of the period as building boomed in the burgeoning metropolis of San Francisco, Taylor established two mills along the creek, one manufacturing paper and the other black powder.

The powder mill was short-lived: It blew up in 1874. The paper mill, however, thrived, especially after a narrow-gauge railroad through the canyon made shipment of Taylor's goods easier. Taylorville, a small town that grew up around the mill and railroad, with its resort hotel and camp, was a popular destination in the 1870s and 1880s.

The 4.5-mile route described here follows the abandoned bed of the Northwest Pacific Railroad, which began in Larkspur and continued up the coast to Tomales and beyond. The rail-trail is also called the Cross Marin Bike Trail, and is a portion of the not-yet-completed Bay Area Ridge Trail.

Beginning at the Platform Bridge Road parking area, cross the lovely old bridge that spans Lagunitas Creek, and turn left (south) onto the trail at the sign that reads CROSS MARIN TRAIL. The path dives under the bridge supporting Sir Francis Drake Boulevard, then cruises through thick bays and scattered redwood groves to a long,

Trees overhang the Sir Francis Drake Bikeway.

open meadow. Towering eucalyptus trees guard the southern reach of the meadow; just beyond, at 1.4 miles, you'll reach the Jewell Trail intersection. From here you can climb steeply onto the Bolinas Ridge Trail, a popular mountain-bike ride.

At about 2 miles, you'll pass a gate that marks the boundary of the state park, and the trail follows a park road through lovely stands of redwoods. Stay straight on the park road, ignoring other roads that branch left and right to housing and other park service facilities. On the north (creekside) border of the trail, in a tiny clearing, a historic marker commemorates the Pioneer Paper Mill, built by the park's namesake, Samuel Taylor, in 1856. The Ox Trail takes off to the east opposite the marker.

You'll pass another creekside marker at the 2.5-mile mark (post 7), which makes note of the first fish ladder on the creek. At 3 miles another gate marks a park boundary; now you are in the park proper, passing campsites, picnic areas, and rest rooms. Stay straight on the park road, again ignoring any roads that depart right or left, passing the Redwood Grove Picnic Area and then through yet another gate. The Pioneer Tree Trail takes off to the south just past the gate.

The rail-trail's surface changes from asphalt to gravel as it heads south to cross the bridge over the highway and creek at 3.5 miles. The Irving Group Picnic Area is on the east side of the bridge. Now a dirt road with a wilder feel, the trail is separated from the highway by the creek and dense walls of redwood and bay. The Ridge Trail, which leads to the summit of Barnabe Peak, leaves from the north side of the railroad grade a half mile beyond the picnic grounds.

A gate and the Kent Lake trailhead mark the end of the route at 4.5 miles. Take the narrow trail on the south side of the grade down to the creek, and head upstream about 100 yards to the cascades that fill swimming holes beneath Shafter's Bridge. This ideal picnic spot is also a great place to watch the salmon and steelhead spawn in winter.

Follow the trail in the opposite direction to return to the Tocaloma trailhead.

Climbing nearly 2,000 feet to the summit of Mount Tamalpais, the Old Railroad Grade boasts some of the best views in the San Francisco Bay Area. The steady grade of the winding dirt track, now frequented by mountain bikers in shiny Lycra, once was a weekend destination of ladies and gentlemen, who would travel by ferry from San Francisco to spend a day in the country.

Activities:

Location: Mill Valley to Mount Tamalpais State Park, Marin County

Length: 9 miles one-way

Surface: Ballast and dirt

Wheelchair access: The trail is not wheelchair accessible.

Difficulty: Hard. As railroad grades go, this one is long and steep, but wonderfully rewarding.

Food: There is no food available along the trail; pack a picnic lunch to eat at the inn or at the summit. Grocery stores are available in Mill Valley, along with a great variety of fine restaurants.

Rest rooms: There are rest rooms at the West Point Inn and at the summit of Mount Tamalpais, but no facilities at the trailhead in Blithedale Park.

Seasons: The trail can be used year-round, but may be muddy or impassable when it rains. Also, the mountain may be swathed in cool—sometimes Minnesotan—fog, even in summer, so be prepared for changing weather conditions.

Access and parking: To reach the Blithedale Park end point from U.S. Highway 101 in Mill Valley, take the East Blithedale Avenue exit and follow East Blithedale Avenue east into downtown Mill Valley, where it ends at the intersection of Throckmorton and West Blithedale Avenue. Turn right (north) on West Blithedale Avenue, and follow the narrow road up through neighborhoods into Blithedale Park. The trailhead is on the right (east) side of the road at a green gate.

To reach the summit of Mount Tamalpais from U.S. Highway 101 in Mill Valley, take the California 1/Stinson Beach exit and head west on California 1 (a.k.a. the Shoreline Highway) to the intersection with the Panoramic Highway. Turn right (north) on the Panoramic Highway, and climb the slopes of Mount Tamalpais to Pantoll Road. Turn right (north) on Pantoll

Road, and keep climbing to its end at the Rock Spring picnic area on Ridgecrest Boulevard. Turn right (east) on East Ridgecrest Boulevard, and follow this to its end in the East Peak parking lot.

Adequate parking is available at both end points, but lots may be packed on weekends or during the summer.

Transportation: Golden Gate Transit buses serve Mill Valley. Contact the transit service at (415) 455–2000 or visit the GGT Web site at www.golden gate.org.

Rentals: No rentals are available along the trail.

Contact: Eric McGuire, Environmental Services Coordinator, Marin Municipal Water District, 220 Nellen Avenue, Corte Madera, CA 94925; (415) 924–4600.

• •

L ike a benevolent but sometimes temperamental goddess, the Pacific Ocean lords over Mount Tamalpais. On clear days, views sweep in every direction for miles—north up the ragged, emerald California coast; east to the snow-capped Sierra Nevada; south over San Francisco Bay and across its glittering city; and west to the ocean itself, past the shadowy Farallon Islands to the endless horizon. Sun bathes the forested slopes of the peak, and the Old Railroad Grade offers the perfect opportunity to bask in these gifts.

But when the goddess shows her temper, allowing the fog to envelop the mountain in cold mists and brisk winds, other gifts become apparent. For despite the peak's location in the midst of a sprawling urban area, a traveler caught on a fog-shrouded ridge may suddenly find him or herself alone in a viewless wilderness, perhaps transported back to the time when the mountain was an escape to the country for San Franciscans.

In those days, around the turn of the twentieth century, the Mill Valley & Mount Tamalpais Scenic Railway Company operated "The Crookedest Railroad in the World" on the mountain. Passengers rode the winding line to the summit, savored the views, and perhaps took a hike along the rolling crest of the mountain, then rode the rails back down to Mill Valley. The line was abandoned in 1930, and the former grade is now a popular hiking and mountain biking route on the mountain.

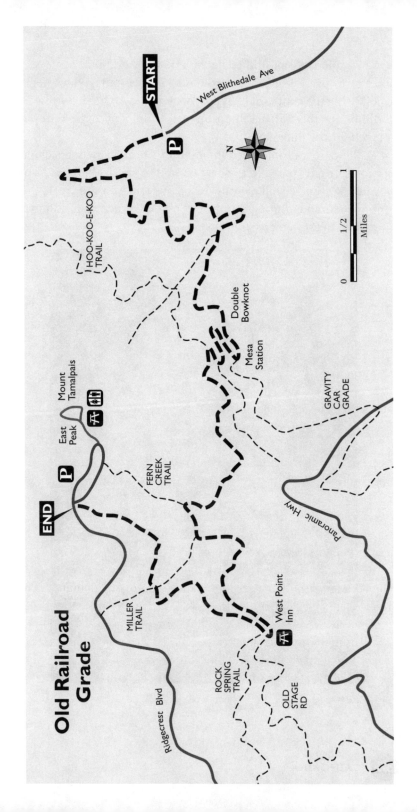

The trailhead is at Blithedale Park on the gated Blithedale Summit/Northridge Fire Road. Green posts line the route, which begins by following the course of heavily wooded Arroyo Creek northward. It climbs steadily for the duration, so set your pace, and prepare yourself for the long haul.

At the first trail intersection, another fire road switchbacks up and to the right (northeast); stay left on the railroad grade. At the next intersection, go left (southwest), down and over the creek, then continue climbing through a forest of bay, oak, madrone, and manzanita that opens a bit as you ascend.

Remnants of track are visible atop the Old Railroad Grade on Mount Tamalpais.

At about 1.5 miles, the trail passes a gate and merges with paved Summit Avenue. Go right (north) on Fern Canyon, enjoying lovely views of San Francisco and the bay, and pass the Temelpa Trail, which breaks off the pavement to the right (north). The pavement ends at a gate posted with watershed signs. Pass the gate to the right (the left road is a driveway), and continue upward on the Old Railroad Grade.

At about the 3-mile mark, near the site of Mesa Station and the start of the Gravity Car Grade, the road reaches a **T** intersection. Go right (east) and up on the switchbacking rail-trail, which negotiates the Double Bow Knot, where the grade gains an incredible 600 feet in elevation. Less than a half mile beyond, pass the Hoo Koo E Koo Road, which breaks off to the right (northeast); stay left (west) on the obvious railroad grade.

As you climb, the forest gives way to low-growing coastal scrub, thick with the blooms of sticky monkey flower and Scotch broom in the spring, dry and silvery in summer and fall. At the Hogback Road intersection, at about the 4-mile mark, stay right (west); above, as you cruise through moist draws that boast waterfalls in winter and spring, pass the Fern Canyon Trail,

EXPLORING MOUNT TAMALPAIS

The Olmsted Bros. Map Company has produced a very nice map of trails on Mount Tamalpais. The map, "A Rambler's Guide to the Trails of Mount Tamalpais and the Marin Headland," is available at local outdoor-equipment retailers and bookstores, or can be acquired by contacting the company at P.O. Box 5351, Berkeley, CA 94705; (510) 658–6534.

The historic West Point Inn offers accommodations for hikers and cyclists wishing to spend the night on the mountain. Contact the inn by writing 1000 Panoramic Highway, Mill Valley, CA 94941 or by calling (415) 388–9955. Reservations can be made by calling (510) 658–6534.

Camping is also available within Mount Tamalpais State Park on a first-come, first-served basis. For more information, contact the park headquarters at Pantoll, 801 Panoramic Highway, Mill Valley, CA 94941; (415) 388–2070.

a water tank, and the Miller Trail, all on the right (north) side of the trail.

At about 6 miles, the trail switches back around the West Point Inn. The inn has offered hospitality to mountain visitors since it was built in 1904, and provides the perfect setting for hikers or cyclists to stop, rest, enjoy the spectacular views, and perhaps, if you are done climbing, to picnic before returning down the same route. A number of other trails also depart from this spot, including the Matt Davis Trail and the Old Stage Road, which leads the Pantoll junction. With a good map and some time, you can explore these other routes.

To continue on the Old Railroad Grade, round the broad switch-back, passing behind the West Point Inn's cabins, and head east, climbing above the wooded canyons that stretch down toward Mill Valley. Another couple of miles of easy climbing, during which you will pass the Miller and Tavern Trail junctions, leads to the end of the grade on East Ridgecrest Boulevard. Go right (east) on the paved highway, which climbs steeply in spots, to the summit area parking lot. A fragment of the railroad is on the west side of the East Peak, which you can climb to stand on the summit and bask in the vistas and a profound feeling of accomplishment.

Unless you've arranged for a shuttle, you must return the way you came, or you can choose one of many alternative trails for the descent.

Tiburon Linear Park

Scanning the western and southern horizons from this shoreline rail-trail, hikers, cyclists, and skaters will be treated to views of Mount Tamalpais, the wooded hills of Sausalito, and the shimmering skyline of San Francisco.

Activities:

Location: Tiburon, Marin County

Length: 2.1 miles of the 2.7-mile trail are on the abandoned railroad grade.

Surface: Asphalt with a walkway of crushed stone running alongside

Wheelchair access: The trail is entirely wheelchair accessible.

Difficulty: Easy

Food: There is no food available along the trail itself, but once you arrive in Tiburon, restaurants, delis, and markets offer a variety of gastronomic temptations.

Rest rooms: There are rest rooms available at the Blackies Pasture trailhead. Public rest rooms are also available in the ferry terminal for the Blue and Gold Fleet in Tiburon.

Seasons: The trail is wonderful year-round.

Access and parking: To reach either trailhead from U.S. Highway 101 in Mill Valley, take the Tiburon Boulevard (California 131) exit. Go east on Tiburon Boulevard to Blackies Pasture Road, which is on the right (south) side of the highway along the waterfront. The Tiburon end point is about 3 miles farther south, also on the waterfront.

There is a large parking area at Blackies Pasture, but extremely limited parking in downtown Tiburon, which is often congested with tourists.

Transportation: Golden Gate Transit buses serve the Tiburon area. Contact the transit service at (415) 455–2000 or visit the GGT Web site at www.golden gate.org.

Rentals: There are no rentals available along the trail.

Contact: Tony Iacopi, Director of the Tiburon Public Works Department, (415) 435–7399. Tiburon Town Hall, 1505 Tiburon Boulevard, Tiburon, CA 94920; (415) 435–7373.

• •

The views from this rail-trail, which winds through Tiburon Linear Park, couldn't be any richer. The trail runs along Richardson Bay, which branches off of San Francisco Bay. Across the bay to the west, the sparkling white buildings of Sausalito glisten among the dark woods that cloak the hills. The tips of the towers of the Golden Gate Bridge rise above these hills, simple and elegant. Beyond Belvedere, its gentle slopes garnished with lavish homes, the jagged skyline of San Francisco glints above the bay waters.

Traveling back along the path, the reclining profile of the Sleeping Lady, Mount Tamalpais, dominates the view. The mountain's lower flanks shimmer with sunlight reflected off the windows of homes tucked into the woods of Mill Valley, and Richardson Bay laps calmly on the beach to the west.

And to the north? Well, the homes of Tiburon, neat and quite lovely, are perched over the trail and bay, allowing residents to live with the spectacular views that visitors only revel in for a short time.

The path follows the route of the Northwestern Pacific Railroad, which provided passenger service through Marin County and points north from the early 1900s to the 1930s. At the south end of the trail, in downtown Tiburon, you will pass the depot, which was just one of many stops on the rail line that ran from San Francisco to Duncan Mills in the north.

The Tiburon Linear Park Trail offers views of Richardson Bay and the surrounding hills.

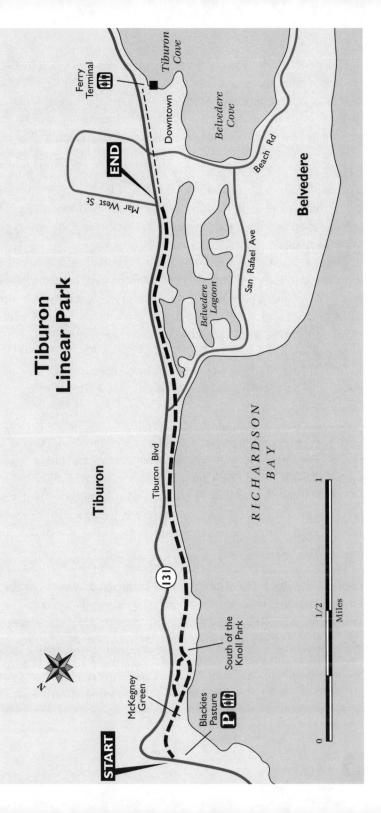

The route is described beginning in Blackies Pasture. The broad path leads across Shapero Bridge at 0.1 mile to McKegney Green, where the trail forks, leading either bayside around the green or up and to the northeast of the broad lawn. A series of interpretive signs, describing the ecology of the bay and its environs, lines this section of the path.

McKegney Green presents the perfect site for a game of Frisbee or kite flying, and also offers a parcourse to those who are interested in a well-rounded workout. The lower trail leads to a trio of benches that look out over Belvedere and San Francisco Bay, then fades to dirt as it skirts a knoll that separates it briefly from the paved path to the northeast.

To remain on the pavement, take the high road, which passes behind the knoll that separates the trail from the bay. Tucked in the lee of the hill is a small park known as South of the Knoll Park. It offers visitors a tot lot and a large grassy area upon which to relax. The lawn gradually narrows until the trail ends up tucked between Tiburon Boulevard and the bay. A strip of beach allows trail users to fish or rest and contemplate the views. Benches, garbage cans, and a couple of water fountains line the trail as it continues south, offering virtually unbroken views for the next mile or so.

At about the 1.5-mile mark, you will cross Lagoon Road at a stoplight. The path continues on the south side of the road, leaving the bay views behind as it dives into a bower of trees and blooming oleander that buffers the trail from the adjacent boulevard.

At 1.9 miles, pass a roadside parking lot and another small green studded with a couple of benches on the west. Just 0.2 mile beyond, the trail splits; stay right, and proceed to the end of the trail proper, at Mar West Street.

You can turn around here, but if you've come this far, you ought to sample the pleasures of downtown Tiburon. A bike route has been delineated alongside the boulevard, and sidewalks offer pleasant roadside walking. At 2.4 miles, you will cross Beach Road, and at 2.6 miles, you will reach the train depot. At trail's end, at 2.7 miles, you will arrive at the ferry terminal for the Blue and Gold Fleet and other transbay lines. Yet another small green overlooks Angel Island and San Francisco in the distance. Follow the same route back to the trailhead.

12 Mill Valley–Sausalito Path

Traveling from the base of Mount Tamalpais in the north to the Sausalito shoreline in the south, the Mill-Valley Sausalito Path traverses the wetlands of Richardson Bay, where egrets, herons and other seabirds forage at low tide. The path also passes the San Francisco Bay Model, a fascinating exhibit that demonstrates the dynamics of the bay.

Activities:

Location: From Mill Valley to Sausalito in Marin County

Length: 3.5 miles one way

Surface: Asphalt with a parallel path of crushed stone in some sections

Wheelchair access: The entire trail is wheelchair accessible.

Difficulty: Moderate, only because of the trail's length

Food: Savory meals are available at either end point of this trail. Both Mill Valley and Sausalito harbor eateries that range from fast-food outlets to gourmet burrito joints to upscale restaurants requiring reservations weeks in advance. It's a diner's delight.

Rest rooms: Facilities are available in the various parks along the bike path, including Bayfront Park in Mill Valley and Earl F. Dunfy Park in Sausalito.

Seasons: The trail can be traveled year-round.

Access and parking: The best parking is at the north end of the rail-trail in Mill Valley, where you will find a small lot at Edna Maguire School, and more parking along the quiet residential streets that bound the school grounds. Limited parking is available at the Sausalito end point: There is a downtown parking lot, but because of the town's popularity with tourists, it is often full.

To reach the northern end point of the trail at Edna Maguire School from U.S. Highway 101 in Mill Valley, take the East Blithedale Avenue exit and follow East Blithedale east for 0.7 mile to Lomita Drive. Turn right (north) on Lomita Drive, and follow it for 0.6 mile to the Edna Maguire School. The parking area is on the left (west), but you can also park on the streets nearby.

To reach the southern end point in Sausalito from U.S. Highway 101 at the north end of the Golden Gate Bridge, take the Sausalito exit and follow Bridgeway through the heart of town to the parking lot at Plaza Vina Del Mar. The lot is on the right (north) side of the road.

Transportation: Golden Gate Transit offers service between Sausalito and Mill Valley. Call (415) 455–2000 or visit the GGT Web site at www.golden gate.org.

Rentals: In Sausalito, the Sausalito Cyclery offers rentals; call (415) 332–3200. For Sausalito Mountain Bike Rentals, call (415) 331–4448.

Contact: Steve Petterle, Parks, Open Space & Cultural Services Department, Marin County Civic Center, San Rafael, CA 94903; (415) 499–6387.

• •

From the base of Mount Tamalpais to the edge of San Francisco Bay, from the quaint neighborhoods of Mill Valley to bustling downtown Sausalito, this rail-trail exemplifies perfectly the contrasts of a trail corridor that is both scenic and urban.

It begins in a forsaken tangle of blackberry and poison oak, skims through the manicured lawns of a neat suburban park, passes the shallow waters of Richardson Bay, where snowy egrets and other waterfowl do their best to ignore the hum of nearby traffic as they forage, then rams through civilization proper, briefly paralleling busy U.S. Highway 101 before plunging into the heart of historic Sausalito. It ends with postcard views of the bay and city of San Francisco, amid the sights and sounds that draw tourists from around the world to the cosmopolitan enclaves surrounding the Golden Gate.

The trail follows the former bed of the Northwestern Pacific Railroad, an interurban rail service that operated throughout the north bay counties of Marin and Sonoma. The electric line operated between 1903 and the early 1940s, and the trail was constructed in the late 1970s and early 1980s.

Keep in mind that cycling on the trail, while infinitely satisfying on the stretches in Mill Valley, is not easy when the trail merges with the crowded sidewalks of Sausalito. If you plan to ride or skate, consider stashing the bikes and the skates once you reach Gate 6 Road.

From the Edna Maguire School end point, a trail sign points you west of the school and onto the path, which is reached in 0.2 mile via a rough paved access road. Once on the paved path, you can either go left (south) toward the Sausalito end point, or head right (north) to the trail's true beginning.

If you choose to start from the beginning, go 0.1 mile north to Vasco Court; there is limited parking and trail access at this inter-

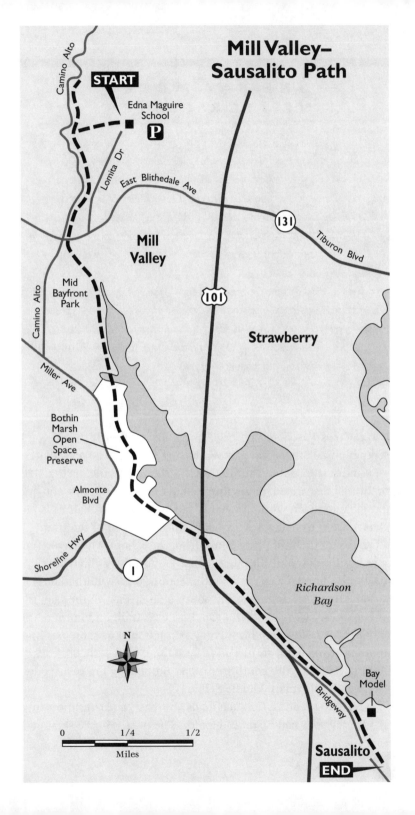

THE BAY MODEL
VISITOR CENTER

Get an inside look at the waterworks of San Francisco Bay by visiting the San Francisco Bay Model, which is located adjacent to the Mill Valley–Sausalito rail trail. This scale-model reconstruction of the bay and its delta allows both scientists and the public to observe the dynamics of tides and other influences on the bay. The model itself, built by the U.S. Army Corps of Engineers in 1956 and expanded in later years, is the centerpiece of the Bay Model Visitor Center, but there are other historic and environmental exhibits at the center as well.

The Bay Model Visitor Center is located at 2001 Bridgeway, but is reached via Harbor Road; follow the small brown-and-white Bay Model signs. The model is open from 9:00 a.m. to 4:00 p.m. Tuesday to Friday, and 10:00 A.M. to 6:00 P.M. on Saturday during the summer; winter hours are 9:00 A.M. to 4:00 P.M. Tuesday to Saturday, except holidays. There is no fee. Call (415) 332–3870 for more information.

section. Cross Vasco and proceed north for another 0.15 mile on a dirt double-track that soon narrows to single-track in an area that remains moist and muddy through winter and into the spring. The Alto Tunnel lies ahead, but is impossible to see from trail's end and impossible to reach without a hardy bushwhack. It's a half mile out and back from the Maguire School to this end point of the trail.

The rest of the trail heads south from the school. The paved trail slopes gently downhill through a shady and flower-filled corridor bordered by homes to a major intersection at East Blithedale and Camino Alto at 0.7 mile. On the south side of East Blithedale, the trail becomes part of the San Francisco Bay Trail, and borders the marsh in Mill Valley's Bayfront Park. At 1.0 mile, pass more parking, for both trail and park, at the end of Sycamore, which can be reached by taking Camino Alto south from East Blithedale and turning left (east) at the Mill Valley Middle School.

Pass a dog run and a trail that leads left (east) and over the bridge to Bayfront Park's ball fields and tot lot. The next 1.5-mile section of trail meanders through the marshes of the park, with glorious views of Mount Tamalpais, the wooded hills overlooking south Mill Valley and Sausalito, and the shimmering waters of Richardson Bay, which are frequented by snowy egrets, great blue herons, and other seabirds.

At 2.5 miles, the trail passes under the Richardson Bridge and emerges next to Highway 101. The route is wedged between the freeway and the bay for a short stint, eventually breaking away from the highway to border Bridgeway, Sausalito's main artery. Looking north toward the waterfront yields views of sailboats and fishing boats bobbing at docks and moorings, and across the bay to the extravagant homes of Tiburon and Belvedere.

At 3.3 miles you'll cross Gate 6 Road. At this point, walking is easier and more pleasant than cycling or skating. Shops and restaurants line Bridgeway, which follows the route of the railroad. At Napa Street (4.6 miles) the sidewalk splits, and riding or skating is a bit easier. Just beyond Napa and to the left (north and bayside) rise the grassy hummocks of Earl F. Dunfy Park, which invites both rest and picnics.

The rail-trail proper ends after 3.5 miles, but if you've come this far, there's no point in missing the action in Sausalito. Reaching the heart of the town is simple—just continue along Bridgeway for another mile and a half. On summer weekends, you'll find the sidewalks crammed with people speaking a mélange of languages and gazing into the dazzling windows of charming bayfront shops. Just beyond the central shopping district, views open of San Francisco Bay and its forested islands, and of the glamorous city that glistens on the hills south of the Golden Gate. You can enjoy these views in greater peace by visiting off-season and during the week, but truly, half the fun is watching the people.

13   Lands End Trail

Riding high on the cliffs overlooking the mouth of San Francisco Bay, the Lands End Trail offers unbeatable views of the Golden Gate Bridge, the most famous landmark of the city by the bay.

Activities:

Note: Mountain biking is limited due to steep staircases around cliff areas that require riders to portage their bikes.

Location: San Francisco, San Francisco County

Length: 2 miles one-way

Surface: Dirt

Wheelchair access: Wheelchair users have access to short sections of the trail at either end point, but the middle of the trail has been damaged by weather, narrows to single-track in spots, and includes a long staircase.

Difficulty: Moderate. The trail isn't long, but it includes steep stairs and uneven trail surfaces.

Food: There is no food available along the route, but San Francisco is famous for its fine dining.

Rest rooms: There are rest rooms at the U.S.S. *San Francisco Memorial* parking lot.

Seasons: The trail can be used year-round, but it is best to avoid Lands End during periods of heavy rainfall. Erosion has already taken its toll on the grade, which suffered quite a bit of damage during the El Niño winter of 1997–1998. Repairs have been made, but erosion, which is always worse when trails are used while muddy, constantly wears away at the spectacular cliffs of these headlands.

Access and parking: To reach the Point Lobos trailhead from the toll plaza on U.S. Highway 101 at the Golden Gate Bridge, take Lincoln Boulevard south and west to El Camino Del Mar. Follow El Camino Del Mar west, passing through the Lincoln Park Golf Course. At Legion of Honor Drive, turn left (south), passing the Palace of the Legion of Honor, to Clement Street. Go right (west) on Clement Street to its intersection with 48th Avenue and El Camino Del Mar. From here, you can go right (north) to the San Francisco Memorial parking area or, to reach the trailhead proper, go left (south) on El Camino Del Mar for less than 0.1 mile to Point Lobos Avenue. Turn right

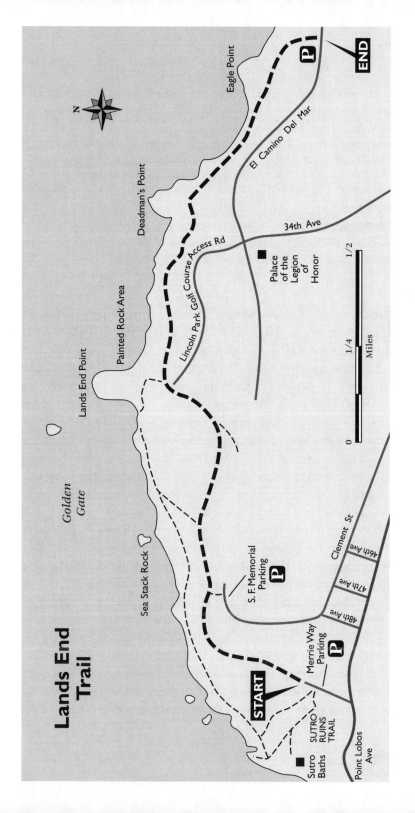

(west) on Point Lobos Avenue, and then turn right (north) almost immediately into the parking lot.

There is limited streetside parking at the El Camino Del Mar end point; it's best to begin at the Point Lobos trailhead, where there is generous parking in the Merrie Way lot.

Transportation: MUNI, San Francisco's municipal rail and bus service, offers transit services to the area, and can be reached by calling (415) 673–MUNI. Golden Gate Transit offers service to the Golden Gate National Recreation area as well; call (415) 455–2000 or visit the GGT Web site at www.golden gate.org.

Rentals: No rentals are available near the trail.

Contact: Mike Percy, Golden Gate National Recreation Area, Fort Mason, Building 201, San Francisco, CA 94123; (415) 561–4512.

• •

I t's not often that a man-made structure can compete with the elegance, grace, and beauty of the natural world. And it is no small feat when such a structure vies honorably with the majestic landscape at the mouth of San Francisco Bay. But the Golden Gate Bridge does just that. Because of its remarkable architecture, it transforms competition into compliment, so that the Golden Gate, lovely as it is, cannot be envisioned without its equally lovely bridge.

Both bridge and landscape are showcased along the Lands End Trail. This trail follows the former bed of a steam-powered railroad that was originally established by Adolph Sutro, one-time mayor of San Francisco. The railroad was operated by a number of companies, including the Cliff House and Ferries Railway, from the 1880s to 1925, when landslides, which had plagued the area for years, finally forced the closure of the line. As former National Park Service ranger Dennis R. Glass notes in the history of the Lands End railroad lines that he has compiled, this closure was "the end of a rail era and the beginning of . . . public access" to the area.

After years of limited public access, the newly established Golden Gate National Recreation Area (GGNRA) cleaned up Lands End and opened the trail to the public in the mid-1970s. To quote Glass: "It is a site historically and presently for re-creation of the spirit."

The path, which circles crumbling cliffs with views of the narrow passage from the Pacific Ocean into San Francisco Bay, is part of the 9.1-mile Coastal Trail maintained by the GGNRA, which spreads north to include the spectacular Marin Headlands and abuts the Point Reyes National Seashore.

From the north end of the Merrie Way parking lot at Point Lobos, head up the wide, obvious grade to the right (north). The open canopies of cypress trees shade the trail and break the incessant wind that blows off the Pacific; the muffled roar of the ocean is a soothing companion for the entirety of the trail. Ignore narrow spur trails that branch off the main path. At the first major trail intersection, less than a quarter mile into the hike, go up and left (north) on the railroad grade.

The trail circles east to a staircase that leads up and south to the parking area at the U.S.S. *San Francisco Memorial*. Views of both the craggy coastline guarding the mouth of the bay and of the Golden Gate Bridge open as the path bends eastward. The hillsides are thick with cypress, but an abundance of wildflowers can be found along the trail, glowing orange and pink beneath the green-bordering-on-black foliage of the evergreens. The trail is laid in a strip of wilderness that separates the city from the wind-whipped edge of the continent.

Cypress trees frame views of the craggy coastline, which can be seen from the Lands End Trail.

Two hikers take a brisk walk on the Lands End Trail.

As you near the half-mile mark, the trail passes below the edifices of the Veterans Administration Memorial Hospital. Spur trails branch left and right; stay on the main, obvious track. A bit further, a paved road drops to the rail-trail; stay left (east and seaward) on the dirt route.

At about 0.75 mile, you'll reach the Painted Rock Cliff, where danger signs warn you to stay on the maintained path. Go up and right (southeast) on a long flight of railroad-tie steps; a bench at the halfway point on the staircase is a nice spot from which to enjoy the views. At the top of the stairs, rest before descending through eucalyptus and spindly Bishop pines to a trail intersection. Go left (northeast), back toward the ocean.

Once on the cliff again, views open of the Golden Gate. Bowers of cypress arc over the path, and the exclusive homes of Sea Cliff, with the beach below, can be seen. It's a bonanza of color on a clear day; the brick-red of the bridge, the pastels of the homes, the smoky green-blue of the ocean, the bleached sails of boats in the bay.

As you approach trail's end at about 2 miles, the path narrows again, and is bounded by thick underbrush. The rail-trail leads to the edge of the Lincoln Park Golf Course near the Palace of the Legion of Honor. A wooden overlook at Eagle's Point offers yet another chance to savor the views before you retrace your steps to the Point Lobos trailhead.

Black Diamond Mines Regional Preserve Railroad Bed Trail

Mount Diablo dominates the skyline of the East Bay, and forms the bedrock upon which the rail-trail in Black Diamond Mines Regional Preserve is built. The trail, short and sweet, leads to an abundance of historic sites within the preserve.

Activities:

Location: Black Diamond Mines Regional Preserve, Contra Costa County

Length: 1 mile one-way

Surface: Dirt

Wheelchair access: The trail is not wheelchair accessible. Although the incline is relatively flat, the trail's surface is very rough.

Difficulty: Easy

Food: There is no food available along the trail or in the park, but ample food outlets, from fast food to restaurants to grocery stores, can be found a few miles east of the preserve in Pittsburg and Antioch.

Rest rooms: Rest rooms are available at the park office, which is near the lower end of the trail. There are no rest rooms at the trail's upper end.

Seasons: The trail is accessible year-round, but the path may be muddy after rains during the winter months.

Access and parking: To reach the park from California 4 in Antioch, take the Somersville Road exit. Go south on Somersville Road for 1.6 miles to where the road enters the Black Diamond Mines Regional Preserve. Go another mile up the canyon to the park entrance station. The lower trailhead for the Railroad Bed Trail is located here, at the south end of the large parking lot on the east side of Somersville Road. Head up the canyon for another mile to reach the upper parking area, where you will also find a good-size parking lot, a corral, and picnic sites. The parking is plentiful at both trailheads.

Transportation: There is no public transportation available within the park.

Rentals: There are no rental facilities in the park.

Contact: East Bay Regional Park District, 2950 Peralta Oaks Court, P.O. Box 5381, Oakland, CA 94605-5381; (510) 544–2611 or 635–0135.

• •

The foothills of Mount Diablo fold into steep, shadowy canyons shaded by the occasional oak tree and carpeted in tall grasses and wildflowers. In the winter, rain feeds these grasses, encouraging them to blush a vivid green; in summer, drought dries them golden and brittle.

This is the setting of the short rail-trail that leads into Black Diamond Mines Regional Preserve. Although the trail itself is not breathtaking, it links with a trail system within the park that is rich in history and natural beauty. Consider it a gateway to a greater adventure or take it on its own merits. Regardless, you'll be delighted.

The railroad that once ran along this grade served the Black Diamond mines. Black diamonds were coal, and millions of tons were extracted from these hills over a forty-year period at the end of the nineteenth century. A thriving mining district blossomed around the mines, including five towns, the remains of which lie within the 5,000-acre preserve. The rail line, operated by the Black Diamond Coal & Railroad Company, ran for nearly 6 miles from Pittsburg to Nortonville, which lies in the western section of the present-day preserve.

After the coal mines were abandoned, sand was mined in the area in the 1920s. And when those mines ceased operation, ranchers took over the hills, using the old mining equipment, including railroad ties, to help outfit their operations.

Because of its ease, this trail is perfect for children and fledgling mountain bikers. It begins beyond the gate at the south end of the parking lot near the park buildings and entrance station. The trail parallels Somersville Road as it heads up and south into the narrowing canyon. The stream that runs seasonally from the higher reaches of the park lies to the west of the road, overhung by pockets of oak trees. The rail-trail itself is entirely open to the sun and the rain, bordered only in grasses, thistles, and wildflowers. Bring plenty of water and wear a hat if you plan to hike during the heat of a summer's day.

The canyon grows ever narrower and the adjacent paved road creeps closer to the trail as you climb toward the Somersville town-

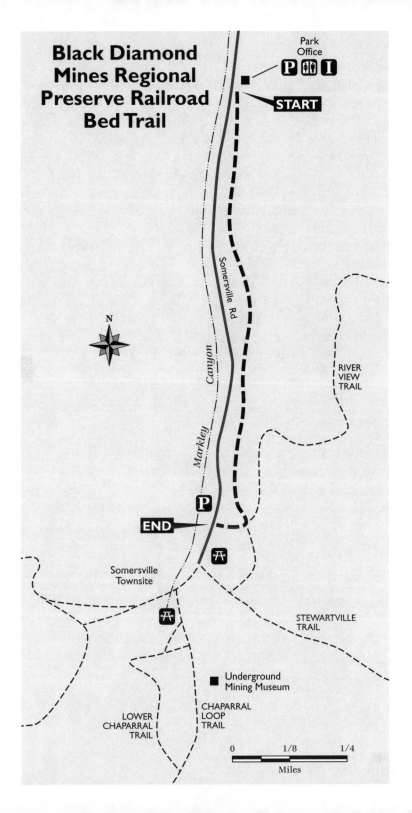

site. At about the 0.7-mile mark, the trail crosses a raised bed of gray ballast and sand. Once past this exposed section of the route, the trail drops below the elevation of Somersville Road, passing a stately shade tree. It fades from open roadbed to double track, and climbs more steeply to the picnic area and corral at 1 mile.

This is the end of the rail-trail, but there is much more to see. Another mile's worth of hiking will allow you to take a tour of the Somersville area, which includes the Underground Mining Museum, the Greathouse Portal, and the powder magazine, where explosives used in the mining process were stored.

The trailhead at the upper end point of the rail-trail also offers abundant opportunities to take longer treks or mountain bike rides into other areas of the park. You can visit the end of the Black Diamond railroad line at Nortonville, stopping at the Rose Hill Cemetery along the way, or head east to the Stewartville townsite. The park brochure, which includes some general interpretive material, is a handy tool for planning other explorations, and is available at the entry station.

Residents and visitors to three East Bay cities enjoy the amenities of this long rail-trail, which offers access to community parks and experimental gardens. The trail also features intimate contact with the modern Bay Area Rapid Transit railway system.

Activities:

Location: Berkeley, Albany, and El Cerrito in Contra Costa County

Length: 5.5 miles one way

Surface: Asphalt

Wheelchair access: The trail is entirely wheelchair accessible.

Difficulty: Moderate. This is a long trail, but it is easily broken into segments, which can reduce the difficulty.

Food: Although there are no restaurants or grocery stores along the path itself, a quick jog onto a neighboring street, especially in Albany and El Cerrito, will land you in shopping districts or malls presenting a parade of culinary outlets.

Rest rooms: There are no public rest rooms along the route.

Seasons: The trail can be used year-round.

Access and parking: To reach the Ohlone Park end point from Interstate 80 in Berkeley, take the University Avenue exit and head east on University Avenue toward the University of California at Berkeley campus. Turn left (north) on Milvia Street, and go two blocks to Hearst Avenue. Ohlone Park is on your left (west). Park along the street.

To reach the Key Boulevard end point from Interstate 80 in El Cerrito, take the San Pablo Avenue exit (California 123). Go south on San Pablo Avenue to Conlon Avenue, and turn left (east). Follow Conlon Avenue east for one block to its intersection with Key Boulevard, and turn right (south) onto Key Boulevard. The trail is located on the right (west) side of Key Boulevard. Again, park along the street.

Transportation: The San Francisco Bay Area Rapid Transit (BART) tracks fly directly overhead, offering the perfect opportunity for folks to travel the rail-trail and then ride the train back to either end point. BART can be reached at P.O. Box 12688, Oakland, CA 94606-2688. The phone number for the Oakland/Berkeley area is (510) 465–2278; for the Richmond/El

Cerrito area, call (510) 236–2278. The Web site is www.bart.gov. A/C Transit also provides service in the area. Call (510) 891–4777 or check the Web site at www.actransit.dst.ca.us.

Rentals: There are no rental shops on the path.

Contact: The trail passes through three cities. The contact for Berkeley is Brad Ricards, Landscape Architect, Parks and Waterfront Department, Park Design Division, City of Berkeley, 2201 Dwight Way, Berkeley, CA 94704; (510) 665–3455. For the Albany section, contact Judy Lieberman, Environment Resources Coordinator, Community Development Department, City of Albany, 1000 San Pablo Avenue, Albany, CA 94706; (510) 528–5766. In El Cerrito, contact Bruce King, Manager of the City of El Cerrito's Maintenance and Engineering Department, 10890 San Pueblo Avenue, El Cerrito, CA 94530; (510) 215–4382.

· ·

Although it has a distinctly urban flavor, the Ohlone Greenway, also known as the Santa Fe Greenway, toys with being a recreational trail. Its utilitarian worth is obvious: The trail allows workers and students to walk or ride from their homes to jobs or the University of California at Berkeley. But on any sunny day, you'll also find joggers, cyclists, families out for a stroll, and people walking their dogs on the route. From diapers to Lycra to three-piece suits, you'll see it all along the Ohlone Greenway.

Except for a short section in Berkeley, the trail runs directly beneath the elevated tracks of the San Francisco Bay Area Rapid Transit (BART). The trains are relatively quiet, but their passage never permits you to forget that you travel on a rail-trail. The route is nicely landscaped for its entire distance, passing through parks and past a couple of community gardens, and is long enough to give those seeking a workout just what they are looking for.

The trail is described here from south (Berkeley) to north (El Cerrito), but it is crossed by numerous city streets, and can be accessed from any of these points.

Ohlone Park, which, like the rail-trail, is named for the native peoples that once populated the Bay Area, is an extremely pleasant origin or conclusion for the trail. Basically a swath of greenery plunked in the middle of a quiet residential neighborhood, it offers a tot lot, basketball courts, and narrow fields that are nonetheless perfectly

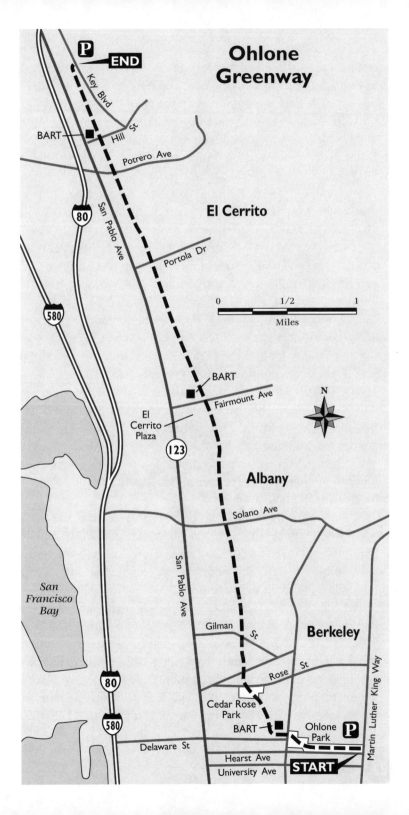

suited for a pickup game of soccer or Frisbee. The asphalt path heads west through the park, weaving back and forth to other meandering paths, until the park ends at the intersection of Delaware and Sacramento Streets, at the North Berkeley BART station.

Follow the bike lane that runs along Delaware Street for two blocks to its intersection with Acton Street, and turn right (north), following the signs for the Ohlone Greenway. Go two blocks along Acton Street to its junction with Virginia Street. The signed Ohlone Greenway takes off from the northwest corner of the intersection at about the 0.3-mile mark.

The trail weaves across several quiet streets, passing basketball courts that ring with the sounds of men and women at play, to Cedar Rose Park at 0.5 mile. Another tot lot and a rolling lawn invite rest and fun.

At about the 0.8-mile mark, you will cross Peralta Avenue and pass two community gardens: The Karl Linn Garden is on the northeast side of the road, and the Peralta Community Garden is opposite, adjacent to the continuation of the trail.

The BART tracks rise up to meet the trail, then climb overhead. You pass underneath them at the intersection of Curtis and Gilman Streets at 1 mile. Cross the busy intersection with care, and continue on the rail-trail into the city of Albany.

At 1.2 miles you will cross Codornices Creek. The street intersections that follow require concentration, especially the Solano Avenue crossing at about 1.7 miles.

The trail is nicely landscaped beneath the shade of the tracks, and features a parcourse for those who want to add a few crunches or pull-ups to their walking or running routine. Pedestrians can avoid bicycle and skate traffic by stepping onto a winding dirt walkway that parallels the main paved route.

Enter the city of El Cerrito at the 2.4-mile mark, and pass the El Cerrito Plaza BART station and the intersection with a link to the Bay Trail at Fairmount Avenue. Although the stretches of trail between street crossings become longer, and the streets seem less busy, these crossings demand you use caution.

Pass a retaining wall painted in splashes of green and blue, and another parcourse that runs along the rail-trail. The trail's character

The Ohlone Greenway begins in lovely little Ohlone Park.

changes as it passes from city to city, with the major difference between the El Cerrito and Albany sections being the landscaping; El Cerrito's is a bit more rustic than Albany's. Instead of manicured plants and shrubs, you'll encounter more opportunistic flora. In spring the trail is sprinkled with the brilliant orange blooms of poppies and the vivid yellows and greens of clover, as well as the riotous colors of calla lilies and other plants that have escaped the confines of gardens. Trail signs become more frequent in El Cerrito as well, pointing the way to the local library and other public facilities that can be reached from the trail.

As you near the 4-mile mark, you will enter a section of trail designated a Dinosaur Forest. No dinosaurs were present when I passed; the name actually refers to some prehistoric-looking plants that grow in the area. The section of trail between Schmidt Lane and Potrero Avenue is the site of another unique plant environment. In the Urban Forest Demonstration Area, a wide variety of exotic trees and shrubs has been planted; they are marked with small interpretive signs.

You will reach Hill Street at the 4.6-mile mark and pass the El Cerrito Del Norte BART station. Beyond the station the trail skirts the parking lot for a neighboring apartment building, then climbs to Baxter Creek, which is nicely accented with small, well-tended flower beds. The creek is the subject of a preservation effort by a grassroots organization called Friends of Baxter Creek. Part of that effort involves promoting an extension of the Ohlone Greenway along the creek to the San Francisco Bay Trail. If you'd like more information about the organization, call (510) 236–5351 or (510) 237–7968.

Until such an extension is reality, however, the trail ends just past the creek on Key Boulevard at about the 5.5-mile mark. Either return as you came or backtrack to the BART station and catch a ride back to Berkeley.

A short description for a trail of this length will, of necessity, resemble the proverbial laundry list. Oak-shaded greenbelts that run through quiet neighborhoods, modern business districts and quaint shopping districts, long stretches that will work the muscles of the most dedicated athlete, sunshine, rolling hills—the Iron Horse Trail adds up to a wonderful recreational experience.

Activities:

Location: Alameda and Contra Costa Counties

Length: 23 miles are currently in place, but plans call for the trail to be extended south to the Dublin–Pleasanton BART station, and then east to the San Joaquin county line, for a total distance of 35 miles.

Surface: Asphalt and concrete with a parallel dirt walkway in some areas

Wheelchair access: The trail is accessible to wheelchairs for its entirety.

Difficulty: Hard if taken as a whole, but when broken into smaller chunks, the rail-trail is easy to moderate.

Food: There are innumerable places to pick up a bite to eat along the northern reaches of the trail. You will find grocery stores, fast-food joints, snazzy restaurants, and coffeehouses at the trail's midpoint in the Danville area. South of Danville, the trail passes through more residential areas; it is not until you reach the mall at Alcosta Boulevard that you again encounter convenient eats.

Rest rooms: There are a few public rest rooms scattered along the trail, at the BART station and Walden Park in Walnut Creek, at Hap McGee Park in Danville, and at the San Ramon Community Center and Park in San Ramon.

Seasons: This paved route is accessible year-round.

Access and parking: The trail parallels Interstate 680 through the towns and cities of Concord, Pleasant Hill, Walnut Creek, Alamo, Danville, and San Ramon. It can be accessed at numerous points along its route. There is limited parking at the Monument Boulevard trailhead, which is located east of I–680 on Monument Boulevard at Mohr Lane. You can also pick up the trail at the Walnut Creek BART station on Treat Boulevard; this too is east of I–680, with parking located to the north of the station on Coggins Drive.

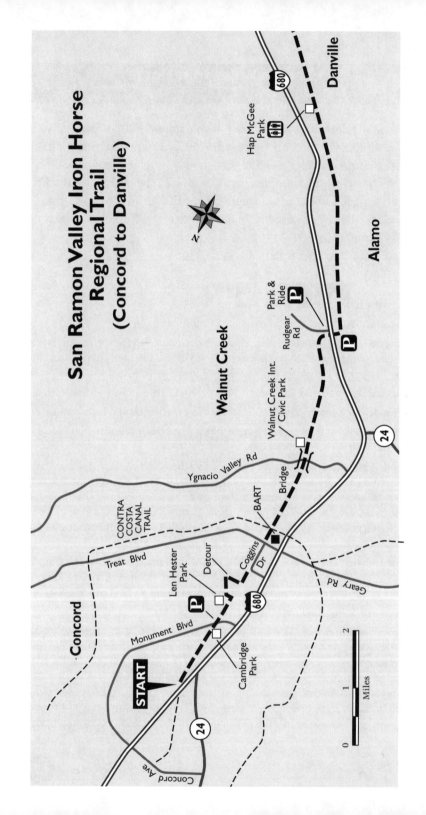

San Ramon Valley Iron Horse Regional Trail
(Concord to Danville)

Danville

Alamo

680

Hap McGee Park

N

Park & Ride

P

P

Rudgear Rd

Walnut Creek

24

Walnut Creek Int. Civic Park

Ygnacio Valley Rd

CONTRA COSTA CANAL TRAIL

Bridge

BART

Treat Blvd

Len Hester Park

Detour

Coggins Dr

Geary Rd

P

680

Monument Blvd

Concord

START

Cambridge Park

24

Concord Ave

0   1   2
Miles

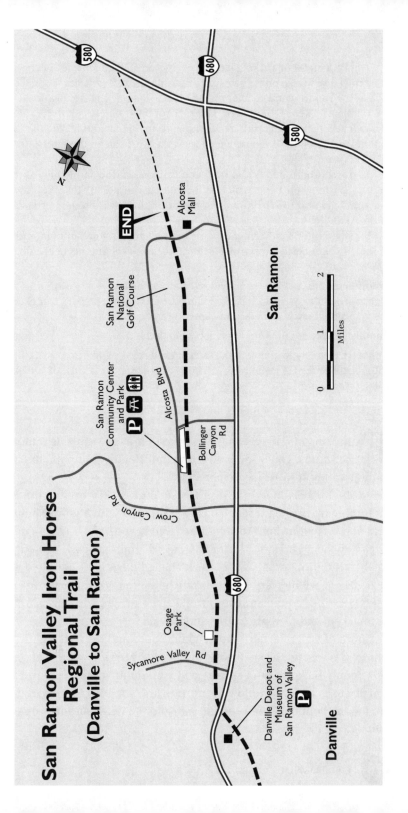

The Park-and-Ride parking lot on the east side of the interstate at Rudgear Road in Danville also offers good parking and trail access. Cross to the west side of the freeway and go about 25 yards north along the frontage road to the trailhead. There is limited parking right at the trailhead at this location. You can also pick up the trail in downtown Danville, near the Danville Depot on West Prospect Avenue, which is on the west side of the interstate at Diablo Road.

At the southern end of the trail, you can park at the San Ramon Community Center and Park, which is located east of I–680. Take Bollinger Canyon Road east toward Alcosta Boulevard; the park is on the north side of the road.

Finally, at the southern end point in San Ramon, you can hop on the trail near the Alcosta Mall, which is located east of the interstate on Alcosta Boulevard.

Transportation: A/C Transit provides service in the area. Call (510) 891–4777 for bus schedules, write to 1600 Franklin Street, Oakland, CA 94612, or check the Web site at www.actransit.dst.ca.us.

Rentals: There are no rentals available along the trail.

Contact: East Bay Regional Park District, 2950 Peralta Oaks Court, P.O. Box 5381, Oakland, CA 94605-5381; (510) 544–2611 or (510) 635–0135; www.ebparks.org.

• •

From Silicon Valley–esque business districts to trailside lemonade stands, you'll see it all along the friendly and popular San Ramon Valley Iron Horse Regional Trail.

At its northern end, the Iron Horse Trail is very urban, almost metropolitan, passing through business districts with high-rise buildings and busy four-lane roads. At its center, in Alamo and Danville (arguably the prettiest section of the trail), the rail-trail passes through wealthy suburbia on a swath of oak-shaded pavement bordered by lush grasses, wildflowers, and well-kept homes on quiet streets. Downtown Danville is quaint and also well kept, outfitted with upscale supermarkets and pleasant coffee shops.

South of Danville, both the neighborhoods and the trail are more exposed. Gone are the shady oaks, replaced by a wide treeless greenbelt upon which the grasses are vividly green in winter and spring, and dry to a crackling yellow in summer and fall. Wooden fences delineate the boundary between the trail and the neighborhoods on either side of it.

Beyond Crow Canyon Road, the trail passes through industrial complexes boxed neatly in glass and masonry, with large parking lots abutting the trail. At its southern terminus, the trail passes through the San Ramon National Golf Course, where trail users are protected from wayward golf balls by a bower of meshlike fencing.

The rail-trail follows the right-of-way of the Southern Pacific Railroad, which established a branch line in the San Ramon Valley in 1890 to serve the farming and ranching communities that had sprung up in the then sparsely populated area. The railroad served the valley and its burgeoning towns for about seventy years, until improved roadways through the region rendered the rail line unnecessary. The tracks were abandoned in 1975, and by the early 1980s, cities in the valley had begun to acquire the right-of-way and set it aside for a trail. By the end of the 1980s, sections of the trail had been constructed, paved, and dedicated, and the Iron Horse Trail was well on its way.

The East Bay Regional Park District (EBRPD) continues to focus on further development of the rail-trail corridor, with plans well underway (and funded) to extend the trail south and east to the San Joaquin county line. Construction on the segment south of Alcosta Boulevard was nearly completed at press time; contact the EBRPD for more information.

As mentioned above, the 25-mile-long trail can be done in its entirety or in segments. I found the section from Rudgear Road to Danville to be the prettiest—and probably the most enjoyable for hikers and runners—with the segment in San Ramon the most conducive to exercise-oriented cycling, running, and in-line skating. Every part of the trail offers wonderful recreational opportunities to neighborhood residents.

The trail is described here beginning in the north at Monument Boulevard in Concord and running southward to Alcosta Boulevard in San Ramon.

The trail crosses Monument Boulevard, heading north for about 0.5 mile, through tiny Cambridge Park and alongside the channel that holds Walnut Creek, to an underpass at Interstate 680. A fence there bars passage under the freeway; traveling this segment is an out-and-back affair.

The streetlight at Mohr Lane offers safe passage across Monument Boulevard, where you pick up the southbound trail. After crossing a railroad bridge, the trail winds south between homes and crosses a neighborhood street. Pass between the yard of a masonry supply business and a cement fence topped with barbed wire to where the formal path temporarily ends on Hookston Road at 1.4 miles.

Go left (east), then quickly right (south) onto Bancroft Road. Follow Bancroft Road south for 0.3 mile to Mayhew, turn right (west) on Mayhew, and continue for 0.3 mile to the trail, which is on the left (south) side of the road. An informational billboard with a trail map is at this junction.

The paved rail-trail proceeds south through a greenbelt between more homes until it ends again, temporarily, at 2.2 miles on Coggins Drive. Follow Coggins Drive south for about 0.5 mile, past the BART station and through the station's parking lot (the route is very well marked) to Treat Boulevard at 2.7 miles. Cross Treat Boulevard; the trail veers left (east) off the sidewalk about 0.2 mile south of this major arterial.

The next intersection is with the Contra Costa Canal Trail (3.0 miles). Continue straight (south) through the greenbelt (or goldbelt once the grasses die off in summer). At 3.1 miles you can turn right (west) to Walden Park, which features a tot lot, picnic tables, water, and rest rooms.

Beyond this trail junction, the rail-trail crosses a couple of quiet neighborhood streets. Head toward the bridge over Ygnacio Valley Road in Walnut Creek at about 4.2 miles; this is followed by a more traditional trestle bridge.

A couple of street crossings come in quick succession at about the 5-mile mark; the first at Mount Diablo Boulevard, the second leading to the west side of Newell Avenue. Beyond Newell, the trail is squeezed between apartment buildings on the west and an ivy-draped wall that serves as a barrier to South Broadway on the east.

At about 6.5 miles, you will arrive at the intersection of Rudgear Road and Interstate 680. The Park-and-Ride parking lot is on the northeast corner of the intersection. Pass under the interstate and cross the frontage road (Danville Boulevard); the trail continues about 25 yards north of the stoplight on the frontage road.

A cyclist climbs a bridge on the Iron Horse Trail.

The setting of the rail-trail now gives the impression of being almost rural, passing through an oak woodland spread with knee-high grasses and wildflowers, and bordered by large homes with tasteful fences and ornamental shrubbery. You will cross a number of small neighborhood roads before the trail's intersection with Stone Valley Road at 9 miles, where the scenery becomes more urban. Cross a bridge at Hemme Avenue. At about 10 miles, you can follow Camille Avenue left (east) to Hap McGee Park, where you will find water and rest rooms.

Cross another small bridge before Hartford Road, then travel south for another mile to West Prospect Avenue, where the Danville Depot and the Museum of San Ramon Valley border the path. The museum is open Tuesday through Friday noon to 4:00 p.m. and Saturday 10:00 a.m. to 1:00 p.m.

Now in downtown Danville, the trail circles the west side of a shopping center and drops you onto the sidewalk alongside Railroad Avenue. The safest crossing is to the north, at the stoplights at Hartz Avenue. From Hartz, backtrack along Railroad Avenue to the trail, which continues south, passing under the interstate at about the 12.5-mile mark.

By the time the rail-trail crosses Sycamore Valley Road at 13.2 miles, it has taken on a decidedly suburban aspect, passing south through a broad greenbelt that resonates with noise from the nearby freeway. From this point to the trail's terminus at Alcosta Boulevard, the rail-trail can be hot and dry—especially in summer—with no water available save that found at the San Ramon Community Center and Park, which is at about the 17.5-mile mark.

Between Sycamore Valley Road and the park, you will cross several streets, including Fostoria Road, where a large "golf ball" and power station adorn the east side of the path. Cross Crow Canyon Road as well, which is also bordered by industrial buildings. You can reach the community park from the trail via either Norris Canyon Road or Bollinger Canyon Road. At 18 miles, you will pass a park with a tot lot at Monte Video Road.

The power poles that have been shadowing the trail since Crow Canyon Road end at Pine Valley Road. At about 19.5 miles, you will reach the San Ramon National Golf Course, passing beneath the arch of fencing that protects trail users from stray golf balls.

As of press time, the trail ended at the 23-mile mark, behind the shopping center at Alcosta Boulevard, where a bridge spans San Ramon Creek. The trail will eventually continue south from the bridge, crossing the Alameda County line and heading off into the golden hills.

Rolling, grassy hills trimmed with spreading oaks form the backdrop for this long, scenic rail-trail. The route links tidy residential communities with St. Mary's College, the community park at Moraga Commons, and the more rustic trails of the neighboring watershed.

Activities:

Location: From Lafayette to Moraga in Contra Costa County

Length: 7.6 miles one-way

Surface: Asphalt and concrete

Wheelchair access: The trail is accessible to wheelchairs for its entire length, with the exception of the dirt Valle Vista Staging Area parking lot.

Difficulty: Moderate, due to the trail's length

Food: The northern part of the trail, through Lafayette's residential districts and past St. Mary's College, offers few gastronomic opportunities. Once you enter Moraga, however, you will find grocery stores and restaurants near the path.

Rest rooms: There are no rest rooms at the Olympic Boulevard Staging Area, but rest rooms are available at the Moraga Commons and at the Valle Vista Staging Area.

Seasons: The trail can be used year-round.

Access and parking: To reach the northern end point in Lafayette, take the Pleasant Hill Road exit from California 24. Go right (south) on Pleasant Hill Road for 0.9 mile to Olympic Boulevard. Go right (west) on Olympic Boulevard for about 0.1 mile to the parking area, which is on the right (north) side of the road. There is ample parking here, and at another lot located about 0.2 mile farther west on Olympic Boulevard.

To reach the Valle Vista Staging Area from California 24, take the Pleasant Hill exit, go south onto Pleasant Hill Road, then turn right (west) on Mt. Diablo Boulevard. Follow Mt. Diablo Boulevard to Moraga Road, and turn left (south). Go south on Moraga Road to St. Mary's Road, and turn left (east). Follow St. Mary's Road, which traces the route of the rail-trail, south to Canyon Road. Canyon Road continues south to the Valle Vista Staging Area parking lot.

Transportation: A/C Transit provides service in the area. Call (510) 891–4777 for bus schedules, write to 1600 Franklin Street, Oakland, CA 94612, or check the Web site at www.actransit.dst.ca.us.

Rentals: No rentals are available along the trail.

Contact: East Bay Regional Park District, 2950 Peralta Oaks Court, P.O. Box 5381, Oakland, CA 94605-5381; (510) 544–2611 or 635–0135, www.ebparks.org.

• •

The beauty of the Lafayette-Moraga Trail sneaks up on you. It has many facets: the neat and quiet neighborhoods of Lafayette, the pastoral setting of St. Mary's College, the playfulness of the Moraga Commons, the relative wildness of the Valle Vista Staging Area. Each of these facets, taken alone, has a certain sparkle, but when combined, the trail glitters with possibilities.

The rail-trail lies on the former bed of the Sacramento Northern Railroad; a scattering of railroad crossing signs hints at its past. But where passengers once let electric trolleys transport them from one destination to the next, these days hikers, cyclists, and in-line skaters propel themselves through the sun-splashed hills.

The trail is described here from north to south, but direction makes no difference, as the trail is an up-and-down affair, with the high point at the "pass" near St. Mary's College.

From the Olympic Boulevard trailhead, go west on the paved path, which meanders among the old trees of an orchard for 0.2 mile to the second parking lot at the intersection of Reliez Station Road and Olympic Boulevard. Cross Reliez Station Road to continue on the trail, which lies within a narrow greenbelt that passes between residences.

At about 0.5 mile, the trail crosses Hawthorne Drive; pass a railroad sign, then cross Foye Drive at about the 1-mile mark. Beyond, the path weaves through the Moraga Pumping Plant complex, crosses a bridge, then proceeds through more neighborhoods. A brief section of the trail is on Brookdale Court, a residential street, but resumption of the rail-trail proper is just ahead.

By the 2-mile mark, intersections with neighborhood streets are spaced a bit further apart. Pass the Las Trampas Pool complex at about 2.5 miles, and continue south.

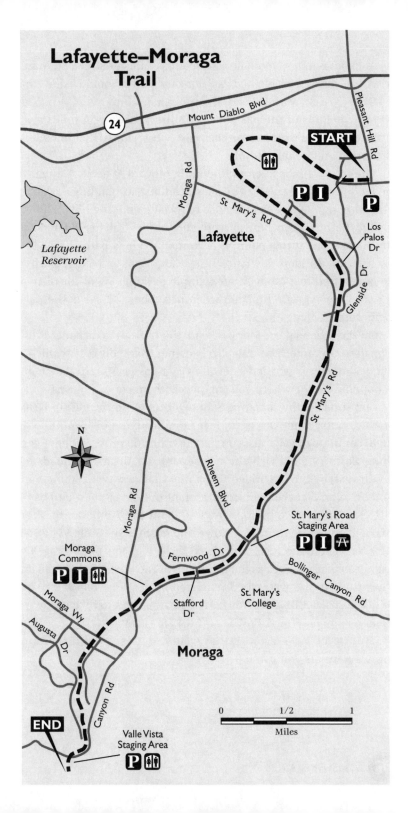

At about 3 miles, you will have to cross a busier street, St. Mary's Road. Parking is available midway along the trail at South Lucille Lane.

Once past St. Mary's Road, the trail passes into more scenic terrain in the folds of the oak-covered hills. At about 3.5 miles a waterfall drips from the rocks on the right (west) side of the trail during the spring and winter months.

The route climbs to cross Rheem Boulevard at about 4 miles. To the left (east) is the St. Mary's College campus, its buildings sparkling white among the greens and golds of the surrounding hills. There is parking for trail users here as well, and the rail-trail itself, which begins its descent at this point, is accompanied by a parcourse.

The trail wanders down to Moraga Commons at 5.5 miles, where users will find rest rooms, water, ample parking, lawns for picnicking, and a playground for the wee ones. The trail skirts the park, then crosses Moraga Road.

On the other side of Moraga Road, the trail surface changes from asphalt to concrete. The trail also becomes markedly less scenic—in fact, it's merely a glorified sidewalk—as it passes Moraga Ranch and a shopping center, where you can purchase groceries if necessary.

Continue southwest along School Street to Country Club Drive. Cross Country Club Drive; trail signs indicate the bike route forks, but to continue to Valle Vista on the rail-trail, you must go right (west) along Country Club Drive to the separate path, which heads left (southwest) before the bridge. The route snakes between homes and a creek to an S-curve behind apartment buildings, then climbs beside Canyon Road to hilltop views at about the 7-mile mark. From this high point, the trail drops down and south to the Valle Vista Staging Area. There are rest rooms here, as well as lots of parking. The staging area also serves as the trailhead for the Rocky Ridge Trail and other trails in the watershed managed by the East Bay Municipal Utility District (EBMUD). You can obtain a permit to hike in the watershed by contacting EBMUD at (510) 287–0469.

Unless you have arranged for a shuttle, this is the turnaround point. Return as you came.

18   Loma Prieta Grade

The trees within the Forest of Nisene Marks are so thick and the environment seems so pristine that it's hard to fathom the rail-trail upon which you tread was once part of an extensive logging operation in the Aptos Creek Canyon.

Activities:

Location: The Forest of Nisene Marks State Park in Aptos, Santa Cruz County

Length: 9 miles round trip

Surface: Dirt

Wheelchair access: The trail is not wheelchair accessible.

Difficulty: Hard. The rail-trail is relative steep, and completing the entire loop will take most of a day.

Food: There is no food or water available along the trail. Pack in what you will need. There are a couple of restaurants in Aptos, and lots of eateries in nearby Santa Cruz.

Rest rooms: The nearest rest rooms are located at the Porter Family Picnic Area, which is 0.2 mile south of the trailhead.

Seasons: The trail is best tackled when dry, between the months of May and October.

Access and parking: To reach the Forest of Nisene Marks State Park from California Highway 1 (the Pacific Coast Highway) in Aptos, take the State Park Drive exit. Go north on State Park Drive for 0.1 mile to Soquel Drive and turn right (east). Go 0.5 mile on Soquel Drive to Aptos Creek Road, which is just before the Aptos Station, and turn left (north). Follow Aptos Creek Road for about 0.7 mile to the Forest of Nisene Marks entrance station, where a fee is levied. The pavement ends at this point. Follow the park road another 1.2 miles to George's Picnic Area, which is the trailhead during the winter season. There is plenty of parking at the picnic area and along the park road. In the summer, you can proceed another 1.1 mile to the Porter Family Picnic Area, where you will find ample parking as well.

Transportation: There is no public transportation available within the park.

Rentals: There are no rentals near the trail. Mountain biking is not allowed on the Loma Prieta Grade Trail.

Contact: The Forest of Nisene Marks State Park can be reached by writing to the California Department of Parks and Recreation, 600 Ocean Street, Santa Cruz, CA 95060; (831) 763-7064. You also can support the park by contacting the Advocates for Nisene Marks State Park at P.O. Box 461, Aptos, CA 95001-0461.

• •

In the Forest of Nisene Marks, nature proves that it can renew itself. The original redwoods and Douglas firs that grew here, thriving on moisture from the nearby Pacific Ocean, were extensively logged in the early 1900s, but you'd never know it now. The evergreens, along with oaks, madrones, and bays, have grown back with a vengeance, creating a jungle that envelops park trails in a translucent green light. This benevolent light even shines on the trail that runs along the grade of the railroad that was used to haul the ancestor trees down and out of the canyon.

That's not to say the landscape doesn't bear the scars of the lumbering operations run by the Loma Prieta Lumber Company. Along the former Loma Prieta Railroad grade, which was used to transport logs out of the forest to the mill site and beyond, you will see a few old railroad ties half-buried in the loamy soils, and stacked at trailside. Other signs of human activity in the Aptos Creek Canyon, like the site of the Porter House and the remnants of the Loma Prieta Mill Site, still huddle in clearings amid the encroaching trees.

The railroad operated in the steep canyon beginning in 1910, and was abandoned in the early 1920s. A Dutch woman named Nisene Marks later purchased the lumber company's property, and under her ownership the forest began to revive. It was her children who donated the area to the California state parks system, in honor of their mother.

The history of the park, both natural and human-made, is documented in interpretive signs scattered along the trails, and in books and materials available from the park and from the Advocates for Nisene Marks.

As if all the logging and railroading and natural beauty weren't enough, the park is also the site of the epicenter of a major earthquake that rocked the San Francisco Bay Area in 1989. One of the other trails that wind through the park takes you past this interesting point of more modern history.

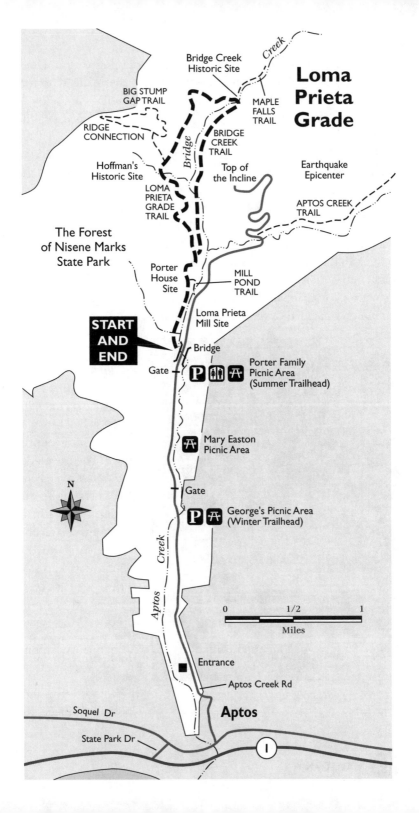

Loma Prieta Grade

Bridge Creek Historic Site

Creek

BIG STUMP GAP TRAIL

MAPLE FALLS TRAIL

RIDGE CONNECTION

BRIDGE CREEK TRAIL

Bridge

Hoffman's Historic Site

Top of the Incline

Earthquake Epicenter

LOMA PRIETA GRADE TRAIL

APTOS CREEK TRAIL

The Forest of Nisene Marks State Park

Porter House Site

MILL POND TRAIL

Loma Prieta Mill Site

START AND END

Bridge

Gate

Porter Family Picnic Area (Summer Trailhead)

Mary Easton Picnic Area

Gate

George's Picnic Area (Winter Trailhead)

N

Creek

Aptos Creek

0   1/2   1
Miles

Entrance

Aptos Creek Rd

Aptos

Soquel Dr

State Park Dr

1

The Loma Prieta Grade Trail is a lollipop loop, starting and ending about 0.4 mile beyond the gate that blocks the roadway to motor vehicles at the Porter Family Picnic Area. No bikes are allowed on the trail, and a bike rack is provided for those who pedal to the trailhead.

The grade takes off past the gate on the left (northwest) side of the main park road, with Aptos Creek running loud and clear to the right (east). The forest chatters in the almost ever present ocean breeze, which stirs the treetops, rattles the limbs, and sends cones and branches tumbling to the ground. The path is soft and duff-covered, muffling the footfalls of those who pass on it, and the shade is so thick that it's almost dark beneath the canopy, even at noon on a bright, sunny day.

Within a quarter mile, the trail narrows to a footpath etched in the mountainside, dropping through a drainage and crossing a small bridge. Climb back onto the railroad grade; a pile of moss-covered railroad ties is stashed on the right (east) side of the trail.

The Loma Prieta Grade trail burrows through a dense forest.

Continue gently upward on the grade. You'll pass a clearing that hosts the Porter House site, with its interpretive sign and bench, at about the 1.5-mile mark. A side trail leads east from here to the Aptos Creek Fire Road, which serves as the main route through the park. The rail-trail then loops through another drainage, using yet another small bridge, to the trail fork at the intersection with the Bridge Creek Trail at 1.8 miles.

You can do the loop in either direction. If you travel to the left (northwest), you will climb first to the Hoffman Historic Site, at 3.7 miles. Named for the man who was camp superintendent, and nick-named Camp Comfort, this logging camp operated between 1918 and 1921. The railroad grade was used to haul huge redwoods out of Big Tree Gulch.

Beyond the camp, the trail continues to the intersection with Big Stump Gap Trail, which leads to the ridge in the western reaches of the park. Remain on the rail-trail, which continues northward and reaches its apex as it leaves the railroad grade and makes a sharp right-hand (eastward) turn.

Drop to the Bridge Creek Historic Site at the 6-mile mark. Not much remains of this logging camp, which was washed downstream by El Niño–strengthened storms that battered California in 1982. A side trail leads left (north) off the loop at this point, and follows Bridge Creek to Maple Falls.

The next leg of the loop, which follows the Bridge Creek Trail down along the creek that bears the same name, won't rejoin the railroad grade until it nears the end of the loop and the Porter House site again. From the Bridge Creek Camp, turn right (south), and fol-low the eastern bank of Bridge Creek, which you will cross about 1.5 miles below the historic site. Pick up the railroad grade again, and continue down to the junction with the Loma Prieta Grade Trail. From here you will retrace your steps back to the trailhead and the Porter Family Picnic Area.

Tucked in a steep canyon in the hills east of San Jose, this rail-trail passes through beautiful country that once attracted visitors not simply with its natural setting, but also with mineral waters that bubbled to the surface near a creek shaded in alders and oaks.

Activities:

Location: Alum Rock Park in San Jose

Length: 1.8 miles of the 2.4-mile Creek Trail is on the abandoned railroad corridor.

Surface: The section from Penitencia Canyon to Quail Hollow Picnic Area is dirt single-track. The surface is paved from Quail Hollow to the dirt road 100 yards west of the railroad bridge, then a broad dirt track to the western border of the developed section of the park near the visitor center. The route is paved past the visitor center and Youth Sciences Institute, then narrows to a dirt track for the last mile, ending at the confluence of Penitencia and Aguague Creeks.

Wheelchair access: The paved portion of the trail is wheelchair accessible.

Difficulty: Moderate, due to the changing trail surface and the trail's length

Food: There is no food available in Alum Rock Park, so bring a picnic lunch. Water is available in the park. Nearby South Bay cities, including San Jose, offer a bonanza of grocery stores and restaurants.

Rest rooms: Facilities are available at the Eagle Rock and Quail Hollow picnic areas in the western part of the park, at the visitor center, and at the Live Oak Picnic Area in the eastern reaches of the park.

Seasons: The paved section of the trail is passable year-round. The dirt section, however, may be difficult or impassable when rains turn the surface to mud.

Access and parking: To reach the park, take the Alum Rock Avenue/California Highway 130 exit from either U.S. Highway 101 or Interstate 680 in San Jose. Go east on Alum Rock Avenue to the park entrance, which is 4.6 miles from U.S. 101 and 3.5 miles from I–680. A small fee is charged to enter the park.

To reach the west end of the rail-trail, turn left (west) at the intersection immediately north of the entrance station onto Penitencia Creek Road, and

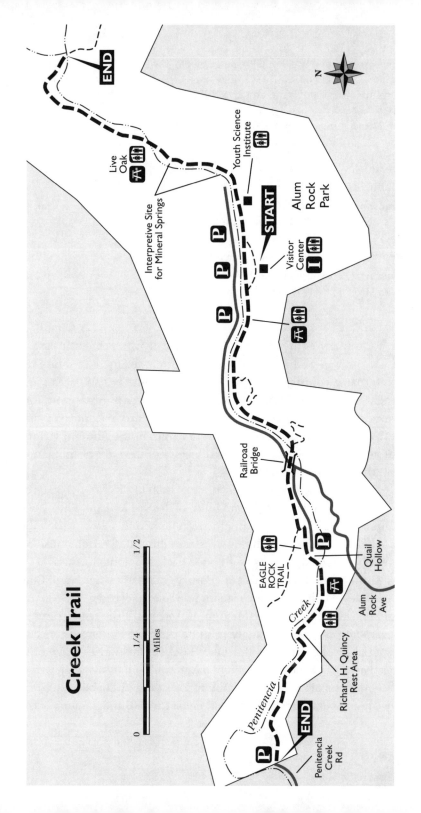

Creek Trail

0   1/4   1/2

Miles

N

END

Live Oak

Youth Science Institute

Interpretive Site
for Mineral Springs

P P

P

P

START

Visitor Center

I

Alum Rock Park

Railroad Bridge

EAGLE ROCK TRAIL

Penitencia   Creek

P

Quail Hollow

Alum Rock Ave

Richard H. Quincy
Rest Area

Penitencia Creek Rd

P

END

drive approximately 0.2 mile to the Quail Hollow Picnic Area. A Creek Trail signpost directs you over the bridge and through the picnic area; the trail continues west along the creek to the Penitencia Creek Road end point. There is plenty of parking at this location.

To reach the east end of the rail-trail, follow the main park road east for 0.6 mile from the entrance station to the large parking lot near the visitor center. The Creek Trail runs along Penitencia Creek on the north side of the visitor center. From this point, you can head either east toward the creek confluence or west toward Quail Hollow.

Transportation: Contact the Santa Clara Valley Transportation Authority by calling (408) 321–2300, or writing 3331 North First Street, San Jose, CA 95134-1906. The Web site is www.vta.org.

Rentals: No rentals are available in the park.

Contact: Rob Reynolds, Alum Rock Park, 16240 Alum Rock Avenue, San Jose, CA 95132; (408) 259–5477.

• •

Alum Rock Park, tucked in a steep canyon in the hills east of sprawling San Jose, has been a retreat for the city-weary for more than a century. Its mineral springs—some infused with soda, others smelling of sulfur—as well as a tea garden, restaurant, and dance pavilion, were among its lures in the early part of the twentieth century. These days, you cannot soak in the mineral waters, but you can enjoy the scenery and history of the park from the rail-trail that rolls through it.

The park was a popular resort from 1890 to the early 1930s. For two bits you could ride the steam trains of the San Jose and Alum Rock Railroad into the park. Apparently, riding up to the resort wasn't too bad, but the open cars behind the "steam dummies," or engines, frequently jumped the tracks on the ride back down into town.

At the turn of the twentieth century, railroad owner Hugh Center converted his Alum Rock steam line to an electric narrow-gauge line, and the railway continued to prosper until the Great Depression, when the line gradually fell into disuse. The hard times culminated for the San Jose and Alum Rock Railroad in 1934, when it was dismantled and the rails and other equipment salvaged.

Remnants of the line that couldn't be salvaged can be seen along the Creek Trail, which follows Penitencia Creek through much of the

Mineral spring grottoes can be found along the Creek Trail.

park. The flat track takes visitors past concrete abutments that once supported the tracks, and across an old trestle near Alum Rock. A forest of great variety, including buckeye, maple, walnut, and alder, lines the shores of the creek, with the steep walls of the Penitencia Creek canyon rising to grassy heights to the north and south.

The best place to begin the rail-trail is at the visitor center. The Creek Trail is the paved path wedged between the creek and the lawns fronting the visitor center. Go west on the trail, past the log

EXPLORING ALUM ROCK PARK

Although the section of the Creek Trail that heads east from the visitor center to the confluence of Penitencia and Aguague Creeks is not entirely on the railroad grade, it makes a fascinating addition to the route.

From the visitor center, follow the trail west past the greens, the Ramada, and the Youth Science Institute to the mineral springs, grottoes, and picnic area. Pools, fonts, and alcoves shelter the different mineral springs, and an interpretive display describes some park history. About a half mile from the visitor center, the trail crosses to the north side of the creek, the pavement ends, and the route narrows to single-track. Follow the gently climbing route for another half mile, amid the crackling shade of the oaks, buckeyes, and maples, to the shady overlook at the confluence of Penitencia and Aguague Creeks.

cabin. The trail's surface changes from pavement to dirt on the west side of the cabin.

The track continues west along the creek, passing intersections with the Woodland Trail at 0.2 mile and 0.5 mile. At both, stay right (west) on the old railroad bed. At about 0.8 mile, you reach the concrete trestle, which arcs around Alum Rock to an intersection with the Eagle Rock Trail. At this point, you leave the railroad bed for about 0.2 mile. Go left (south), then right (west) in a quick switchback down to Penitencia Creek Road, and follow this west to the Quail Hollow Picnic Area at 1 mile.

At Quail Hollow, cross the creek on a ramshackle bridge, then head west to pick up the trail at the western edge of the picnic area. The route narrows to single-track as it winds down the south side of Penitencia Creek, passing a couple of concrete abutments and a section of trail supported by a lovely stone retaining wall.

At about 1.8 miles, the trail leaves creekside and enters an open, rustic picnic area. A steep dirt-and-railroad-tie staircase leads down to the parking area on Penitencia Creek Road. Return along the same route to the visitor center.

MORE RAIL-TRAILS

D Larkspur–Corte Madera Path

From the banks of estuarine Corte Madera Creek to the tangled undergrowth that has wrapped itself around the long-unused Alto Tunnel, the Larkspur–Corte Madera rail-trail runs through a lovely slice of Marin County that illustrates why the area has become a desirable (and expensive) place to live.

Activities:

Location: Larkspur, Marin County

Length: 1.7 miles one-way

Surface: Asphalt and dirt

Wheelchair access: Most of the trail is paved and wheelchair accessible. The extreme southern end of the trail is dirt and narrows to overgrown single-track as you approach the Alto Tunnel.

Difficulty: Easy

Food: The trail passes through downtown Larkspur, where you will find grocery stores and both upscale and café-style dining establishments.

Rest rooms: No rest rooms are available along the route.

Seasons: The trail is passable year-round, but the dirt section of the route may be muddy during and following winter rains.

Access and parking: Parking is limited at both trailheads. To reach the southern trailhead from U.S. Highway 101 in Corte Madera, take the Tamalpais Drive exit, and head west on Tamalpais Drive, which becomes Redwood Avenue, to Corte Madera Avenue. Turn left (south) on Corte Madera Avenue, which merges into Montecito Drive. Continue south on Montecito Drive, following it for about 0.3 mile to a dirt parking area that is wedged between the roadway and the dirt trail.

To reach the northern trailhead from Highway 101 in Larkspur, take the Sir Francis Drake Boulevard exit. Go left (west) on Sir Francis Drake Boulevard to Bon Air Drive. Turn left (south) on Bon Air Drive, and go over the bridge; a paved trail takes off to the north from the right (west) side of the road. The rail-trail begins on the left (east) side of Bon Air Drive on the far side of the bridge, heading south.

Transportation: Golden Gate Transit operates buses in this area. Contact the transit service at (415) 455–2000 or visit the GGT Web site at www.golden gate.org.

Rentals: There are no rentals along the route.

Contact: Ed Manassee, Associate Planner, Town of Corte Madera, 300 Tamalpais Drive, Corte Madera, CA 94925; (415) 927–5064.

. . . .

Passing through the heart of the hip little town of Larkspur, this short rail-trail has style. It is primarily a neighborhood path; venture onto it, and you'll see folks walking their dogs, taking a brisk stroll, or teaching their kids to ride a bike or roller-skate. The trail also links with other recreational paths in the area, including one that heads west along Corte Madera Creek into Kentfield, and routes that head east toward Point San Quentin.

The trail follows the abandoned bed of the Northwestern Pacific Railroad, which was used primarily to move people around Marin County prior to the explosion of road construction that followed completion of the Golden Gate Bridge in the 1930s.

The trail is described here beginning at its southern end. To reach the north portal of the Alto Tunnel, a massive concrete gateway shuttered by huge metal doors, you must head south for about a quarter mile from the parking area. The route narrows quickly from a broad dirt track to narrow single-track overgrown with blackberries and thick riparian brambles. It dead-ends at the base of the portal in a shady clearing.

Unless you've a hankering to visit this spot, you will, like most folks, head north from the parking area on the wide rail-trail. The route passes two sets of posts that serve as barriers to motorized traffic, then makes a straight shot between neighborhood streets to the Old Corte Madera Square kiosk, where you will find benches and a water fountain. Cross Redwood Avenue, head through the parking lot adjacent to Montecito Drive, and swing to the right (east) onto the path, which continues northward.

The trail is a bit wilder once you leave Old Corte Madera behind, bordered by a thick hedge of blooming shrubs. At about the 0.5-mile mark, you will pass under an old concrete bridge. After crossing a couple of neighborhood streets (William Avenue and Ward Street), the trail passes along the backside of the businesses that line Magnolia, Larkspur's busy main road.

At 1 mile, you will reach the Larkspur Station, with the warming house on the east side of the trail and the station on the west. Both buildings now house private businesses, but they bear historical emblems that briefly describe what they once were, and when they were built. They are also recognizable to any railroad buff, having a distinctive architecture that bespeaks small-town railroad depots from the early twentieth century.

Beyond the station, you will cross the access road to a shopping center, pass through a small park, then cross Doherty Drive at the signaled arterial. Follow the sidewalk that borders Magnolia for about 75 yards north of Doherty Drive to a trail fork. Although the railroad ran alongside present-day Magnolia, it is more scenic to follow the asphalt path that runs roughly parallel to the grade, looping around residences that have views of Corte Madera Creek. Both the rail-trail and the asphalt path end on Bon Air Road at about 1.7 miles.

To continue west on the creekside trail, which is a delightful addition to this route and offers the opportunity to visit both a tot lot and view the wildlife

The Larkspur Station on the Larkspur rail-trail is a classic small-town railroad depot.

that thrives in this tidal creek, carefully cross to the north side of Bon Air Drive using the pedestrian crosswalk. Head north, over the bridge, to the trailhead. The tot lot lies to the north, and a parcourse parallels the asphalt track, which is also bordered by a dirt walkway. The trail continues north until the creek is forced into a concrete channel in Kentfield. Downtown Kentfield and the College of Marin lie 1 mile west of Bon Air Drive, and the bike route continues west from there, heading on road and separate paths through San Anselmo to Fairfax.

E Bol Park Bike Path

The Bol Park Bike Path is a charmer that threads through a peaceful neighborhood in the hills south of San Francisco. At its heart is Bol Park, a strip of playground and lawn laid alongside Matadero Creek.

Activities:

Location: Palo Alto, Santa Clara County

Length: 1.5 miles one-way

Surface: Asphalt

Wheelchair access: The entire trail is wheelchair accessible.

Difficulty: Easy

Food: No food is available along the trail, but you can find restaurants and grocery stores in nearby areas of Palo Alto.

Rest rooms: There are no rest rooms available along the route.

Seasons: The trail can be used year-round.

Access and parking: There is very limited parking along the road at the Hanover Street end point. Parking lots in the area are for private businesses. To reach this end point from the Interstate 280 near Palo Alto, take the Page Mill Road exit and go north on Page Mill Road for about 1.5 miles to Porter Drive. Turn right (southeast) on Porter Drive, which bends to the northeast and becomes Hanover Street. Drive a total of about 0.9 mile to the trailhead, which is wedged between the parking lots of two businesses on the right (southeast) side of Hanover Street.

There is parking at Bol Park itself, which can be reached by continuing down Page Mill Road to El Camino Real. Turn right (southeast) on El Camino Real and follow it to Matadero Avenue. Turn right (southwest) on Matadero

Avenue, and proceed to Laguna Avenue. Go left (southeast) on Laguna Avenue for a short distance to the park.

Transportation: Contact the Santa Clara Valley Transportation Authority by calling (408) 321–2300, or writing 3331 North First Street, San Jose, CA 95134-1906. The Web site is www.vta.org.

Rentals: No rentals are available along the trail.

Contact: Gayle Likens, Senior Planner, City of Palo Alto, P.O. Box 10250, Palo Alto, CA 94303; (650) 329–2136.

• •

Bol Park, a pleasing strip of open space amid a peaceful neighborhood in Palo Alto, is the centerpiece of this stretch of rail-trail. The park features a tot lot (often crowded with squealing young ones), expanses of grass that are perfect for picnicking, and a shady portion of Matadero Creek, which forms the park's eastern border and supports a lush riparian habitat.

The trail follows the former rail bed of a Southern Pacific passenger line that continued southwest to the Los Gatos area. Both the rail-trail and the park were named in honor of Dr. Cornelis Bol, a physicist at Stanford University, whose heirs donated pastureland for use as a park. The park and the abandoned railroad grade were dedicated in the 1970s.

The route begins on Hanover Street, wedged between fences that border parking lots. It heads south along the fenceline, then makes a couple of sharp turns before tumbling onto Laguna Avenue at the northern corner of Bol Park.

At Bol Park, you'll find the playground, picnic facilities, benches, and a dirt track that runs adjacent to Matadero Creek. The paved rail-trail is on the west side of the park, and becomes more rustic as you continue south, traveling through a broad greenbelt of grass and sparse shade trees. At about the 0.5-mile mark, you will cross a bridge spanning the creek. The trail meanders through a narrow, quiet meadow for another half-mile before it forks at the Gunn High School ball fields. Stay left (southeast); a wall of toyon sporting vivid red berries in the autumn screens the school grounds.

The trail ends just south of the school grounds on Miranda Avenue. Return as you came.

F Shepherd Canyon Trail

The Shepherd Canyon Trail follows Shepherd Canyon Road up into a residential area in the hills above Oakland.

Activities:

Location: Oakland, Alameda County

Length: 1.25 miles of the 3-mile trail is on a former railroad grade.

Surface: Asphalt

Wheelchair access: The trail is wheelchair accessible.

Difficulty: Easy

Food: No food is available along the route, but Oakland hosts a variety of restaurants and markets.

Rest rooms: There are no rest rooms along the route.

Seasons: The trail can be used year-round.

Access and parking: To reach the Shepherd Canyon Park access point, which lies near the midpoint of the trail, from California 13 in Oakland take the Park Boulevard exit. Head east (uphill) on Park Boulevard to Mountain Boulevard and go left (north), paralleling the freeway. At the first stoplight, go right (east) on Snake Road. Follow Snake Road to where it splits, and go right (southeast) on Shepherd Canyon Road. Follow Shepherd Canyon Road to the light at the fire station; Shepherd Canyon Park, with parking, is northeast of the fire station on the right (south) side of Shepherd Canyon Road. Walk or ride about a quarter-mile farther up Shepherd Canyon Road to Paso Robles Road, and cross to the left (north) side of Shepherd Canyon Road. When this guide went to press, a housing development was under construction at this site, but a trail easement allows access to the rail-trail.

Transportation: A/C Transit provides service in the area. Call (510) 891–4777 for bus schedules, write to 1600 Franklin Street, Oakland, CA 94612, or check the Web site at www.actransit.dst.ca.us.

Rentals: There are no rentals along the trail.

Contact: Martin Matarrese, Parkland Resources Supervisor, City of Oakland, 3590 Sanborn Drive, Oakland, CA 94602; (510) 482–7857.

• •

The Shepherd Canyon Trail, which heads east into the Oakland hills along a grade established by the Sacramento Northern Railroad, is primarily a neighborhood trail, providing local residents with an easy and scenic path into the oak woodlands from which the surrounding city drew its name.

The trail ascends a steep canyon carved by Shepherd Creek (which now runs under the adjacent roadway), heading east toward Skyline Boulevard and the crest of the ridge. The Sacramento Northern Railroad operated this line as part of an extensive interurban electric rail system that originated in Sacramento and branched east to San Francisco, as well as north to the Chico area. When the railroad abandoned the line, the tracks were pulled up, and the area was used as a dumping ground for a time.

When plans to plow a freeway up the canyon fizzled, the East Bay Regional Park District, which owns the rail bed, and the city of Oakland developed an operating agreement that allowed for construction and maintenance of the trail, which was completed in 1984.

The rail-trail begins down and west of the Shepherd Canyon Park, above the shopping center and parking garage at Montclair Village. It crosses Snake Road, then proceeds east up the canyon on the north side of Shepherd Canyon Road.

The separate trail ends where Shepherd Canyon Road meets Escher Drive. If you wish to continue on the trail, cross Shepherd Canyon Road and head east on the streetside trail, which ends at Saroni Drive. Another streetside bike path extends north along Saroni Drive to Skyline Boulevard.

Ⓖ Los Gatos Creek Trail

This short, unpaved rail-trail follows Los Gatos Creek from the historic Forbes Mill Museum to the spillway at Lexington Reservoir.

Activities:

Location: Los Gatos, Santa Clara County

Length: 1.6 miles one-way

Surface: Dirt

Wheelchair access: The trail is not wheelchair accessible.

Difficulty: Moderate. There two steep sections: one that takes you down onto the railroad grade, and another that leads up to the pedestrian bridge across the spillway.

Food: The trail begins in charming downtown Los Gatos, where you will find a selection of restaurants. There is no water available along the trail, so be sure to bring what you'll need.

Rest rooms: There are no rest rooms along the route.

Seasons: The trail is accessible year-round, but it may be muddy during and after winter and spring rainstorms.

Access and parking: To reach the trailhead from California 17, take the Los Gatos/Saratoga/California 9 exit. Go south on California 9 to where it ends on Los Gatos Boulevard (if you are coming west from the San Jose area, you can only head north on California 9, so you will have to make a U-turn). Turn right (southwest) on Los Gatos Boulevard, which becomes East Main Street. The trailhead is 0.8 mile south of California 9 at the intersection of East Main and Maple Lane. Parking is available along the street and on the bridge.

Transportation: Contact the Santa Clara Valley Transportation Authority by calling (408) 321–2300, or writing 3331 North First Street, San Jose, CA 95134-1906. The Web site is www.vta.org.

Rentals: There are no rentals along the trail.

Contact: Tim Boyer, Park Maintenance Supervisor, Town of Los Gatos, Parks and Public Works Department, P.O. Box 949, Los Gatos, CA 95031; (408) 399–5770.

• • • • • • • • • • • • • • • • • • • •

The Los Gatos Creek Trail offers a quick study in water management. It follows a short section of Los Gatos Creek, from where the creek spills out of Lexington Reservoir at the base of the Santa Cruz Mountains to where it flows east into a concrete channel just above the heart of the town of Los Gatos.

The creek, though obviously altered from its natural state, nonetheless retains its charm, draped with a thick riparian undergrowth and tumbling in small cascades over ledges in the channel. Popular with local residents who take short walks, runs, or mountain bike rides on the route, the path offers access to other trails within the area of Lexington Reservoir.

The trail runs along a railroad grade built by the South Pacific Coast Railroad, which constructed a narrow gauge line that ran from Alameda through Los Gatos to Santa Cruz. The line was the brainchild of James G. Fair, who had made his fortune in mining and retired to the San Francisco Bay Area for his health. The railroad

The Lexington Dam is visible from the Los Gatos Creek Trail.

company was established in 1876, and the line through to Santa Cruz, built primarily by Chinese labor, was completed in 1880. It ferried passengers who previously traveled to the coast via stage lines.

The trail begins by diving from the southwestern corner of the bridge spanning both the creek and neighboring California 17 to the railbed proper. Los Gatos Creek flows on the left (southeast) side, and the highway abuts the trail's northwest edge.

To visit the historic Forbes Mill Museum, a nice start to any hike or ride on the trail, turn right (east) on the dirt track, which leads under the bridge and through an overgrown garden of trees and grasses to the old stone building. Originally four stories tall, the mill was built in 1853 and 1854 and was served by a spur of the South Pacific Coast Railroad. The two-story structure that houses the museum today was built in 1880. The museum is open from noon to 4:00 p.m. Wednesday through Sunday and can be reached by calling (408) 395–7375.

To enjoy the longer section of the rail-trail, backtrack to the steep access trail and go left (south) on the dirt track, heading upstream along the creek, which is safely housed in its V-shaped channel.

At 0.4 mile, the concrete channel ends, and the highway has begun to climb up and away from the path. At 0.7 mile, an old flume pipe appears on the right (northwest) side of the path, its rusted casing adding a shade of russet to the muted greens and browns of the route.

At 1.2 miles, the trail climbs steeply off of the railroad's easy grade and away from the creek, and views open across the canyon to the earth-faced dam of Lexington Reservoir. Climb to the intersection with a paved patch of road at the base of a tall metal retaining wall. The pavement leads right (northeast) for about 50 yards to a fenced area, and curves left (southwest) toward the towering spillway. Although now you are clearly off the railroad grade, you can continue on the scenic trail, which crosses the spillway on a pedestrian bridge, then switchbacks up the face of the dam to the reservoir. Return via the same route to the trailhead.

Rails-to-Trails

SIERRA NEVADA

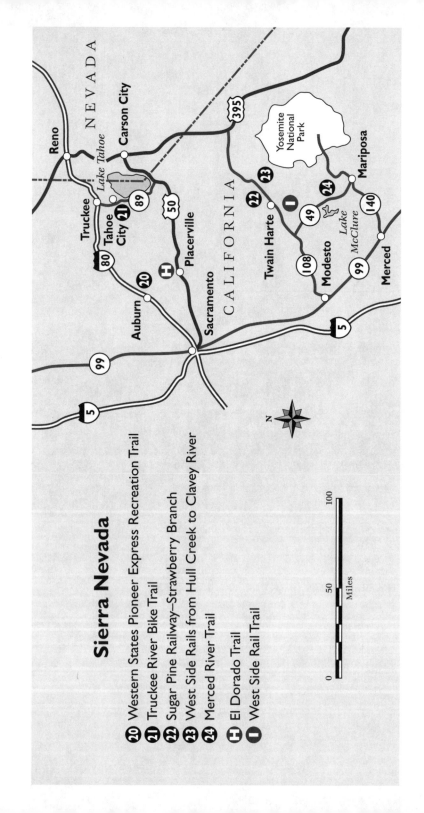

20 Western States Pioneer Express Recreation Trail

The abundant riches of California's Mother Lode surround this rail-trail. Not the riches that are ripped from the ground, mind you, but the wealth of wilderness, which in this case encompasses spectacular vistas of the American River and its canyon, and the peace that comes with hiking on the secluded trail that runs alongside it.

Activities:

Location: El Dorado and Placer Counties near Auburn

Length: 2 miles of the trail are on the railroad grade. The entire Western States Pioneer Express Recreation Trail is 100 miles long; you can get more information about it by calling the Western States Trail Foundation at (530) 823–7282.

Surface: Gravel and dirt

Wheelchair access: None. The trail is rough and quite narrow in places.

Difficulty: Moderate

Food: No food is available along the trail, nor is there potable water, so pack in what you will need.

Rest rooms: There are no rest rooms along the trail.

Seasons: The trail is passable year-round, although you may find snow on the trail in the winter and early spring.

Access and parking: To reach the trailhead at the American River bridge on California 49 from Interstate 80, take the California 49/Placerville and Grass Valley exit in Auburn. Go south on California 49, following the signs through the quaint downtown area. Just out of town, California 49 dives into the American River Canyon. Drive 2.3 miles down the canyon to near riverside, and veer right (south) over the bridge. It's a total of 3.3 miles from Auburn to the bridge parking area.

The section of trail on the former railroad grade ends 2 miles downriver; at this point the trail climbs steeply to a gravel road that leads west toward Auburn and east into the other areas of the Auburn State Recreation Area. The unmaintained railroad grade continues west from this point. The best access to this end point is from the American River bridge trailhead.

Parking for the section of trail on the railroad grade is available on the south side of the bridge on California Highway 49 just beyond its intersection with Foresthill Road. If there is no parking available here, you can park in the small lot 0.2 mile east of the intersection along Foresthill Road. Be cautious crossing the bridge as there is no pedestrian walkway or shoulder.

Transportation: None available.

Rentals: Bikes and boats may be rented in Auburn. This section of trail, however, is off-limits to mountain biking.

Contact: Greg Wells, State Park Ranger, California Department of Parks and Recreation, P.O. Box 3266, Auburn, CA 95604; (530) 885–4527 ext. 21.

• •

The American River is one of California's major arteries, nourishing the fertile soil of the Central Valley and carrying the wealth that spawned the great formative event of the mid-nineteenth century: the Gold Rush.

This rail-trail follows a portion of the Mountain Quarry Railroad, which carried limestone from quarries on the Middle Fork of the American River to Auburn and the Southern Pacific line that continued to Sacramento. The railroad's future—as well as the future of the entire Auburn State Recreation Area—was thrown into limbo when plans to build the Auburn Dam were announced in the 1960s. But the dam was never built, and the canyons that were to be part of a reservoir were developed as a recreational area instead. The railroad grade is now part of an extensive trail system within the Auburn State Recreation Area, a large section of Gold Country mined these days for the pleasure of hikers, mountain bikers, anglers, paddlers, and other outdoor enthusiasts.

The rail-trail begins on the south side of the bridge spanning the American River. There is no sign, but the route is obvious, heading west down the river. You'll pass a trail intersection at 0.1 mile: The left (south) trail leads 3.1 miles to the hamlet of Cool. You want to stay right (west) and cross the bridge that spans the river. Heed the

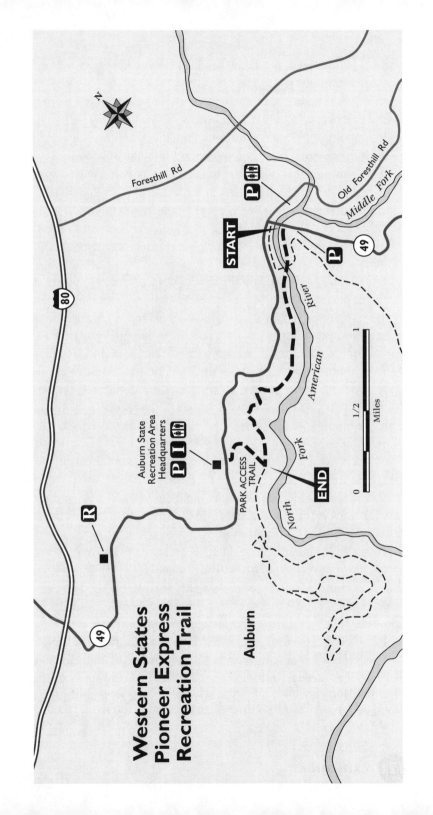

Western States
Pioneer Express
Recreation Trail

warning signs posted on the bridge for safety reasons. It's 4.2 miles to Auburn from here.

The trail is broad and easy, with open and dynamic views of the river and canyon. A gravel road breaks off to the left (south and to the riverside) at 0.6 mile. Continue straight (west) on the very obvious railroad grade, hiking along the south-facing hillside above the river. In summer this hillside is hot and dry, covered with a sparse scrub that grows in sharp contrast to the dense evergreen forest thriving on the moister north-facing slope of the river canyon.

At a Western States Pioneer Trail sign, a path merges onto the rail-trail from the right (north). Stay left on the grade; beyond here the path narrows.

Round a bend marked by the first of several concrete buttresses that were the foundations of short trestles that spanned ravines along the river. The trail narrows to single-track and loops through the gully. Pass the second foundation on the other side; the date 1921 is inscribed in the concrete. The path widens briefly, and then plunges through another drainage where the foundation is dated 1915.

At about 1.2 miles, you'll dip through a third foundation-bordered drainage. This one hosts a lovely waterfall that flows in spring and early summer; it is thick with undergrowth that includes poison oak, so watch your step.

Climb away from the waterfall, passing yet another trestle foundation, to a trail marker. The trail continues west, about 100 feet above the river, which flows green and deep in its bed. As you walk beneath a towering black-streaked rock formation, views of the river are unimpeded by brush or trees.

Pass a mile marker that reads 2.5 miles. At this point, the rail-trail ends on the concrete foundation to the left (west). The Western States Recreation Trail arcs sharply right (north), leaving the railroad grade behind. Efforts are afoot to restore the former railroad grade into Auburn; contact the trail manager for more information.

If you choose to continue on the Western States Pioneer Trail, follow switchbacks that lead steeply up the sun-baked hillside before the trail dips through a brush-choked creek bed. Continue up past two more switchbacks and a trail sign to a dirt road that is 0.5 mile above the end of the railroad grade. Go left (west) on the road to reach Auburn; heading right (east) will lead to California 49 between the Auburn State Recreation Area headquarters and the town itself. Either return as you came, or enjoy other trails and activities in the recreation area.

Hikers walk their dog on the Western States Pioneer Trail.

Boisterous. If a single word could describe the Truckee River Trail in summer, that would be it. The trail hums with activity during the height of the summer season, as colorful rafts packed with paddlers spill down the Truckee River, and hikers, cyclists, and skaters trace a parallel course downstream on the rail-trail that also originates on the shores of Lake Tahoe.

Activities:

Location: Tahoe City, Placer County

Length: 4 miles one-way

Surface: Asphalt

Wheelchair access: The entire trail is wheelchair accessible, but snow precludes wheelchair use during the winter months.

Difficulty: Moderate, due only the trail's length

Food: There are two grocery stores and a number of restaurants in Tahoe City, at the eastern end point of the trail. River Ranch, near the trail's western end point, also offers the opportunity for riverside dining.

Rest rooms: Rest rooms are available at the Tahoe City end point, at various locations along the trail, and at River Ranch.

Seasons: The trail can be used year-round.

Access and parking: To reach the trailhead from the intersection of California Highways 89 and 28 in Tahoe City, follow California 89 south for 0.2 mile to the trailhead, which is on the right (west) side of the road. To reach the western end point from the Tahoe City intersection, follow California 89 west, toward the town of Truckee, for 3.6 miles to Alpine Meadows Road. The trail crosses the Alpine Meadows Road at River Ranch. Limited parking is available along the roadway.

There is a huge parking lot at the Tahoe City end point, but this lot may be packed during the summer season, when both trail users and river rafters flock to the Truckee River.

Transportation: TART, the Tahoe Area Regional Transit organization, provides bus service in the area. TART may be reached by calling (530) 550–1212.

Rentals: Several shops in the Tahoe City area rent bicycles. Consult the local telephone directory for shop names and telephone numbers.

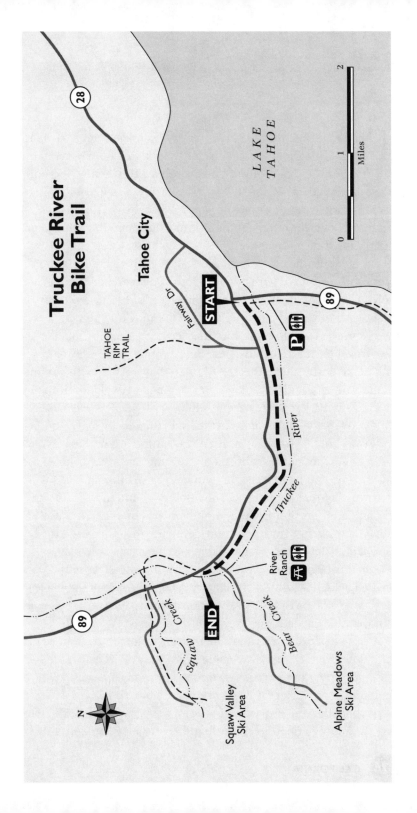

Truckee River
Bike Trail

Tahoe City

LAKE TAHOE

28

89

START

P

Fairway Dr

TAHOE RIM TRAIL

Truckee River

River Ranch

A

END

89

Squaw Creek

Bear Creek

Squaw Valley Ski Area

Alpine Meadows Ski Area

N

0   1   2
Miles

Contact: Cindy Gustafson, Director of Resource Development, Tahoe City PUD, P.O. Box 33, Tahoe City, CA 96145; (530) 583–3796.

• •

T he Truckee River has carved an easy passage from Lake Tahoe to the historic town downriver that shares the river's name. The Truckee, though swift moving, is remarkably gentle, sweeping in broad meanders along the floor of a heavily wooded valley. This placid but invigorating demeanor has made the river the destination of an army of river rafters in the summertime, and the site of a rail-trail of unparalleled popularity.

On any summer weekend, the Truckee River rail-trail and the river itself are packed with brightly clothed recreationalists. The rafts are vivid orange, sunburst yellow, and electric blue, accented by the bright garb of those bouncing along, whooping and singing, inside them. On the trail, the folks are dressed with equal brilliance, and they travel by many modes—walking, cycling, or in-line skating— with equal enthusiasm. It is the ultimate family trail, with strollers, training wheels, and dogs on leashes as much in evidence as the Lycra and intensity of more serious athletes.

If you feel the urge to forsake the trail temporarily for the translucent waters of the Truckee, by all means, jump in. The water is clear and reflects the mottled browns of the sand and river cobbles that pave its bed, fading to a cool blue in deeper swimming holes.

It was the relative flatness and apparent gentleness of the river that no doubt made it inviting to the railroad operated by the Lake Tahoe Railway and Transportation Company that once used the bed upon which day hikers, dog walkers and bicyclists now play.

The trail begins on the west side of the Truckee River access parking area, which is located off California 89 just south of the main intersection in Tahoe City. Cross the bridge, then go left (west), following both the highway and the river downstream.

A couple of driveways and side roads intersect the trail in its first mile, then the trail drops riverside. The Truckee initially is hidden in a dense cover of riparian vegetation, but soon comes into view as the rail-trail passes a scattering of private homes.

Beyond, the trail is uninterrupted for a long stretch. For the most part the route is open to the sun and river views, broken only by

Rafters can be seen from the Truckee River Trail.

brief shady stretches overhung by evergreens and crowded with willows and lush riverside undergrowth. Portable rest rooms are placed at intervals along the route, and short side trails lead to beaches where you can rest or swim.

It's not until about the 3.5-mile mark that the scenic routine is broken. At that point, you climb a short hill and pass through a parking/staging area for Truckee River rafting companies. By now, having watched the antics and overwhelming joy of those floating downriver, you are probably more than intrigued by the prospect of trying a rafting excursion yourself, so you might want to jot down the names of the companies using the area.

This is just the beginning of a busy and often crowded stretch of trail, so proceed with courtesy and caution. River Ranch and Bells

Landing lie just downstream; from the trail you can observe the bustle of bodies and rafts, a bonanza of color and activity, at the landing. Patrons of River Ranch watch from the deck of this riverside resort, which lies at the intersection of California 89 and Alpine Meadows Road.

To continue on the rail-trail, cross Alpine Meadows Road. The trail changes demeanor immediately, as though the gate that marks the beginning of this portion of the path is more than a barrier to cars. Although still paved, the trail is wilder and seems more secluded: There are no bodies on the river, and the highway noise fades a bit as the trail drops below its grade. It's a lovely stretch, complete with rest rooms and paved ramps that offer access to the Truckee. Pass the 4-mile marker as you approach what is currently trail's end, at the highway bridge that spans the Truckee.

In the summer of 2000, a trail extension leading down to the entrance to Squaw Valley will open. The extension is not on the former railroad grade. When completed the trail will be 5 miles long.

This segment of rail-trail, which follows the historic Sugar Pine Railway, is captured within the forested gorge of the South Fork of the Stanislaus River. It is lined with interpretive signs keyed to a brochure that describes the logging operations that were carried out here in the early and mid-1900s.

Activities:

Location: Strawberry, Tuolumne County

Length: 3 miles one-way

Surface: Gravel and dirt

Wheelchair access: The trail is not wheelchair accessible.

Difficulty: Moderate

Food: Although there are no food outlets along the trail, you can find eateries and grocery stores by traveling west on California 108 to Twain Harte. Bring food and water and you can picnic along the route.

Rest rooms: There are no rest room facilities at either trailhead or along the trail. The nearest facilities are in the Fraser Flat Campground, which is located about a half mile farther down the forest service road.

Seasons: The trail is accessible year-round. Hiking and mountain biking are best in the spring, summer, and fall; you may cross-country ski on the trail during the winter months when snow permits.

Access and parking: Access to the trail varies depending on the time of year. In summer, you can reach the Fraser Flat trailhead by heading east from Twain Harte on scenic California 108 to Stanislaus Forest Road 4N01, which is well signed. Turn left (north) on 4N01 and follow the winding road for about 2.5 miles to the bridge over the South Fork of the Stanislaus River. The trailhead is on the right (east) side of the road before you cross the river.

The eastern trailhead serves as the only access to the trail in the winter months. To reach this end point, continue on California 108 to Old Strawberry Road, which is about 2 miles east of the turnoff to Fraser Flat. Turn left (north) on Old Strawberry Road, and go about 2 miles to the trailhead, which is on the left (west) side of the road and is marked by a couple of posts that can be difficult to see from the roadway.

Transportation: There is no public transportation to the trailheads.

Rentals: There are no rentals in the area.

Contact: Chuck James, Recreation Technician, or Katie Coulter, District Archaeologist, Mi-Wok Ranger District, P.O. Box 100, Mi-Wuk Village, CA 95346-0100; (209) 586–3234.

· ·

The Stanislaus River gains momentum in the canyon traced by this section of the Sugar Pine Railway, tumbling with the vigor of an adolescent through a narrow passage cut from smoky granite. Evergreen trees—timber to those who built the railroad to harvest lumber—grow thickly on either side of the river, enveloping the route in shade and insulating it from signs of civilization clustered in villages along California 108.

This is but a short section of the Sugar Pine rail-trail, which currently spans approximately 16.5 miles from Twain Harte to Strawberry, and, if all proceeds as planned, will eventually extend for about 30 miles. Indeed, an extensive web of rail lines and spurs winds through this neck of the woods. The Sugar Pine Railway alone included about 70 miles of mainline and approximately 400 miles of spurs, branches, and sidings. The rails were laid down in the rugged foothills just after the turn of the twentieth century, and were used to transport harvested old-growth trees, which then were hauled to sawmills for processing. The railroad ceased operation in 1965. The abandoned grades—including the grade spanned by this segment of the rail-trail—are very mild, belying the steepness of the terrain that surrounds them.

The rail-trail is lined with interpretive posts, which are keyed to an informational packet that is available from the Mi-Wok Ranger District in Mi-Wuk Village.

The trail makes for fine hiking; the mountain biking, especially for the beginner, is sublime. The trail is described here climbing northeast from the bridge that spans the Stanislaus near the Fraser Flat Campground to Old Strawberry Road, but can be traveled in either direction easily. This is the optimal starting point for an out-and-back journey, however, because it is all downhill on the return trip.

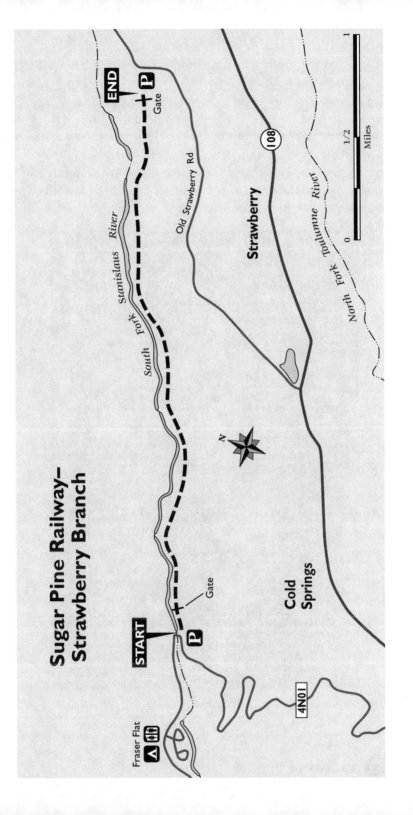

Begin on the south side of the bridge over the Stanislaus River. An informational billboard is posted at the trailhead and the route is barricaded to prohibit use by motorized vehicles.

Posts 1, 2, and 3 are passed within a third of a mile of the trailhead, calling your attention first to the old logging camp at Fraser (now the Fraser Flat Campground), then to Camp Lowell, another logging camp used for a single season in the early twentieth century, and finally to the rigors of building a railroad in the foothills. The path is a gentle roller coaster, dipping through shallow gullies as it

A family enjoys the Sugar Pine Railway Trail.

climbs through thick stands of conifers. You can catch glimpses of the South Fork of the Stanislaus in the canyon to the left (north) from brief openings between the trunks of the trees.

At about the 1.1-mile mark, the gorge deepens, and the remains of a flume appear on the opposite side of the canyon. Called the Philadelphia Ditch, the flume was used by gold miners a century ago. Less than a quarter of a mile beyond, you will pass post 4 and a diversion dam, which is still used for power generation.

At about the 1.5-mile mark, you will pass a green gate, then continue up through the lovely woodland to post 6, where the forest opens a bit and filtered sunlight illuminates the glistening river. The grades split here; remain on the main (and obvious) path that continues northeast to the Old Strawberry Road trailhead. The trail veers away from the riverside at about the 2.5-mile mark and crosses through yet another of the gullies that lend the trail its rolling profile.

You will continue in an easterly direction to post 8. This marks the remnants of research projects conducted within the U.S. Forest Service's Stanislaus–Tuolumne Experimental Forest, which served as a laboratory for foresters and other scientists from 1927 to 1969. The research station is located across the South Fork of the Stanislaus and now houses forest service employees.

Post 8 stands at the edge of a small meadow, which the trail crosses before returning to the woods. At the trail intersection at 2.8 miles, go right (northeast) and up on the narrow footpath. The railroad grade can be seen heading off to the left (north), but it's not well maintained.

The path leads up steeply to Old Strawberry Road, where two orange-and-brown trail posts mark the trailhead. Although these are obvious from the path, they aren't easily seen from the roadway, as they are tucked below grade. Unless you have arranged a shuttle, this is the turnaround point; return as you came.

The foothills of the Sierra Nevada are expansive and remarkably untouched by modern life. The West Side rail-trail travels into the depth of this isolation, winding through dense stands of timber on a track that once rang with the squeal of wheels on track and now rings only with the songs of the wind and the birds.

Activities:

Location: Southeast of Long Barn in Tuolumne County

Length: 8 miles one-way

Surface: Dirt

Wheelchair access: The trail is not wheelchair accessible.

Difficulty: Hard

Food: There is no food or water available along the trail, so bring all you'll need. There are restaurants and grocery stores in Twain Harte and other villages along California 108.

Rest rooms: There are no rest rooms along the trail. Practice leave-no-trace principles by burying waste at least 8 inches underground and packing out toilet paper.

Seasons: The trail is accessible year-round. Hiking and mountain biking are best in the spring, summer, and fall; you may cross-country ski on the trail during the winter months if snow permits.

Access and parking: An absolutely gorgeous road leads to the remote trailheads for this route. To reach the Hull Creek end point from California 108 in Long Barn, turn east off the highway at the Merrell Springs turnoff, where there are signs for Hull Creek and Clavey River. Turn right (south) onto Long Barn Road, and go 0.1 mile to Forest Service Road 3N01 (also known as Stanislaus County Road 31 and North Fork Road). Follow 3N01/County Road 31, cross the North Fork on the Tuolumne River at 2.0 miles, then continue for about 6.3 miles to Forest Service Road 3N07, which sports a sign for the West Side Rail Tour.

Turn right (south) on Forest Service Road 3N07. This well-graded dirt road leads for about 3 miles (9.3 miles from California 108) to an intersection; stay on 3N07, which leads to a second road fork 0.1 mile farther, at the William R. Rolland Memorial Plantation. Go left (east) on Forest Service

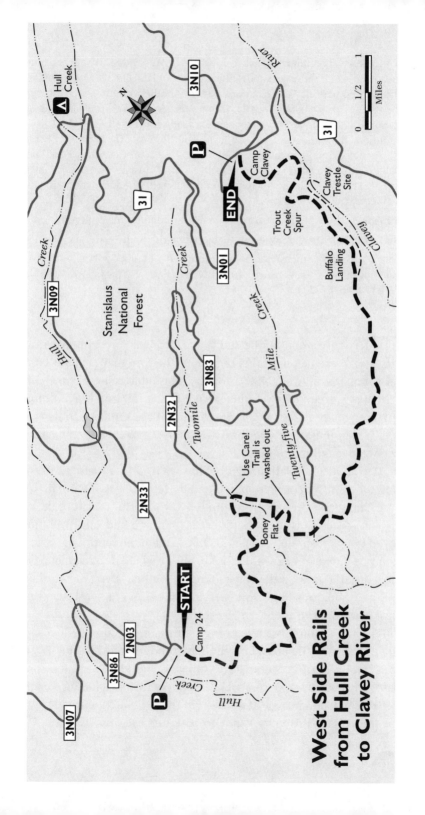

West Side Rails
from Hull Creek
to Clavey River

Road 3N86; a sign indicates that parking for the West Side Rail Tour is 2 miles ahead. The trail begins just above the crossing of Hull Creek, where you will find limited parking. You can continue for another mile to a parking pull-out at post 2, the site of Camp 24, which was home to a thriving logging operation until 1960. Several forest service roads converge here.

To reach the Clavey River trailhead, continue past the turnoff at Forest Service Road 3N07, traveling a total of 15.5 miles on the North Fork Road (3N01/County Road 31) to its intersection with Forest Service Road 3N86 at Camp Clavey. This is the terminus of the rail-trail. There is parking in pull-outs along the dirt road.

Transportation: There is no public transportation to this rail-trail.

Rentals: There are no rentals available along the trail.

Contact: Chuck James, Recreation Technician, or Katie Coulter, District Archaeologist, Mi-Wok Ranger District, P.O. Box 100, Mi-Wuk Village, CA 9346-0100; (209) 586–3234.

· ·

The dense woods of the Stanislaus National Forest impose thorough seclusion on this section of the former West Side Lumber Company railway. Now a rough-and-tumble rail-trail tucked in a thick evergreen blanket, this stretch of the rail line is even more untamed today than it was at the height of the lumberjack days. It is so far out there that you surely would be the only one to hear if a tree were to fall in the forest.

The Stanislaus National Forest has revived this segment of the West Side line, which was abandoned in the 1960s, as a recreational trail. The forest service has compiled a wonderful brochure detailing the route via a good (and necessary) map and interpretation keyed to signposts along the trail. Quite a bit of the route can be traveled in a passenger car, still more in a four-wheel drive vehicle, but the heart of the rail-trail is best managed on foot. Even the hardiest mountain bikers will be sorely tried by the several washouts that have obscured the grade.

The rail-trail follows a leg of one of the four railroads that provided access to the abundant timber in the region. Like its neighbors, including the Sugar Pine Railway, the West Side Railroad Company laid down a remarkable amount of track, including a mainline that reached nearly 70 miles from the town of Tuolumne south toward the Hetch Hetchy Valley in Yosemite National Park.

The West Side Rails were a narrow-gauge line, which made it easier to carve into steep mountainsides but resulted in less stability for the trains on the tracks. The width of the grade these days, however, is perfect for hikers, cyclists, or equestrians who wish to travel side by side, discussing the railroad history that unfolds at their feet while enjoying spectacular views of the high country. The rail-trail doubles as Forest Service Road 3N86.

Interpretation begins just above Forest Road 3N86's intersection with Hull Creek, where signpost 1 marks one of the railroad's sidings. But the best parking is at signpost 2, at about the 1-mile mark,

A mountain biker speeds along on the West Side Rails near Clavey River.

which was the site of Camp 24, once a bustling hub and now little more than a wide spot in the road.

The route continues across open, scrub-covered hillside, passing post 3 at the site of an old oil tank. You leave the open ground for the duration of the rail-trail once you enter the forest, with views opening occasionally southward as you traverse the mountainside.

At about 2.5 miles, you will pass posts 4 and 5, which direct your attention to various types of railroad paraphernalia and to the meadow at Boney Flat. Just beyond, you reach two large stakes that stand on either side of the trail, forming a rustic portal. If you are still in a passenger car, this marks the end of the line for you; if you're in a four-wheel vehicle, you've got another mile and a half or so to travel before you will have to bail out.

The route cuts a broad switchback around Boney Flat. You have to negotiate an easy detour around a missing bridge at the Twomile Creek crossing, which is at about 3 miles. The trail also intersects Forest Road 2N32, which is signed. At this point, the track is no longer passable to motor vehicles. Arc south on the gently inclining rail-trail, which dips into another drainage that is washed out and clogged with fallen logs.

At post 6 you reach the halfway point of the rail-trail. The post marks the site of Camp 25, as well as the washout at Twenty-Five Mile Creek, which you negotiate via rustic stairs.

The rail-trail curves back to the east beyond the creek and winds through the woods to its intersection with Forest Road 3N83 (also signed). This service road branches off first to the right (south), and then to the left (north) at signpost 7 (about 5.5 miles). A cedar tree bearing the scars of chains used by steam donkeys, large machines that pulled logs from where they were cut to where they could be loaded onto railroad cars, is the focal point of this interpretive post.

The trail gently meanders to the northeast beyond Forest Road 3N38, winding through a pleasant forest that opens to offer fleeting views down into the Clavey River drainage. You will cross the occasional creek, usually dry by late summer, and pass a few interpretive signposts. Post 8 points up the difficulty these seasonal streams posed to railroad builders, post 9 marks the location of yet another logging camp, and post 10 brings your attention to the telephone line that served the loggers and railroad workers, sections of which now lie on the ground along the route.

Just before you reach post 11, at about the 6.5-mile mark, you will encounter a final washout. The post itself marks the start of the Trout Creek Spur, which will lead you to trail's end at Camp Clavey—again, an old logging camp. But it's worth your while to branch off to the right (northeast), dropping from Buffalo Landing, once the site of feverish logging activity, toward the Clavey River, where you can view the remains of the Clavey River Trestle. The wooden trestle, which stood more than 75 feet above the river, has burned, but its foundations are still visible. An old flatcar also remains on the site.

To finish the hike, climb up to Camp Clavey via the Trout Creek Spur, which ascends more steeply than the rest of the grade before topping out among the evergreens that encroach upon the clearings at Camp Clavey. The end of the rail-trail (and of Forest Service Road 3N86) is at its intersection with Forest Service Road 3N01 at about the 8-mile mark.

Unless you have arranged a shuttle, the quickest return is along the same route. But a web of forest service roads winds through the woods, offering wonderful opportunities for exploration for those with a good map, a compass, and the wits to use them both.

As rough and tumble as the river it follows, as enchanting as the canyon that cradles it, the Merced River Trail is one of the most challenging and most beautiful of California's rail-trails.

Activities:

Location: West of Yosemite National Park in Mariposa County

Length: 16 miles round-trip; there is no bridge at the Bagby end point.

Surface: Original ballast and dirt

Wheelchair access: None.

Difficulty: Hard

Food: There are no restaurants or stores along the route, but food is available in the nearby town of Mariposa, at the lodges located east of Briceberg along California 140, and in Yosemite National Park.

Rest rooms: Rest rooms are available at Briceberg, in the campgrounds that lie at the end of the gravel access road, and at the campground in Bagby.

Seasons: The trail can be traveled year-round. Hiking and cycling are best in the summer and autumn months. You can cross-country ski on the trail during the winter when there is a sufficient covering of snow. The trail is least hospitable when wet and should be avoided if flooded.

Access and parking: Parking is available at both end points, but it is not easy to do this trail as a one-way shuttle venture because there is no bridge spanning the Merced River at Bagby. Most travelers on the trail begin at the Briceburg end point and travel downstream along the Merced River to where the path ends on the opposite side of the river from the campground at Bagby. To reach the Briceburg end point, head east on California 140 from Mariposa for almost 12 miles to the Briceburg Information Center. Ample parking is available at the picnic area that is wedged between the Briceburg building and the Merced River.

To reach the Bagby end point from Mariposa, follow California 49 north for about 16 miles to Bagby, which is located at the east end of Lake McClure. Turn right (east) into the Bagby recreation area; a small fee is levied here. Follow the campground road for 0.7 mile to the campground area. The river is reached by following the camp road to its end at the southern bank. The only way to reach the trail from here is by fording the river, which is only feasible in late season when water levels are low, and arguably is unsafe at any time of year.

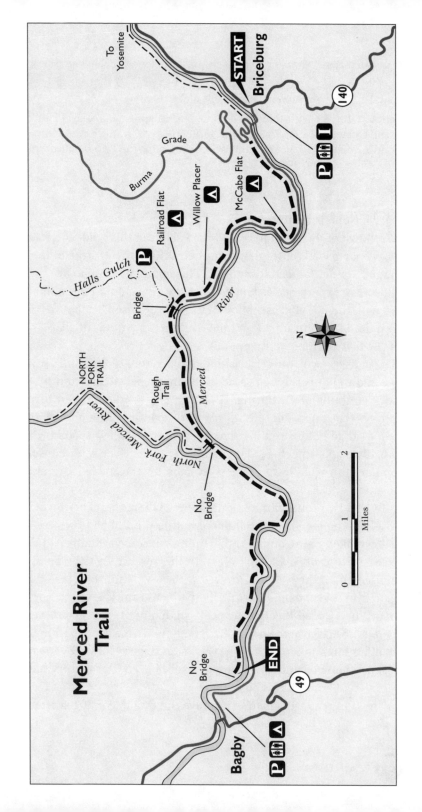

Merced River Trail

START Briceburg

To Yosemite

Burma Grade

Railroad Flat

Willow Placer

McCabe Flat

Halls Gulch

Bridge

P

Merced River

NORTH FORK TRAIL

Rough Trail

North Fork Merced River

No Bridge

140

N

0   1   2
Miles

No Bridge

END

49

Bagby

P

Transportation: There is no public transportation available between the end points.

Rentals: There are no rentals available along the trail.

Contact: Jim Eicher, Recreation Planner, Bureau of Land Management, 63 Natoma Street, Folsom, CA 95630-2671; (916) 985–4474. During the summer months, you can also get information by contacting the Briceberg Information Center at (209) 379–9414.

• •

T his one is far from tame.

Most of the rail-trails you'll read about in this guide are relatively easy paved routes that earn their difficulty by virtue of their length. Not the Merced River Trail. This comes as close to a wilderness experience as you will find on any rail-trail in California, with the possible exception of the Bizz Johnson Trail. And even the Bizz Johnson doesn't present the same kinds of challenges that the Merced River Trail does.

Lest I scare you off, rest assured that this trail is eminently passable and wanders through some of the most spectacular country in the mountains of California. It follows the scenic Merced River Canyon east of Yosemite National Park, passing through a steep-walled gorge before spilling into a wider river valley shaded with spreading oaks and cloaked in wildflowers. The river is immensely popular with white-water rafters, so look for these adventurers in the summer season.

But I'd be remiss not to mention its challenges, most of which have been created by the whims of nature. The El Niño winter of 1998 wreaked havoc on the trail, wiping out some sections and depositing heaps of rubble on others. In the autumn of 1999, a mile-long section of the trail was littered with rocks—no, boulders—that made it no more than a narrow footpath. You must ford the north fork of the Merced River at the trail's midpoint. *And be forewarned:* There is no bridge at the Bagby end point, rendering the trip a round-trip affair totaling 16 miles. The river may be forded at Bagby in late season, when flows are low, but only experienced backcountry travelers should attempt this crossing.

The trail managers plan to improve the trail in coming seasons,

THE BOUNTIFUL
MERCED RIVER VALLEY

The area surrounding the Merced River Trail positively blossoms with opportunities to enjoy the outdoors. Hiking, mountain biking, and horseback
riding on the rail-trail are just a few of the possibilities. More than 70 miles
of the river have been designated "wild and scenic," and all along its upper
sections you will find high-caliber white-water rafting and fishing. The rustic
campgrounds west of Briceberg, which are managed by the Bureau of Land
Management (BLM), cradle delightful sites that front on the river. And
Yosemite National Park, undoubtedly one of the most spectacular places on
earth and the birthplace of the Merced, lies less than 20 miles upstream.

There is also abundant history to be explored in the canyon, including
the unimproved portion of the old Yosemite Valley Railroad, which continues along the north side of the Merced into Yosemite National Park. The
Briceberg Information Center itself is a historic site, having served as a store,
a post office, and a regular stop for the railroad (among other incarnations),
before it was sold to the Bureau of Land Management in the late 1980s. The
quaint stone structure was restored to its pristine condition, and has since
served as a public information center and gateway to the wonders of the
Merced River valley.

To learn more about this area, contact the BLM's Mariposa Visitor Center at (209) 966–3192.

so conditions will be different, and undoubtedly better, in the future.
Contact the trail manager or check at the Briceberg Information Center to learn more about the status of the trail.

The rail-trail follows the right-of-way of the Yosemite Valley Railroad. Trains ran through the Merced River valley into Yosemite National Park from 1906 to 1945, serving the logging, mining, and
tourist industries in the scenic canyon. The railroad began to fall
into disuse once California 140 was completed in 1926. Both Briceburg at the east end of the trail and Bagby at the west end, where

The Merced River Trail winds through a steep-walled gorge.

the Merced flows into Lake McClure, were once way stations along the railroad.

In the summer season, you can either begin at the Briceberg Information Center, where you will find ample parking, or you can drive 4.5 miles down the good gravel road to the trailhead at Railroad Flat Campground, where you will find more limited parking. If you are planning on bicycling the route, the road from Briceberg to Railroad Flat is an enjoyable warm-up. It too follows the old railroad grade and offers wonderful views of the neighboring river.

The trail proper begins at the west end of the Railroad Flat Campground, beyond the white gate. The trail reaches a bench at about the quarter-mile point, at the bridge that spans Halls Creek. A private home is perched on the north slope of the river canyon beyond the creek crossing, and another little bridge spans a seasonal stream just below the house. The trail narrows to single-track amid a jumble of rocky debris from the flood. Stay straight (west) on the riverside track at the switchback that leads up toward the residence. At about the 0.6-mile mark, you will reach a Merced River Trail sign.

The footpath winds through the narrowing gorge, with steep cliffs overhanging the route on the north. Unless you are an exceptionally skilled mountain biker, you'll be walking your bike through this section. The walk is absolutely wonderful, because the slower pace—and the diminished fear of crashing and burning—will permit you to truly enjoy the lovely canyon.

The bike portage/single-track/rock jumble hike, accented by the occasional dogwood tree, continues for about 1 mile. Skirt a rather major rock slide, then the canyon opens a bit and you can look across to the rusted flume that traces the canyon's southern wall.

The rail-trail, now bordered by thin grasses, continues its gentle descent through the broadening canyon, to the confluence of the North Fork of the Merced River at about the 3-mile mark. There is no bridge here; you must ford the brisk river, which is deep even in late season, and may be impassable when the runoff is high. The trail leads to the most obvious ford. The concrete remains of the trestle that spanned the confluence are at the mouth of the North Fork; upstream (north) of the trestle and ford are the remains of a rustic stone structure. This makes a fine picnic and turnaround point for those seeking a pleasant day hike.

Once across the North Fork, you can use one of two routes to climb back onto the railroad grade. The right (northern) route leads directly to the path, the left (southern) leads about 50 yards to an inviting clearing in which you will find the sun-splashed pilings for the defunct trestle, then goes up and west to the rail-trail.

The route west of the North Fork of the Merced is broad, pebbly, and bordered by grasses that grow blonder as the summer progresses.

A narrow creek, which may be dry in late season, spills down from the north to cross the trail at about the 5-mile mark.

Farther downstream, the path pulls northwest, away from the Merced, and is shaded by a sparse canopy of thin pines. Brush and shade encroach on the route before it spills back into the more open river basin, where the Merced threads through channels that it has carved in its cobbled bed. The canyon now wears the mantle of the lower foothills, including shady oak and buckeye trees and thickening grasses peppered with wildflowers. These tufts of grass squeeze the trail, confining it to a narrow swath on the broader grade.

The rail-trail ends at the remains of the bridge that used to span the stream that spills from Solomon Canyon into the Merced. To the west, the river thickens into an arm of Lake McClure. This is the trail's turnaround point, unless you have arranged a shuttle and it is reasonably safe to ford the Merced to the road that leads into the campground at Bagby.

MORE RAIL-TRAILS

Ⓗ El Dorado Trail

The El Dorado Trail, like so many rail-trails in California and else-where, is a route in transition. About half of the trail is in place, a nice path that wanders through the oak woodlands east of downtown Placerville that serves, for the most part, local residents. But plans are afoot to extend the route.

Activities:

Location: Placerville, El Dorado County.

Length: 1.7 miles are currently in place, but the trail will be 4 miles once the pedestrian bridge over U.S. Highway 50 is completed, and 8 miles in length when the entire project is finished.

Surface: Asphalt (with a parallel dirt path) and ballast

Wheelchair access: The paved portion of the trail, which is in place, is wheelchair accessible.

Difficulty: Easy. The trail has a 3 percent grade.

Food: Restaurants and grocery stores are available in Placerville.

Rest rooms: There are rest rooms along the trail.

Seasons: The trail can be used year-round. Despite its location in the foothills of the Sierra Nevada, the elevation is too low to maintain adequate snow cover for cross-country skiing in winter.

Access and parking: To reach the Jacquier Road staging area from U.S. Highway 50 in Placerville, take the Broadway exit. Go left on Broadway and follow this to Smith Flat Road. Turn left (east) on Smith Flat Road, and follow it to Jacquier Road. The trailhead is on the west side of Jacquier Road. The Jacquier Road staging area provides access both to the section of trail already in place, which heads west to Mosquito Road, and the section that heads west to Snows Road, which is expected to be in place by the fall of 2000.

To reach the Mosquito Road end point, take the Broadway exit from Highway 50 and go right (west) on Broadway to Mosquito Road. Go right (north) on Mosquito Road, under the bridge. Continue left (north) on Mosquito Road for about 25 feet; the trailhead is on your right.

Transportation: There is no public transportation serving the trail.

Rentals: There are no rentals available along the trail.

Contact: Ron Mueller, Recreation and Parks Director, City of Placerville, 549 Main Street, Placerville, CA 95667; (530) 642–5232.

• •

The El Dorado Trail rambles through the oak woodlands that surround the charming foothill town of Placerville. The nearly 2-mile-long section of the trail that is currently in place functions as a nice route for folks commuting within Placerville and as a short recreational romp for the community at large. But when planned extensions are completed, lengthening the trail east along the railroad grade to Camino, the El Dorado Trail will doubtless earn a reputation as a premier recreational trail.

The El Dorado Lumber Company originally built the grade upon which the trail rests at the turn of the twentieth century. Like many railroads in the foothills, this one was used to transport logs from forest to sawmill, which in this case was located in Camino. The line was sold to the Michigan-California Lumber Company, which abandoned it in 1950. The grade was unused until the County of El Dorado purchased it; the section of trail from Mosquito Road to Jacquier Road was completed in 1992.

From Jacquier Road, the path descends gently toward downtown Placerville, buffered by the shady flora of the surrounding oak woodland, which includes not only oaks but Digger pines, and supports a colorful understory of walnut, buckeye, squawbush, and, of course, pesky poison oak.

The paved trail begins in a semirural environment, with Smith Flat Road, Hangtown Creek, and the freeway paralleling the trail on its south side. You will cross a street, then the trail is uninterrupted for more than a mile until it is crossed by Schnell School Road. Cross several more residential streets before reaching the western end point of the rail-trail on Mosquito Road at 1.7 miles, where there is limited parking.

The trail extension that is slated to be completed by September 2000, which heads east from Jacquier Road, will cross a pedestrian bridge over U.S. Highway 50 and proceed up into the foothills for another 1.5 to 2 miles. When the entire project is built out, the path will climb from the oak forests surrounding Placerville into the dense mixed conifer forests that surround the mountain village of Camino.

❶ West Side Rail Trail

This trail follows one of the many railroad lines plowed through the foothills of the Sierra Nevada by the West Side Lumber Company.

Activities:

Location: Tuolumne City, Tuolumne County

Length: 5.5 miles one-way

Surface: Dirt and original ballast

Wheelchair access: This rough path is not wheelchair accessible.

Difficulty: Hard, due to the trail's length and rough surface

Food: There is no food available along this rail-trail, but restaurants and grocery stores are available in Twain Harte and other towns along California 108. No water is available along the trail either, so be sure to pack plenty.

Rest rooms: There are no rest rooms available along the trail. Practice leave-no-trace principles by burying waste at least 8 inches underground and packing out toilet paper.

Seasons: The trail is accessible year-round. Hiking and mountain biking are best in the spring, summer, and fall; you may cross-country ski on the trail during the winter months if snow permits.

Access and parking: To reach the trailhead from the Mi-Wok Ranger Station in Mi-Wuk Village, follow California 108 west for 2.9 miles to Tuolumne Road. Go left (east) on Tuolumne Road, and follow it for 6.7 miles to Cottonwood Road (a.k.a. Stanislaus Forest Road 1N04/Forest Route 14). Go left on Cottonwood Road for 0.2 mile to the trailhead parking area, which is located at the intersection of Miramonte Road and Buchanan Road.

Transportation: There is no public transportation to this rail-trail.

Rentals: There are no rentals near the trail.

Contact: Chuck James, Recreation Technician, or Katie Coulter, District Archaeologist, Mi-Wok Ranger District, P.O. Box 100, Mi-Wuk Village, CA 95346-0100; (209) 586–3234.

Like its sister rail-trail, the West Side Rails from Hull Creek to Clavey River (Trail 23), this portion of the abandoned West Side Lumber Company railroad system features wonderful hiking and mountain biking through a dense mixed conifer forest.

This portion of the railroad system was part of the company's Hetch Hetchy and Yosemite Valleys Railway, which was used to bring lumber from the surrounding forests to the company's sawmill in Tuolumne (formerly called Carters). The awesome job of carving the grade out of the mountainside was done by Chinese and Native American laborers at the turn of the twentieth century. More information about the line and its construction is available from the trail manager at the Mi-Wok Ranger District office.

The trail begins at Miramonte Road and heads up along the south-facing wall of the steep canyon that cradles the North Fork of the Tuolumne River. The route is exposed and lovely, dipping in and out of steep drainages and offering wonderful views of the canyon and surrounding foothills as it climbs. Traces of the West Side line, including rails and ties, can be seen along the rail-trail. The route ends on Cottonwood Road, which roughly parallels the rail-trail, at 5.5 miles near a campground.

Rails-to-Trails

CENTRAL CALIFORNIA

Central California

25 Monterey Peninsula Recreational Trail
26 Ventura River Trail
27 Ojai Valley Trail
1 Fillmore Trail
K Fresno Sugar Pine Trail and Clovis Old Town Trail

PACIFIC OCEAN

N

Fresno
Clovis
41 K
99
5
Salinas
Monterey 25
101
San Luis Obispo
101
Santa Barbara
1
Ventura
Ojai 27
26
Fillmore 126
1

0   50   100
Miles

TOP RAIL-TRAILS

25 Monterey Peninsula Recreational Trail

This rail-trail immerses you in the culture of the sea. If you are lucky, otters will be frolicking in the kelp off the coast of Pacific Grove when you pass. There is no doubt that sparkling sailboats will be moored in Monterey Bay near Fisherman's Wharf, and seabirds take wing over the estuary at the trail's northern end in Seaside.

Activities:

Location: Pacific Grove, Monterey, and Seaside in Monterey County

Length: 4.8 miles one-way

Surface: Asphalt and concrete, with a dirt walking path alongside the paved trail in Pacific Grove

Wheelchair access: The entire trail is accessible to persons with disabilities.

Difficulty: Easy

Food: You will find an abundance of restaurants along the trail in Monterey's Cannery Row and Fisherman's Wharf areas.

Rest rooms: There are no rest rooms located at either end point of the trail, but facilities can be found in parks, beaches, and private business establishments along the route.

Seasons: The trail can be used year-round. Although temperatures are usually moderate, Monterey Bay is subject to the marine influence, and the fog can be dense and cold when it is in. Be prepared for swift changes in temperature.

Access and parking: To reach the parking lot at Lovers Point in Pacific Grove, follow U.S. Highway 1 to the California Highway 68 exit. California 68 leads into Pacific Grove. After about 2.2 scenic miles, the highway veers left (south) onto the famed 17-Mile Drive; stay right (straight) on Forest Avenue. Follow

Forest Avenue about 2 miles to Lighthouse Avenue. Turn left (south) on Lighthouse Avenue, go two blocks to 17th Street, and turn right (west). Follow 17th Street for about 0.3 mile to the Lover's Point parking lot, which is on the right (north) side of the road about 100 yards before the big pink Lovers Point Inn.

To reach the Pacific Grove/Lovers Point trailhead from downtown Monterey, head toward the ocean to Del Monte Avenue. From the intersection of Del Monte Avenue and Washington Street, which is north of Cannery Row and the Monterey Bay Aquarium, head south on Del Monte Avenue, through the tunnel, to the first road fork. Ignore the signs for Cannery Row and the aquarium, staying south on Lighthouse Avenue. Once you enter Pacific Grove, stay left (south) on Central Avenue to 17th Street. Turn right (west) on 17th, and go down toward the bay for about 0.2 mile to the trailhead on the right (north) side of the road.

To reach the Seaside trailhead from U.S. Highway 1, take the Seaside/Del Rey Oaks exit. Go east on California Highway 218 (Camino Del Rey), drive about 50 yards, and turn right (south) onto Roberts Avenue and into the parking lot, which faces a small estuary. The bike path that begins here leads to the rail-trail, which is located on the far (east) side of the estuary.

There are parking areas at both end points.

Transportation: Monterey–Salinas Transit serves the area. MST can be contacted by writing 1 Ryan Ranch Road, Monterey, CA 93940, or by calling (831) 899–2555 or 424–7695. The Web site is www.mst.org.

Rentals: Bay Bike Rentals (831–646–9090) has shops on the rail-trail at both Cannery Row and Fisherman's Wharf in Monterey.

Contact: For the portion of the trail in Monterey, contact Kay Russo, Director of the Monterey Recreation and Community Service Department, 546 Dutra Street, Monterey, CA 93940; (831) 646–3866. For the section of trail in Pacific Grove, contact John Miller, Director of the Pacific Grove Recreation Department, 515 Gunipero Avenue, Pacific Grove, CA 93950; (831) 648–3130.

• •

There are some who might gaze with longing upon the gingerbread dollhouses that overlook the craggy shoreline of Pacific Grove. There's no denying it: The folks who live in these historic homes reside in an area of unsurpassed scenic and cultural beauty. But the sea otters have it pretty darn good too. From the sun-splashed kelp beds on which they lounge, the views are just as spectacular, and because they work from home, they get to enjoy it day in and day out. That's living!

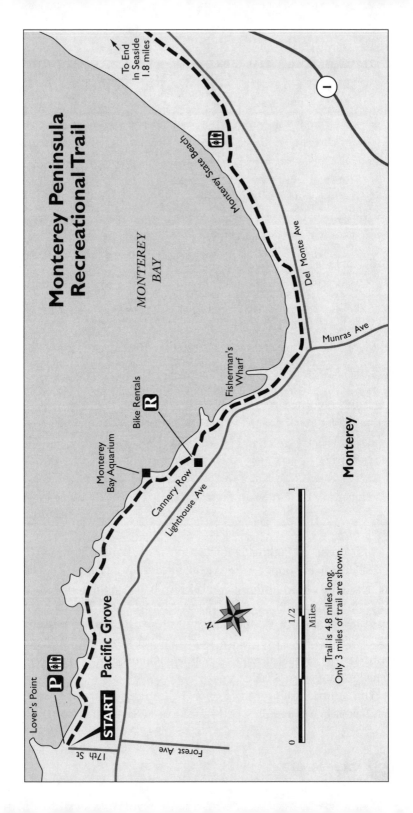

PEEK INTO THE DEEP

Luminous jellyfish that look like egg drops. Leopard sharks and sunfish that fly from inky darkness to blue light in a tank that holds a million gallons of seawater. Otters that play, eat, and rest in kelp that grows two stories high. Anchovies that spin a silvery web overhead.

The Monterey Bay Aquarium is home to some incredible creatures, offering glimpses into a mysterious world and displaying animals and plants that thrive in a realm we can only visit and admire from behind glass.

This amazing aquarium, which shelters and provides a forum for study of the wildlife protected within the Monterey Bay National Marine Sanctuary, is located one block south of the Monterey Peninsula Recreation Trail in Monterey's Cannery Row. From the trail you can enjoy the flat, glittering expanse of Monterey Bay and the wildlife that abides on or near its surface. Within the aquarium, you can observe the environment below the bay's surface, from the magic of tide pools to the mysterious depths of the Monterey Canyon.

The aquarium is open from 10:00 A.M. to 6:00 P.M. daily except Christmas Day, and from 9:30 A.M. to 6:00 P.M. from Memorial Day through Labor Day and during major holiday periods. Ticket prices are $15.95 for adults, $12.95 for seniors, and $6.95 for children ages 3 to 12 and for the disabled. Contact the aquarium at (831) 648–4888 for more information, or visit the aquarium's Web site at www.mbayaq.org.

The Monterey Peninsula Recreation Trail affords hikers, cyclists and skaters many opportunities to check out the sea otters—and the sea lions, and the seabirds—as well as the chance to sample the many other amenities offered by the popular resort town. The path wanders through historic Cannery Row, past the eateries and museums of Fisherman's Wharf, along the beaches at San Carlos Park and Monterey Bay Park, and through a colonnade of eucalyptus to a seabird-speckled estuary in Seaside.

The rail-trail follows the former bed of a Southern Pacific line that began in Spanish Bay and ran north to San Francisco. During the heyday of the area's fisheries, in the 1930s and 1940s, the line served the canneries, taking goods to the markets in the north and bringing supplies back south to Monterey. It also served as a passenger line, with a turntable located at Lovers Point in Pacific Grove.

You can begin at either end point, but the trail is described here starting at Lovers Point. The spectacular rocky shoreline borders the path on the west; on the east, the charming Victorians of Pacific Grove overlook the bay. Head north up the rail-trail; bicyclists and in-line skaters are restricted to the paved portion, while hikers and walkers stroll along the dirt walkway that parallels the pavement. At 0.3 mile, pass a mural on the east (right) that describes the history of the area; to the west, the lumpy crags poking out of the bay host cormorants, seagulls, and pelicans, and clumps of kelp serve as beds for the frolicsome otters. A small park, with manicured grass and benches shaded by cypress, lies at the half-mile point.

At 0.8 mile, historic homes give way to historic warehouses, and the trail passes the Hopkins Marine Station of Stanford University on the west. Cross Eardley Avenue at 1 mile, and enter Cannery Row proper. The trail is now concrete, and walkers, cyclists, and skaters share the same path. A series of street crossings follows. Pass the

This cyclist enjoys a marina view along the Monterey Peninsula Trail.

Monterey Bay Aquarium, the cannery buildings, the carousel in the Edgewater Packing Company building, and the Southern Pacific railway cars that house the Cannery Row Welcome Center.

The route continues north to San Carlos Beach and Fisherman's Shoreline Park at 1.5 miles. A sloping lawn shaded by cypress drops to a blue bay dotted with sparkling fishing and sailing vessels. Pass a small beach. At 2.0 miles, the trail deposits you on Fisherman's Wharf in the square that fronts the Custom House Museum.

Beyond the wharf, the trail splits briefly, with hikers staying waterside, while users on wheels are shunted east around a parking lot. The bike path crosses Washington Street and parallels Del Monte Avenue to Monterey Bay Park at 2.5 miles.

The rail-trail, now asphalt again, veers left (west) into the park, rejoins the walking path, then heads north between the small dunes sheltering the beach on the west side and a large lawn on the east. Beyond the park, the path is used primarily by local residents. It passes between warehouses and businesses into a strip of eucalyptus that serves as a barrier between it and the adjacent roadway. At 3.5 miles a boardwalk offers access to the tall dunes to the west of the path; there is no dune access for the next half mile or so, as the beachside property belongs to a U.S. Naval installation with restricted access. The railroad tracks, unseen to this point except in Cannery Row, reappear to the east of the trail, cross beneath it, and pop in and out of view as the route continues north.

The trail rolls beneath a couple of overpasses, then enters the city of Seaside at 4.1 miles, near the intersection of Del Monte Avenue and Roberts Avenue. The emergent railroad tracks pass through a small bower of cypress; the paved trail runs alongside them for another 0.2 mile to the trail's end at Camino Del Rey. The rail corridor—perhaps the site of a trail extension someday—continues ahead, running between shopping centers and the busy thoroughfare. Unless you have arranged a shuttle, you must return as you came.

While hardly the most scenic trail in this guidebook, the Ventura River Trail is definitely one of the most fascinating. More than any other, this route points up the intriguing and provocative juxtaposition of what the railroads often bring to a community—namely, industry—and what they leave behind when they are abandoned.

Activities:

Location: City of Ventura, Ventura County

Length: 6.3 miles one-way

Surface: Asphalt

Wheelchair access: The trail is wheelchair accessible. There aren't many easy ways to access the trail other than at the end points, however, so all users, whether in wheelchairs or not, should be prepared to go the distance or travel only a portion of the trail.

Difficulty: Moderate, due only to the trail's length

Food: There is no food or water available along the trail, so pack what you will need. Picnic tables are available at Foster Park. You can find restaurants and stores in Ventura, if you want to stock up at that end point.

Rest rooms: There are no rest rooms at the Ventura end point, nor are there any along the trail. Rest rooms are available at the Foster Park end point.

Seasons: The trail is accessible year-round.

Access and parking: To reach the Ventura end point from the southbound lanes of U.S. Highway 101 in Ventura, take the Main Street exit. Turn right (east) on Main Street and follow it less than a quarter mile to the trailhead parking lot, which is on the right (south/ocean) side of the road opposite Peking Street and before the California 33 overpass. From northbound 101, take the California 33/Ojai exit. Head north to Main Street. Turn left (west) on Main Street and follow it to the parking lot.

To reach Foster Park, continue northeast on California 33 for about 5.5 miles to the Casitas Vista/Foster Park exit. The park is adjacent to the freeway on its northwest side. There is plenty of parking available.

Transportation: The Ventura County Transportation Commission runs the VISTA bus system, which can be reached by dialing (800) 438–1112 within the local calling area, or (805) 642–1591. The Web site is www.goventura.org.

Rentals: Bikes can be rented from Cycles4Rent Inc., which is near the trailhead at 239 West Main Street in Ventura. The phone number is (805) 652–0462; the Web site is www.cycles4rent.com.

Contact: Jill Dolan, Marketing Specialist, City of Ventura, 501 Poli Street, P.O. Box 99, Ventura, CA 93002-0099; (805) 654–7800.

• •

S tretching from ocean to mountain, like the river that lends it its name and the railroad that preceded it, the Ventura River Trail presents a conundrum. This unusual route showcases both the natural world and the industrial, presenting an interesting and contradictory visual tableau. There is the willow-lined Ventura River and there are the rusted scraps of industry. There is the noisy freeway, and there are the rugged mountains that frame the valley. There are lemon trees, and there are tractors. It's a little boy's dream come true, and a provocative and very worthwhile journey for a thoughtful traveler.

The rail-trail cuts through Ventura's industrial underpinnings. Oil wells sucking black gold from the earth nod a slow hello to passersby; the tanks that store the crude rise adjacent to the trail in stark, fenced yards; tractors and trucks, which will burn the oil once it is refined, are parked in orderly rows awaiting dispatch. The Ventura River, a sluggish flow in a broad bed bordered by a fragile veil of riparian plants, writhes in and out of view on the northwest side of the rail-trail, not dominating the scene until the trail bends toward its finish in the Ojai Valley. And all along the route, artists have placed evocative works—a sculpture of an egret, a scattering of "oranges," animals set in bas relief on the trash cans—that draw from nature. Most striking of these are the "Midden Markers," etched with sayings that are as thought-provoking as the setting. More art projects are planned for this trail, which is very new to the California rail-trail system.

The trail follows the lower portion of the former Ventura and Ojai Rail Road, which was purchased in 1890 by the Southern Pacific Railroad Company. Fighting a losing battle with flood damage to the rails, Southern Pacific began to abandon the line, a process that started in the 1960s and wasn't completed until the late 1980s. The right-of-way was acquired as open space, and the trail was opened to the public in October, 1999.

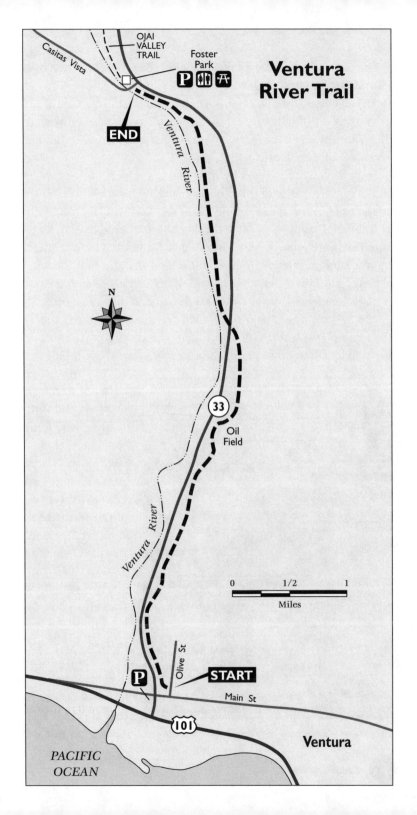

The rail-trail begins by following the on-street bike lane east down Main Street, passing under California 33 to Olive Street. Turn left (north) on Olive Street; there is a Ventura River Trail sign here. Turn left (north) off of Olive Street at Dubbers Street (marked with another Ventura River Trail sign). The obvious trail begins at the sharp curve in Dubbers Street.

The paved path, marked by mile and kilometer markers and accented with the "Midden Markers," is wedged between the freeway and the ball fields and community center at West Park, then spills into the industrial complexes. At 1.4 miles, the trail crosses Stanley Avenue. The neighboring freeway is screened by eucalyptus for a stretch, then the trail pulls away from the busy roadway as it winds through a series of gates that offer access to various industrial operations. Watch for trucks, and walk bicycles around the gates if they are closed.

The first oil rigs appear on the left (northeast) at about the 2.5-mile mark. Cross a series of small access roads as you pass through the oil fields, then cross under the freeway again at 3.4 miles.

A dilapidated bridge spans the Ventura River Trail.

The trail is now adjacent to the willow-screened Ventura River, which runs seasonally, and may be completely dry in summer and early fall. On the east side of the trail rise the storage tanks, painted a pastel green and accented with rust and drips of oil.

The route takes on a more rural aspect as you continue inland toward the Ojai Valley, with orchards decorating the slopes of the nearby mountains,

A TALE OF TWO TRAILS

The Ventura River Trail and its older sibling, the Ojai Valley Trail, lie on the former right-of-way of the Ventura and Ojai Rail Road Company. This railroad, which traveled between Ventura and Ojai carrying both passengers and freight, including the succulent citrus of the region's ubiquitous orchards, was established in 1898, and was purchased by Southern Pacific less than a year after its completion.

But floods, scourge of roadways and railroads throughout California into modern times, beset the rail line. The Ventura and Ojai line washed out many times before Southern Pacific decided to discontinue passenger service in the early 1930s. By the time record rains drenched the area in the late 1960s, the tracks had been damaged so many times that Southern Pacific decided it wasn't worth the fight and abandoned all but a limited section of track that served the oil industry in Ventura. Eventually floods damaged that last link as well, and the line was completely abandoned by the late 1980s.

The Ojai Valley Trail, which runs from Foster Park to Ojai, was built over a period of nearly ten years, and completed in 1989. The Ventura River Trail, also ten years in the making, opened in October 1999. Linking the trails makes for a fantastic bike ride, totaling more than 20 miles and encompassing all of the fascinating scenery from the mountains surrounding the Ojai Valley to the flatlands near the Pacific Ocean.

and a few lemon trees growing adjacent to the trail. Cross a bridge at 4.6 miles, where you will be treated to the best views of the Ventura River.

By the 5.4-mile mark, the trail again runs adjacent to the freeway but has curved away from Ventura into the scenic Ojai Valley. The mountains, with a scrappy covering of grayish green scrub, rise steeply away from the river bottom. Pass a trail entrance at 5.7 miles and stay straight on the obvious route.

The trail ends in Foster Park, with its picnic tables, tot lot, lawns, and other amenities, at 6.3 miles. This is the turnaround point, unless you plan to continue on the Ojai Valley Trail, which begins here.

27 Ojai Valley Trail

Though it sits on the edge of Los Angeles, a metropolitan area that is ever-changing and expanding, the Ojai Valley has retained its rural charm. Part of that charm is the rail-trail that follows the Ventura River into the valley, passing broad open spaces and wonderful views of the surrounding mountains as it climbs.

Activities:

Location: From Foster Park to Ojai in Ventura County

Length: 9.5 miles one-way

Surface: Asphalt, except for a short section from Fox Street in Ojai to the Soule Park Golf Course, which is dirt and limited to equestrian and pedestrian use

Wheelchair access: Except for the brief unpaved section from Fox Street in Ojai to Soule Park Golf Course, the trail is wheelchair accessible.

Difficulty: Hard. The trail is long, and climbs steadily from Foster Park to Ojai.

Food: You will find fast food and a market near the midpoint of the trail, when it briefly parallels California 33 in Oak View. There are plenty of restaurants and stores in downtown Ojai, at the trail's northeastern end point.

Rest rooms: There are public rest rooms at Foster Park. No other public facilities are available along the trail.

Seasons: The trail can be used year-round, but the portion of the path that crosses the Ventura River may be flooded during and after winter and spring rains.

Access and parking: To reach the Foster Park end point from California 33 northeast of Ventura, take the Casitas Vista/Foster Park exit. The park is adjacent to the freeway on its northwest side. There is plenty of parking available here.

To reach the Fox Street end point, continue on California 33 into the town of Ojai. At the intersection of California 33 and California 150 in Ojai, go right (east) on California 150 and proceed through the charming downtown area. Fox Street intersects the highway on the east side of town; turn right (south) and drive a couple of blocks to the trail. Limited parking is available along the residential streets.

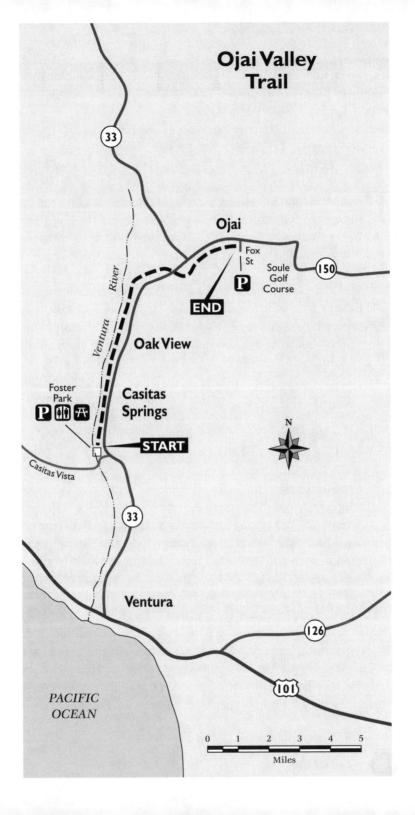

Transportation: The Ventura County Transportation Commission runs the VISTA bus system, which can be reached by dialing (800) 438–1112 within the local calling area, or (805) 642–1591. The Web site is www.goventura.org.

Rentals: There are no rentals available along the route.

Contact: The Ventura County Reservations and Information Office, 800 South Victoria Avenue, Ventura, CA 93009; (805) 654–3951.

• •

The spectacular Ojai Valley, cradle of the Ventura River, is surrounded—you might even say insulated—by the sharp, dry peaks of Los Padres National Forest. Carpeted with grasses that are verdant in winter and spring and golden in summer, the valley fended off suburban sprawl, retaining the rural, agricultural atmosphere that once dominated the coastal valleys in Southern California.

The Ojai Valley Trail, awarded the Cal-Trans Award for Excellence in Transportation Facilities in 1989, is the perfect path from which to enjoy the valley. At its southern end, Foster Park offers all the amenities, including riverside picnicking and a playground for the wee ones. The trail dips away from busy California 33 into the wildlands bordering the river for an infinitely appealing mile or so, then climbs into quiet neighborhoods as it approaches Ojai. Within the quaint town itself, the trail, a shady pathway frequented by local residents walking dogs and pushing strollers, offers a wonderful alternative to the bustling main street.

The rail-trail lies on the bed of the former Ventura and Ojai Rail Road, which followed the Ventura River from Ojai to the oceanside town of Ventura. The railroad carried passengers and freight between the two towns from the turn of the twentieth century to the 1930s. When Southern Pacific, which acquired the railroad shortly after it was completed, decided to abandon the line, the county of Ventura purchased it and installed the trail, which was completed in 1989.

The trail begins in Foster Park, which is also the end point of the Ventura River Trail; combining these two routes makes for an extremely pleasant, lengthy bike ride. The first half mile of the trail borders the park, passing the picnic areas, tot lot, and ball fields. Beyond, the trail passes through a bower of eucalyptus, then cruises by the open backyards of homes wedged between the trail and California 33, which the route roughly parallels. A dirt walkway, ideal for horses and trail runners, parallels the paved path, but is separated by a rustic fence.

At the 1-mile mark, the trail curves east to parallel the two-lane highway through Casitas Springs for a half mile, crossing several side streets. On the north side of the town, the trail hooks back west toward the river, bordered on one side by the broad, rocky channel and on the other by dense brush and oaks. Climb a short hill onto the railroad grade proper and wind through the oak woodland to a low, concrete-covered culvert that bridges the river at 1.8 miles. This section is subject to flooding during and after rainstorms.

The splendid seclusion ends at the 3-mile mark, where the trail slowly makes the transition from relative wildness to the tameness of the quiet neighborhoods of Oak View. Cross Santa Ana Boulevard, then Monte Via, where you will find a small parking area.

The rail-trail passes behind Oak View Community Park, with its lawns, playground, and ball field, then climbs onto an exposed stretch of grade that offers commanding views of the river valley. Beyond the elevated section, the trail drops into a shady gully and continues through area neighborhoods.

Here pavement and railroad grade meet along the Ojai Valley Trail.

At 5.3 miles, the trail again bends eastward to parallel the highway. At the Woodland Avenue intersection in Oak View, you have easy access to fast food and a market. The trail crosses a number of side streets before it reaches a large meadow that opens on the left (northeast) side of the trail near the 6.5-mile mark. This lovely open space, with its scattering of oak trees, stretches to the wooded mountains in the distance.

At the 8-mile mark, the trail crosses the major intersection of California Highways 33 and 150 in Ojai; there is a large shopping center at this juncture. Use traffic signals to cross California 150 safely, then pick up the obvious trail on the south side of the highway.

The rail-trail plunges back into a peaceful neighborhood, cruising through the greenbelt that separates these Ojai backyards. At 9 miles you will pass through Libbey Park, which offers parking, an amphitheater, rest rooms, picnicking, and access to a trail leading north to the downtown area.

The paved trail ends in a cul-de-sac at Fox Street, although horseback riders and those on foot can continue on the dirt track to Soule Park and Golf Course. Unless you have arranged a shuttle or plan to return to the trailhead via public transportation, you will return as you came. It's all downhill from here!

MORE RAIL-TRAILS

J Fillmore Trail

This short rail-trail begins at the Fillmore end of the historic Fillmore & Western Railway. The dynamic collection of railroad cars clustered around the station—including one that houses a museum—is the highlight of the route.

Activities:

Location: Fillmore, Ventura County

Length: 2 miles one-way

Surface: Asphalt

Wheelchair access: The rail-trail is wheelchair accessible in its entirety.

Difficulty: Easy

Food: There are no restaurants located on the trail, but you can find restaurants and markets nearby in downtown Fillmore.

Rest rooms: There are rest rooms at the Fillmore City Hall trailhead.

Seasons: The trail can be used year-round.

Access and parking: To reach the Fillmore Central Station Park from California 126 (Ventura Street) in Fillmore, head north for one block on Central Avenue to City Hall. Parking is available in the designated lots off of Main Street and along the street itself.

Transportation: The Ventura County Transportation Commission runs the VISTA bus system, which can be reached by dialing (800) 438–1112 within the local calling area, or (805) 642–1591. The Web site is www.goventura.org.

Rentals: There are no rentals available on the trail.

Contact: Bert Rapp, City Engineer, City of Fillmore, 524 Sespe Avenue, Fillmore, CA 93015; (805) 524–3701.

Fillmore is a train town. Nowhere is this more in evidence than at the Fillmore Trail's eastern end point at the Fillmore Station, which doubles as the end of the line for the historic Fillmore & Western Railway Company.

The Fillmore rail-trail runs along the tracks of the Fillmore & Western Railway.

Railcars of various descriptions line the tracks fronting the old Fillmore Station and the Fillmore City Hall building. The concrete trail, impeccably landscaped and separated from the tracks by a quaint iron railing, runs the length of the rail yard, passing the old station house, a museum and gift shop, and the Red Caboose, where you can purchase tickets for a ride on the historic train.

The Fillmore & Western is a major player in the area. In addition to offering visitors the opportunity to ride a variety of vintage railcars on its line between Fillmore and Santa Paula—trains upon which you can solve a murder mystery or travel to a secluded location to enjoy dinner and dancing—the railroad also serves the movie industry and participates in the annual Rail Festival, which is sponsored in part by the Santa Clara Valley Railroad Historical Society.

For more information on the Fillmore & Western Railway, you can call (805) 524-2546 or write P.O. Box 960, Fillmore, CA 93061. Reservations can be made by calling (800) 773-TRAIN. The Web site is www.fwry.com.

The heart of the rail-trail is the half mile that runs by the station complex, but the rest of the path is also pleasant. Between Central Avenue and A Street the trail runs adjacent to the existing railroad tracks, wedged between private homes and warehouses. At A Street, the trail bends northwest and parallels Old Telegraph Road as well as the tracks. Sycamores shade the route, which continues for another mile to Shiells Park, on the left (south) side of the road. You'll find more parking, picnic facilities, ball fields, and rest rooms in the park. A Sunkist plant is opposite the park, a stopping point for the massive amount of citrus that grows in the orchards that surround Fillmore.

Fresno Sugar Pine Trail and Clovis Old Town Trail

The development of the Fresno and Clovis route exemplifies how community support can foster the birth and growth of an urban rail-trail. The path passes through Old Town Clovis, and, when completed, will connect with trails along the San Joaquin River in northern Fresno.

Activities:

Location: Fresno and Clovis in Fresno County

Length: The Clovis Old Town Trail is currently 5 miles long, and the Fresno Sugar Pine Trail is 3 miles long. When the two trails are completed in 2001, the route will total 13 miles.

Surface: Asphalt

Wheelchair access: The paved route is wheelchair accessible.

Difficulty: The two sections, taken independently, are easy, but the entire route, when completed, will qualify as moderate due to its length.

Food: Restaurants, grocery stores, and fast food outlets are available throughout the Fresno and Clovis areas.

Rest rooms: There are no public facilities located on the trails.

Seasons: The trail can be traveled year-round.

Access and parking: To reach the southern end point of the Clovis Old Town Trail from California 99, take California 41 north to California 180. Follow California 180 west to California 168 to Clovis/Huntington Lake (also known as the Sierra Freeway). Take the Ashlan Avenue exit off California 168. At the stoplight turn right (west) on Ashlan Avenue and go about 3 miles to its intersection with Clovis Avenue. Go right (south) on Clovis Avenue and proceed to Dakota Avenue; the trailhead is on your left at the Clovis Recreation Center.

Transportation: The Clovis Transit Stageline can be reached at (559) 297–2482. You can also visit the City of Clovis website at www.ci.clovis.ca.us.

Rentals: There are no rentals along the route.

Contact: Mark Keppler, Coalition for Community Trails, P.O.Box 1313, Clovis, CA 93613-1313; (559) 323–0892. His e-mail address is mkeppler@csufresno.edu. The Fresno City Parks and Recreation Department is at 2326 Fresno Street, Room 101, Fresno CA 93721; (559) 498–4239. For the section of trail in Clovis, contact John Lovejoy, construction manager with the Clovis Engineering Department, 1033 Fifth Street, Clovis CA 93612; (559) 297–2354.

• •

It may not look like much now, but when the nearly 5,000 trees that were planted in 2000 reach maturity, this is going to be one shady—and lovely—urban rail-trail.

This evolving addition to California's rail-trail system follows the Clovis Branchline/Pinedale Spur railroad corridor through Old Town Clovis and northern Fresno. It is the product of a concerted community effort spearheaded by the Coalition for Community Trails, which has worked diligently in cooperation with other nonprofit and public agencies to get the trail in place.

The rail-trail actually includes two railroad corridors—the Clovis Old Town and the Fresno Sugar Pine—which were purchased by Fresno and Clovis from Union Pacific in 1997. Two separate segments are currently in place, and when the connection between these is completed, the trail will be about 13 miles long.

The first segment begins at the intersection of Clovis and Dakota Avenues and heads north through the heart of Old Town Clovis for about 5 miles to the intersection of Peach and Alluvial Avenues. When this guidebook went to press the trail ended here, but by 2001, the route will be linked to the second existing section, which begins at the intersection of Willow Avenue and Shepherd Avenue and curves west to end at Nees Avenue and California 41. This 3-mile section of the rail-trail skirts Woodward Park, on the banks of the San Joaquin River, and ends at the River Park at Market Place Mall.

The trail is basically urban in nature, primarily serving as a commuter route for local residents. But the thirty-three different varieties of trees that were planted in the spring of 2000 will doubtless go a long way toward beautifying both the route and the surrounding community.

Rails-to-Trails

SOUTHERN CALIFORNIA

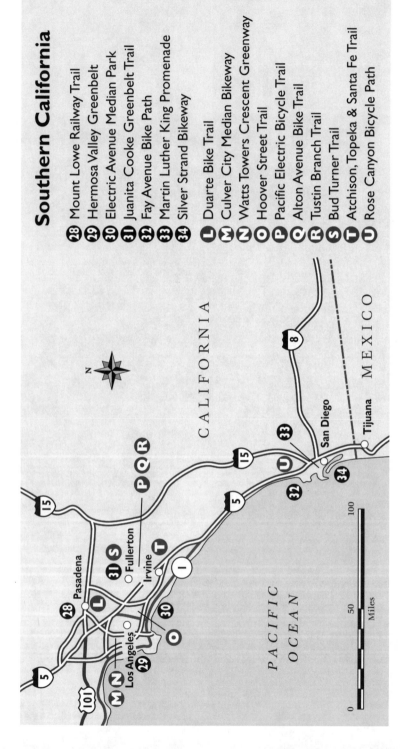

Southern California

28 Mount Lowe Railway Trail
29 Hermosa Valley Greenbelt
30 Electric Avenue Median Park
31 Juanita Cooke Greenbelt Trail
32 Fay Avenue Bike Path
33 Martin Luther King Promenade
34 Silver Strand Bikeway

L Duarte Bike Trail
M Culver City Median Bikeway
N Watts Towers Crescent Greenway
O Hoover Street Trail
P Pacific Electric Bicycle Trail
Q Alton Avenue Bike Trail
R Tustin Branch Trail
S Bud Turner Trail
T Atchison, Topeka & Santa Fe Trail
U Rose Canyon Bicycle Path

Southern California's

TOP RAIL-TRAILS

<table>
<tr><td>28</td><td>Mount Lowe Railway Trail</td></tr>
</table>

This rail-trail lies on the bed of one of the most famous and historic rail lines in the Los Angeles area. The Mount Lowe Railway, which featured a remarkable incline up Rubio Canyon to the Echo Mountain House, and a circular bridge that was world renowned as an engineering landmark, stopped transporting passengers up the mountain in 1939, but the route continues to thrill modern visitors with its scenery and views.

Activities:

Note: Camping and backpacking opportunities exist along other routes in the Angeles National Forest. A Forest Adventure Pass, available for a small fee at sporting goods outlets throughout the Los Angeles area, is required to use this trail.

Location: West of Pasadena in Los Angeles County, in the San Gabriel Mountains and the Angeles National Forest

Length: 4 miles on the railroad grade, but you must hike or bike up the very steep access road for 2.2 miles before you reach the rail-trail. The round-trip totals 12.4 miles.

Surface: Ballast and dirt

Wheelchair access: The trail, given its steep grades and rough surface, is not suitable for wheelchairs.

Difficulty: Hard

Food: There are no food or water sources along the trail, nor are there any along the steep access road that leads to the trail. Be sure to pack in all you need. There are plenty of restaurants and grocery stores in Pasadena, Altadena, and the other cities that lie at the foot of the mountains.

Rest rooms: There are no rest rooms at the trailhead, nor are there any along the route.

Seasons: The trail can be used year-round but may be muddy during and after winter rainstorms. The trail and access road also may be off-limits during periods of high fire danger.

Access and parking: There is no easy way to get to the Mount Lowe Railway Trail. Arguably the easiest, however, is to follow the paved access road up to the rail-trail near its Echo Mountain end point.

To reach the access road and trailhead from Interstate 210 in Pasadena, take the Lake Avenue exit. Head north on Lake Avenue for 3.7 miles to Loma Alta Drive, which is at the base of the steep massif. Turn left (west) on Loma Alta Drive and go for 1.1 miles to Chaney Trail; a flashing yellow light marks the road. Turn right (north) on Chaney Trail and follow this for 1.4 miles, passing a display about the Forest Adventure Pass, to a gate. If the gate is open, you can proceed for another 1.1 miles to a saddle where you will find another gate and the beginning of the paved access road. There is limited roadside parking.

Transportation: There are no transit services directly to this trail, but public transportation is available to Pasadena. Transit services in Los Angeles County may be obtained by calling (800) COMMUTE in the Los Angeles calling area. The Los Angeles Metropolitan Transportation Authority Web site is www.met.net.

Rentals: There are no rentals along the trail.

Contact: Mike Alarid, Los Angeles River Ranger District, Angeles National Forest, 4600 Oak Grove Drive, La Canada, CA 91011; (818) 899–1900.

• •

Rising in stark contrast to all the other rail-trails in Southern California, the Mount Lowe Railway Trail is fabulously wild. From an airy perch on this route, which winds through the tight, arid folds of the San Gabriel Mountains, you look down on the sprawling urbanity that makes the Los Angeles basin both famous and infamous.

On a clear day, the views from much of the railroad grade are, as you might expect, sublime, extending westward across the city to the Pacific Ocean and beyond. But even on hazy days you can enjoy vistas of the shimmering city below. Silver and gray and black like an orchestra in a pit, its cacophony muted to white noise by the time it reaches these heights. From Echo Mountain, site of the ruins of the once grand Echo Mountain House, you can enjoy the same panorama that enticed folks to ride the famous Mount Lowe Railway a century ago.

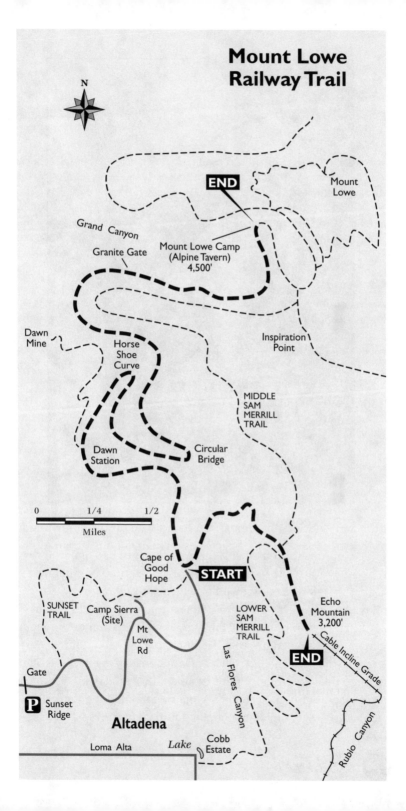

A cyclist pedals up the Mount Lowe railroad grade.

The railway was remarkable for more than just its wonderful views. It, like the rail-trail that now lies in its bed, featured breathtaking exposure, writhing like a sidewinder with a bellyache. It ran for 4 steep miles from the Echo Mountain House to the Alpine Tavern at the Mount Lowe Camp, but was fairly mellow compared to the incline railroad that climbed up from Altadena to Echo Mountain via Rubio Canyon, which ascended 1,500 feet via a 32 to 69 percent grade. Standing amid the foundations of this incline railway today invokes a feeling of incredulity—how could anyone ride up (and then down) such a ferocious grade, much less build a railroad on it?

The Mount Lowe Railway and its accompanying incline railway were built in the early 1890s. The railroad was a tourist attraction for about forty years and was abandoned in 1940. But the route has never totally lost its appeal: The railroad grade continues to draw recreationalists today and is included on the National Register of Historic Places. Interpretive signs placed along the trail help explain the railroad's complex and fascinating history.

Whether on foot, on wheels, or on horseback, you'll do most of the work just getting to the trail. You will climb more than 2,000 feet as you ascend from the trailhead to the Mount Lowe Camp, so plan on a full day, bring plenty of food and water, keep a reasonable pace, and enjoy.

From the trailhead, you will set out on the paved access road, which climbs past an interpretive sign with a map of the railroad. At 0.3 mile, you will pass the first intersection with the Sunset Ridge Trail; the second lies near the road's intersection with the rail-trail.

The paved road is nipped into gullies and tucked behind ridges on the west face of the brush-covered mountainside. At about 1.5 miles, the road forks; stay right (east) on the main track, ignoring the road to the left (north), which leads to the site of Camp Sierra. Just beyond the intersection, at 1.7 miles, pass a gate at a switchback that swings the roadway north into the mountains.

At 2.2 miles, you will pass the second intersection with the Sunset Ridge Trail, which departs from the paved road to the left (west). Within 100 yards of this intersection, you will reach the Cape of Good Hope, where the portion of the rail-trail leading to Echo Mountain breaks off to the right (east).

Although it's clear the rail-trail continues straight ahead, take the time to visit the ruins of the Echo Mountain House. Turn right (east) onto the dirt track, which is lined with interpretive signs and narrows to single-track where it has been washed out. Railroad ties are embedded in the blond soil, and concrete foundations mark where trestles once spanned gullies that are slashed into the mountainside.

The trail leads gently downhill for 0.5 mile to the ruins, which command an awesome panorama of the Los Angeles basin. From a broad arcing staircase to a rusting bed frame, from potsherds to a large cistern to old track and other detritus of the railroad, the site is a history fanatic's dream come true. You can even shout into the Echo Phone and see if the mountains talk back to you. Interpretive signs include a discussion of the builders of the railroad and a map of the railway.

Once you've absorbed all you can, backtrack to the pavement at the Cape of Good Hope, passing the Sam Merrill Trail as you climb. The mileages that follow begin from the Echo Mountain House ruins.

Once on the paved road at 0.5 mile, turn right (north) and continue up the railroad grade, which turns to dirt about 100 yards beyond the Echo Mountain trail. As you climb to Dawn Station at 0.7 mile, you will pass three more interpretive signs, including one that notes that in the next 3.5 miles the railroad negotiated 127 curves. Benches shaded by a gazebo make this a perfect spot for rest and contemplation.

Continuing northward, the trail switchbacks through a major wash that is floored with concrete, then climbs to the upper end of the famed circular bridge, which lies on a switchback at the 1-mile mark.

The winding rail-trail gains altitude gently as it meanders through shady gullies and across sun-washed faces, until it arcs onto the backside of the mountain at about 2 miles. Gone are views of the basin; now you skirt a steep-walled canyon—the "Grand Canyon of the Millard"—which wears a sparse cloak of desert scrub and trees, and offers views only of more mountains rising to the east. At 2.5 miles, pass through the portal of the famed Granite Gate, which was blasted through an outcrop of granite.

In late afternoon, when the sun settles behind the mountains to the west, this section of the track is washed in welcomed shade, making the remainder of the journey quite pleasant. At the 4-mile mark you will arrive at the site of the Mount Lowe Alpine Tavern, which lies at the end of the line at a lofty 4,500 feet above sea level. The tavern suffered the same fate as the Echo Mountain House, burning to the ground in September 1936.

There are many options for exploration in the area of the Angeles National Forest served by the access road and the Mount Lowe Railway Trail, and you can use one of these other trails—such as the Sunset Ridge Trail—to return to the trailhead. If you return as you came, you'll have traveled a total of 12.4 miles.

Meticulously landscaped and popular with local residents and visitors alike, this rail-trail runs through a lovely strip of greenery that links two beachfront towns.

Activities:

Location: Manhattan Beach and Hermosa Beach, Los Angeles County

Length: 4 miles one-way

Surface: Wood chips

Wheelchair access: Although the route is flat and has numerous access points, its wood chip surface would make it a challenge for wheelchair users.

Difficulty: Moderate, due to the trail's length and soft surface

Food: Restaurants are available very near the rail-trail, but there are no food outlets directly on the trail.

Rest rooms: There are no rest rooms on the trail itself, but you may find them at Live Oak Park, located about 1.1 mile south of the trail's northern end point at Rosecrans Avenue.

Seasons: The trail can be used year-round, but it may be soft, and possibly muddy, during and after rainstorms.

Access and parking: To reach the northern trailhead from Interstate 405 in Manhattan Beach, take the Rosecrans Avenue exit. Head west on Rosecrans Avenue for 1.5 miles to a point just before its intersection with Sepulveda Boulevard. Turn left (south) into the large parking area that serves both the trailhead and the large shopping center on Rosecrans Avenue. The lot stretches toward the trailhead, which is at the far south end, and is well signed.

There is no good parking at the rail-trail's southern end point. To reach this end point from Interstate 405, take the 190th Street exit and follow it west (it becomes Herondo Street) for 4.8 miles. The trail is on your right (north) at the intersection of Herondo Street and Valley Drive.

Transportation: Transit services in Los Angeles County may be obtained by calling (800) COMMUTE in the Los Angeles calling area. The Los Angeles Metropolitan Transportation Authority Web site is www.met.net.

Rentals: There are no rentals along the route.

Contact: Mike Flaherty, Public Works Superintendent, City of Hermosa Beach, 1315 Valley Drive, Hermosa Beach, CA 90254; (310) 318–0214.

Although never in sight, the Pacific Ocean's influence bathes the Hermosa Valley Greenbelt. In summer, the fog rolls over it, smothering it in coolness and taking the edge off the sunlight. And the weak winter's sun seems just a bit brighter reflected off the surface of the water nearby. Regardless of the season, the rail-trail is washed in the smell of salt carried by sea breezes.

The path is set in a gorgeously landscaped greenbelt that runs south from Manhattan Beach to Hermosa Beach between Valley Drive and Ardmore Avenue. The soft mottled browns of the wood chips, along with the generous greenery provided by evergreen shrubs and palm trees, conspire to create a comforting insulation from the roadways on either side of the rail-trail. Not that this is needed: Both Manhattan Beach and Hermosa Beach present well kept murals of pastel-colored homes along the trail, appropriate for a Southern California beach town.

The trail follows an abandoned Atchison, Topeka & Santa Fe line that once served the oil refineries in El Segundo, to the north of Manhattan Beach. This freight line was abandoned more than fifteen years ago, and the land was purchased by the neighboring cities as open space, but because of political and monetary concerns the rail-trail wasn't built for several years after the abandonment. Local residents voted to tax themselves to pay for the construction of the greenbelt, and although you can still enjoy the shade of trees that were planted before the trail was formalized, the cities have worked for the last two years to update the landscaping and add a second path that runs parallel to the main route. The trail is clearly a source of pride for the community, and rightfully so.

The route, also called the Veterans Parkway, begins at the south end of the Rosecrans parking lot, heading south under an overpass and into a wide swale lined with fledgling trees and low-growing flowering plants. It passes peacefully between the carefully tended yards of bordering homes. The dirt track runs alongside the wood chipped path, and benches, trash cans, and water fountains are available along the route.

You will reach the first trail intersection at 0.4 mile, crossing 27th Street. Next comes the Pacific Avenue crossing at 0.6 mile, then, at about 1 mile, the 15th Street crossing. Live Oak Park, with its tot lot,

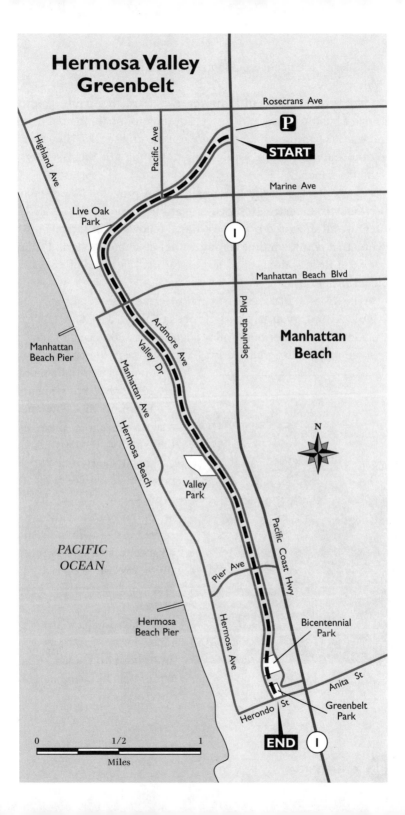

ball fields, picnic facilities, and ample parking, is on the north side of Valley Drive.

The trail takes on a different demeanor at this point, passing through a bustling business district. The crossing at Manhattan Beach Boulevard is complex; take care and use the crosswalks. If you have the time and inclination, a quick detour to the right (west) will take you to the beach.

A parcourse joins the greenbelt as you proceed. There is another busy intersection to negotiate at First Street, but the trail is peaceful and sheltered from the parallel roadways for the most part beyond that point, winding through quiet neighborhoods and sporting quaint little staircases built with railroad ties that offer access to local residents.

At the 2.3-mile mark, you will enter Hermosa Beach; just beyond, at Gould Avenue, you will pass Hermosa Valley Park. The next major landmark is the Hermosa Valley High School and skate park, which is passed at about 3 miles. Palms have given way to eucalyptus by this point, with the shade a bit thinner but more fragrant.

The Hermosa Valley Greenbelt is covered with wood chips and is beautifully landscaped.

The route dips down into a swale between Ardmore Avenue and Valley Drive again as it nears the Herondo Street end point at 4 miles. What appears to be a tiny parking lot at the end of the path is reserved for folks living in the adjacent residential complex. If you choose to park at this end, you'll have to do so on the street.

Unless you have arranged for a shuttle to pick you up and take you back to Manhattan Beach, head back the way you came.

If you believe the setting makes the trail, you won't quibble with the brevity of the Electric Avenue Meridian Park rail-trail. The path is ensconced in a beautifully maintained linear park and offers easy access to a spectacular Southern California beach.

Activities:

Location: Seal Beach, Orange County

Length: 1 mile one-way

Surface: Concrete

Wheelchair access: The trail is accessible to wheelchair users.

Difficulty: Very easy

Food: There is no food available along the trail, but Seal Beach boasts a number of restaurants, many of which are near the route. There are several picnic benches along the route.

Rest rooms: There are rest rooms in the Mary Wilson Branch of the Orange County Library, which is about 0.1 mile south of the trail's northern end point at Marina Drive.

Seasons: The trail can be used year-round.

Access and parking: To reach the Electric Avenue Median Park from Interstate 405, take the Seal Beach Boulevard exit. Go west on Seal Beach Boulevard for 2.9 miles, crossing over the Pacific Coast Highway (California 1) to Electric Avenue. Parking is available along the street for the length of the route, and you can hop on it at any point. To reach the northern end point, follow Electric Avenue north for 1 mile to Marina Drive, and again, park along the street. Electric Avenue is one-way on either side of the median park.

Transportation: For transit information, call the Orange County Transportation Authority (OCTA) at (714) 636–RIDE (7433), or write OCTA, 550 South Main Street, P.O. Box 14184, Orange, CA 92868-1584. Transportation information is also available by calling (800) COMMUTE in the Los Angeles area.

Rentals: There are no rentals available along the trail.

Contact: Nancy Beard, City of Seal Beach, 211 Eighth Street, Seal Beach, CA 90740; (562) 431–2527.

The Electric Avenue Median Park is exceptionally brief, but the setting is sublime, and it offers the best coastal access to the beach of any rail-trail in the Los Angeles area. The warm sands of Seal Beach are but a block to the west, reached via a paved path that breaks off from the trail's southern end point or via any of the streets that cross the route. On the beach, in addition to wonderful sunbathing and friendly wave sports, you'll find an immensely popular playground and a public pier.

The trail itself is a clean strip of asphalt that winds through manicured grass beneath the filtering shade of sycamore and eucalyptus trees. Brickwork laid into the asphalt accents the trail's intersections with cross streets, as well as its two end points. In addition, a Red Line Car of the old Pacific Electric Railway, on whose bed the trail lies, now serves as the Red Car Museum, run by the Seal Beach Historical and Cultural Society. The red car is on the south side of the Mary Wilson library branch. Call the museum at (562) 683–1874 for its hours.

Walk the trail, visit the museum, go to the library and check out a good book to read on the beach, then finish the day with a meal in one of the local restaurants. Who could ask for anything more?

The trail is described here beginning at the Marina Drive end point. Start at the brick roundabout; the wide concrete trail breaks off to the south, and passes the library and Red Car Museum after 0.1 mile. Just beyond is the only major street intersection that you'll find along the trail—it's at Main Street and does require caution.

There are other streets to be crossed as you continue, but they are comparatively minor. The path meanders southward, edged in soft, verdant lawn and shaded by sheltering trees, with fine residences bordering the far sides of Electric Avenue.

The trail ends at about the 1-mile mark at a covered picnic table. You can return as you came, but if you want to walk, skate or ride to the beach, you can do so by continuing south, across Seal Beach Boulevard, to the paved path that skirts charming homes that front on the beach. The path arcs to the north, and proceeds to Eisenhower Park and the municipal pier. You can follow Main Street east for a couple of blocks to return to Electric Avenue, or, again, return as you came.

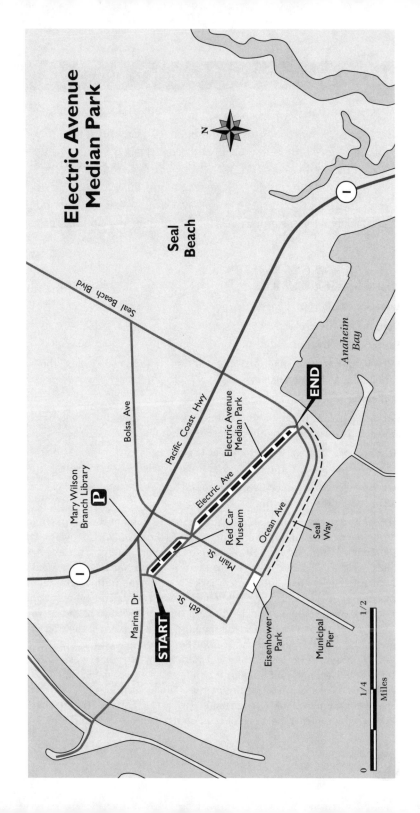

31 | Juanita Cooke Greenbelt Trail

A broad swath of open space set among the residential areas of northern Orange County, the Juanita Cooke Greenbelt does double duty as a recreational trail and a regional commuter route. From the small lake at Laguna Lake Park near the trail's northern end point to the shady lane that skims busy Harbor Boulevard near its southern terminus, the trail presents a corridor that is ideal for easy mountain biking, hiking, and trail running.

Activities:

Location: Fullerton, Orange County

Length: 3.5 miles one-way

Surface: Wood chips and dirt

Wheelchair access: Given the rough and sometimes soft surface, the trail is not suitable for wheelchairs.

Difficulty: Moderate

Food: There are no food outlets along the trail, but you will find grocery stores and restaurants in other areas of Fullerton.

Rest rooms: There are rest rooms at Laguna Lake Park, which is near the northern end point of the trail.

Seasons: The trail can be used year-round but can be muddy and very soft during and after rainstorms.

Access and parking: To reach the southern end point at the North Orange Municipal Court Building from California 91 (the Riverside Freeway), take the Harbor Boulevard exit. Head north on Harbor Boulevard for about 1.7 miles to North Berkeley Avenue. Turn left (west) on North Berkeley and go about 0.1 mile to the large, signed parking lot for the municipal building, which is on the corner as Berkeley bends northward. The Juanita Cooke Greenbelt Trail is the obvious path that heads northwest from the curve.

To reach Laguna Lake Park and the northern end point of the trail from the Riverside Freeway, take the Harbor Boulevard exit and head north on Harbor Boulevard for 3.8 miles to Hermosa Drive. Turn left (west) on West Hermosa Drive, and go for about 0.2 mile to Laguna Lake Park, which is on the south side of West Hermosa Drive. The trail crosses West Hermosa Drive near the park. There is streetside parking along this part of the park's boundary, and formal parking lots can be reached by circling the park on

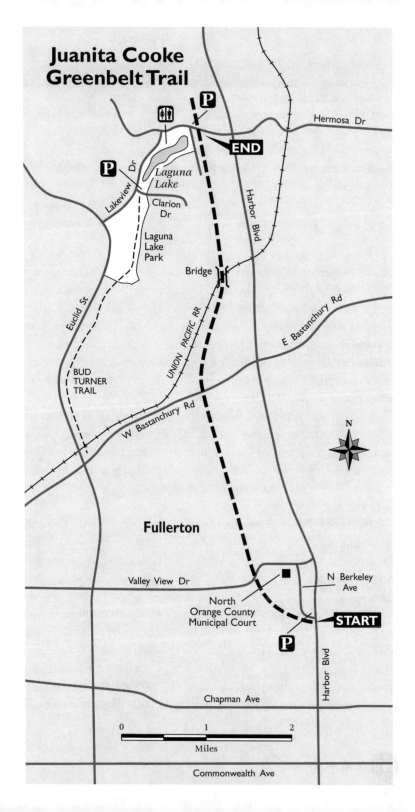

Juanita Cooke
Greenbelt Trail

P

Hermosa Dr

END

Lakeview Dr

Laguna Lake

Clarion Dr

Laguna Lake Park

Harbor Blvd

Euclid St

Bridge

UNION PACIFIC RR

E Bastanchury Rd

BUD TURNER TRAIL

W Bastanchury Rd

Fullerton

Valley View Dr

North Orange County Municipal Court

N Berkeley Ave

START

P

Harbor Blvd

Chapman Ave

N

0   1   2
Miles

Commonwealth Ave

Lakeview Drive to the southwestern side of the lake.

Transportation: For transit information, call the Orange County Transportation Authority (OCTA) at (714) 636–RIDE (7433), or write OCTA, 550 South Main Street, P.O. Box 14184, Orange, CA 92868-1584. Transportation information is also available by calling (800) COMMUTE in the Los Angeles area.

Rentals: There are no rentals along the trail.

Contact: Community Services Department, City of Fullerton, 303 West Commonwealth Avenue, Fullerton, CA 92832-1710; (714) 738–6575, www.ci.fullerton.ca.us.

• •

Thank the powers that be for the Juanita Cooke Greenbelt, and other greenbelts like it. In the midst of dense urban sprawl, where open spaces are swallowed by homes and businesses before people think twice, these strips of relatively undeveloped land are heartwarming and rejuvenating. The Juanita Cooke Greenbelt, shrouded in greenery and relatively insulated from the hectic highways and endless neighborhoods of Fullerton, offers hikers, mountain bikers, and equestrians a relatively long track upon which to forget they are in the midst of modern Los Angeles.

The trail was built on a former Red Car Line run by the Pacific Electric Railway, which was a primary mover of people throughout the Los Angeles basin in the early years of the twentieth century. Today, there are few signs along the trail that harken back to its origins, save where it crosses over the existing Union Pacific tracks, at about the midway point.

The trail begins in the welcome shade on the western side of the municipal court building. At about 0.2 mile, you will cross the first of many, mostly quiet, streets. Head up the little hill, passing a gate and trail sign and ignoring the single-track path that breaks off to the right (east).

At 0.5 mile, cross another residential street; the sign here indicates you are on the bridle path. The route is obvious, passing through bowers of eucalyptus beneath which the flowering bougainvillea thrives, and leading to an underpass, with trails from neighborhoods merging with the railroad grade on either side of the structure.

You will drop steeply to Bastanchury Road at Morelia Avenue at about 1 mile. Carefully cross Bastanchury, using the signal, and follow the dirt path that heads north alongside Morelia Avenue for about 0.3 mile to Laguna Road. The rail-trail proper resumes beyond the gate on the north side of Laguna Road.

Gone is the eucalyptus, leaving this stretch of trail open to the desert sun. At about 1.7 miles, the trail crosses a quaint trestle bridge. A single-track path arcs right (northeast), down off the trail, to parallel the Union Pacific line that runs below, quickly bending out of sight. The rail-trail continues straight (north), across the bridge.

Shade and sun trade off as the trail proceeds through neighborhoods. The next landmark is at 2.3 miles, where you will emerge at Laguna Lake Park. Ducks swim in its still green waters, and benches and picnic tables invite trail travelers to sit and rest a spell. This is a nice turnaround point, although the trail does continue north from the park for a short distance.

To complete the route, cross West Hermosa Drive, which borders the park's northeastern edge, and follow the obvious railroad grade as it dips beneath an overpass. The rail-trail has a decidedly urban conclusion, ending at 3.5 miles on a raised bed between stark apartment complexes at the lip of a cement canal.

Laguna Lake Park is the trailhead for the Bud Turner and Juanita Cooke Trails.

32 Fay Avenue Bike Path

Gazing out across the Pacific Ocean from the heights of the Fay Avenue Bike Path, you can't help but be struck by the gentle beauty of La Jolla. The easy trail, spectacular setting, and wonderful weather conspire to make this a wonderful, if brief, adventure.

Activities:

Location: La Jolla, San Diego County

Length: 1 mile one-way

Surface: Asphalt and dirt

Wheelchair access: All but about 0.2 mile of the trail, at its southern end, are paved and wheelchair accessible. The short section that's not—it's rough dirt—is between Via Del Norte and the Mira Monte end point.

Difficulty: Very easy

Food: Although there is no food available on the trail itself, you'll pass a number of restaurants and a grocery store in downtown La Jolla as you drive to the trailhead.

Rest rooms: There are no rest rooms along the route.

Seasons: The trail can be used year-round, but the dirt section of the rail-trail may be muddy during and immediately following winter rains.

Access and parking: To reach La Jolla from northbound Interstate 5, take the Ardath Road exit. Follow Ardath Road west for 1.2 miles to its intersection with Torrey Pines Road. Stay left (west) on Torrey Pines Road for 1 mile to Prospect Street. Turn right (west) on Prospect Street, which runs through the heart of downtown La Jolla, for 0.6 mile to Fay Avenue. Turn left (south) on Fay Avenue, and follow it to its end at Nautilus Street. There is ample parking in the La Jolla High School lot fronting Fay Avenue. The trailhead is on the south side of Nautilus Street opposite the stoplight at the end of Fay Avenue.

Transportation: The Metropolitan Transit System provides a variety of transportation services as well as links to other transportation authorities and services throughout the San Diego County. The MTS can be reached by dialing (800) 266–6883 (north county) or (619) 233–3004 (south county). You also can get information about San Diego transportation services at www.sandag.cog.ca.us/sdmts.

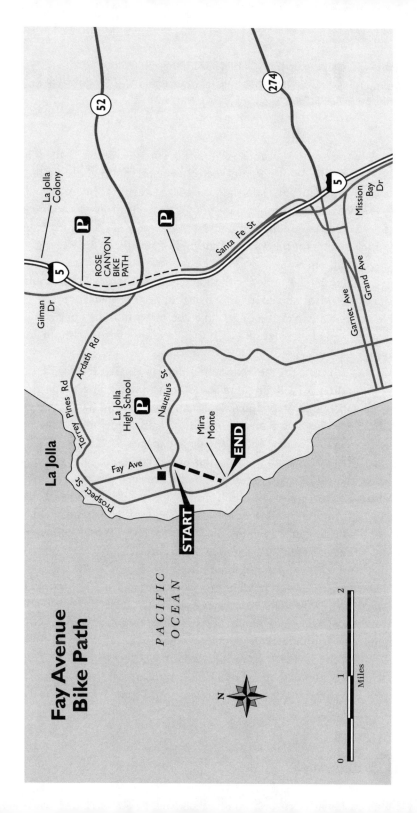

Fay Avenue
Bike Path

PACIFIC
OCEAN

La Jolla

START

END

Prospect St

Fay Ave

La Jolla High School

P

Nautilus St

Mira Monte

Torrey Pines Rd

Ardath Rd

Gilman Dr

5

La Jolla Colony

P

ROSE CANYON BIKE PATH

P

Santa Fe St

52

274

5

Mission Bay Dr

Garnet Ave

Grand Ave

N

0   1   2
        Miles

Rentals: There are no rental outlets near the trail.

Contact: Joel Rizzo, Bike Coordinator, City of San Diego, 1010 Second Avenue, Suite 800 MS609, San Diego, CA 92101; (619) 533–3110.

• •

Quintessential Southern California, spread before you in all its sunbathed glory. Robin's-egg blue skies, melting into a glassy ocean a few shades darker and greener. Towering palms overlooking the beachfront. Immaculate homes with clean lines and broad expanses of glass creeping inland from the edge of the water. From the high points on the Fay Avenue Bike Path, these are the sights that you will enjoy.

The panorama, coupled with the extreme ease of this short route, make it the ideal choice for the visitor or resident who is short on time but has a hankering to get out. The rail-trail is also perfect for families, a good number of which will be found on the path on any sunny weekend.

The path runs on the abandoned line of the San Diego, Pacific Beach, and La Jolla Railroad, a standard-gauge passenger line that was established in 1889 and abandoned in 1919. The trail was built in the late 1970s, and plans to extend the trail southward for another 1.2 miles are funded and in the design stages.

Heading south from the Nautilus Street end point, you will first climb a short hill to where the paved trail breaks out from under the trees at about 0.1 mile. The climb crests with spectacular views. Looking west from here, and from along the trail for the next half mile or so, you will no doubt so enjoy the vistas to the west that you won't notice much else about the trail, which traverses a shrubby hillside above a row of nicely maintained homes.

The trail begins to head gently downhill to a bridge, which is crossed at 0.4 mile. The views are gone by the time you reach and cross Via Del Norte at 0.7 mile. Signs indicate that the bike path continues on Beaumont Avenue, but it's clear that the former railroad grade, and the rail-trail, continue straight.

Now dirt, the path continues southward until it drops behind a small park to the cul-de-sac at Mira Monte at 1 mile. While this is the

A father and son enjoy the Fay Avenue Bike Path in tandem.

formal end point, again, it is clear that the grade continues southward, passing through a parking lot, across La Canada, and following the power lines to La Jolla Hermosa Avenue at 1.3 miles. Bike route signs indicate you can continue south along La Jolla Hermosa, but this is a good turnaround point—as is the Mira Monte cul-de-sac, and the end of the pavement at Via Del Norte, for that matter. Whichever you chose, return along the same route.

Promenade along this rail-trail, which follows the existing railroad tracks along Harbor Boulevard in downtown San Diego, and you'll have easy access to some of the best this delightful city has to offer: wonderful shopping, delightful restaurants, the historic Gaslamp district, maritime exhibits, bayside parks, and more.

Activities:

Location: San Diego, San Diego County

Length: 1.5 miles

Surface: Concrete and asphalt

Wheelchair access: The entire trail is wheelchair accessible.

Difficulty: Very easy, given the trail's short length.

Food: There is a plethora of restaurants in the downtown San Diego area, as well as a number of other cultural amenities, including theaters, museums, and shopping.

Rest rooms: There are no public rest rooms in evidence along the trail.

Seasons: The trail can be used year-round.

Access and parking: The trail can be reached via a number of streets in downtown San Diego. In addition to parking in commercial lots, ample on-street parking is available.

The downtown area is crisscrossed by one-way streets, so it is helpful to have a good map. There are a number of exits of Interstate 5 feeding into the downtown area. Take any of these and head south to Harbor Drive. Eighth Street is south of the heart of town, but you can pick up the trail anywhere along Harbor Drive.

Transportation: The Metropolitan Transit System provides a variety of transportation services, as well as links to other transportation authorities and services throughout the San Diego County. The MTS can be reached by dialing (800) 266–6883 (north county) or (619) 233–3004 (south county). You also can get information about San Diego transportation services at www.sandag.cog.ca.us/sdmts.

Rentals: There are no bike or skate rental outfits located on the trail in the downtown area.

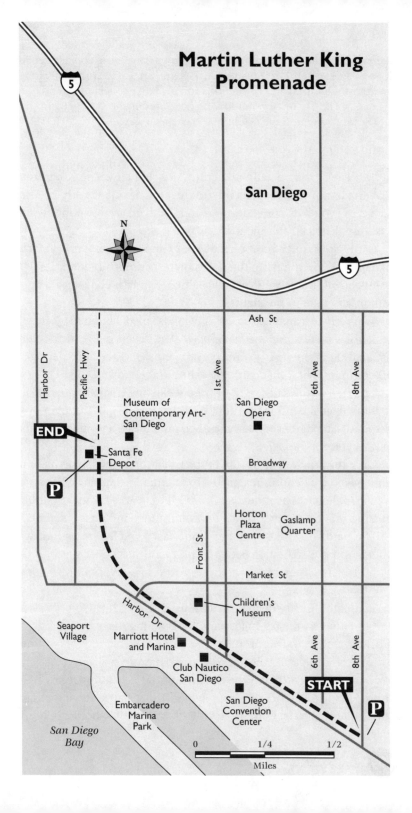

Contact: For the section of trail in downtown San Diego, contact the Port of San Diego, P.O. Box 120488, San Diego, CA 92112; (619) 686–6200, www.portofsandiego.org. For information on trail connections to other areas of San Diego, contact Joel Rizzo, Bike Coordinator, City of San Diego, 1010 Second Avenue Suite 800 MS609, San Diego, CA 92101; (619) 533–3110.

· ·

San Diego is a visually and culturally rich city. The King Promenade rail-trail reaches into to the core of this wealth, offering access to the city's convention center, Embarcadero, shopping and Gaslamp districts, and piers.

Calling the trail a promenade is very appropriate. While you can bike or skate on the path, the downtown section truly lends itself to a slow stroll, a leisurely pace at which you can chat with a companion and take in the sights.

The path downtown is beautifully landscaped, bordered by charming fences and old-fashioned lampposts. The towers of the surrounding city sparkle in the nearly omnipresent sunshine, the stimulating architecture offering shade and pleasure to the viewer.

The trail follows the right-of-way of existing tracks for the Coaster, San Diego's commuter train, and the San Diego Trolley. Given the popularity of these lines, you are bound to see a number of trains pass as you promenade.

Only the downtown section of the trail is described in detail here, but a paved trail continues north from Santa Fe Station. What it loses in visual charm as it heads toward Mission Bay it gains in utility, offering safe off-street passage for commuters and area residents.

The path's Eighth Street end point has a rough, almost industrial feel. You are right alongside the railroad tracks, just south of the center of the city, where warehouses and low-rise buildings dominate the landscape.

The path quickly becomes more urbane as it heads north along Harbor Drive. By the 0.5-mile mark, the buildings have become cleaner and architecturally complex, and patches of lawn, plots of flowers, and shady palm trees border the concrete walkway. At Fifth Street, you can detour to the north into the Gaslamp Quarter National Historic District, with its wonderful restaurants and shops. The Gaslamp district borders Horton Plaza as well, where you'll find

A trolley rolls down the tracks beside the Martin Luther King Promenade.

yet more to tempt your tummy and your pocketbook. To the south of Harbor Drive at Fifth Street, you can walk to Marina Park.

North of Fifth Street, the San Diego Convention Center dominates the left (southwest) side of the trail, with its accompaniment of hotels. At about the 1-mile mark, where the rail-trail bends north away from the convention center at a San Diego Trolley station, you will reach Kettner Boulevard, which offers access to an additional pair of cultural attractions: Seaport Village and Embarcadero Marina Park lie to the left (southwest).

The path crosses Kettner Boulevard and heads north on its west side to the Santa Fe Depot, which is on the left (west) side of the trail at 1.5 miles. San Diego's Museum of Contemporary Art is on the right (east). Continuing north to Ash Street, you can take a side trip to the west to visit the Maritime Museum and the Star of India, as well as other piers along Harbor Drive.

If you wish to continue past the end of the rail-trail, you can continue to Ash Street (the limit of the scenic center of San Diego), or travel north on the paved path to Mission Bay.

34 Silver Strand Bikeway

The Silver Strand occupies a unique niche, arcing into the Pacific Ocean at the southwestern tip of the United States. The bikeway that runs along it offers fascinating views of this end of the line, including Coronado Bridge, the skyline of San Diego, and, of course, the endless Pacific.

Activities:

Location: San Diego and Coronado, San Diego County

Length: 9 miles one-way

Surface: Concrete and asphalt

Wheelchair access: The entire trail is wheelchair accessible.

Difficulty: Hard. Walking, cycling, or skating the trail—especially out and back—is an all-day proposition. Arranging a shuttle or tackling shorter sections of the trail reduces its difficulty.

Food: There are grocery stores and restaurants in Coronado at the north end of the trail and in Imperial Beach at the south end, but there is nothing in between. Water is available at either end point and at Silver Strand State Beach.

Rest rooms: There are public rest rooms at the Coronado ferry complex, and at Tidelands Park. You can also use rest rooms, as well as other facilities, at the Silver Strand State Beach, located at the trail's halfway point. There are no public rest rooms at the Imperial Beach end point.

Seasons: The trail can be used year-round. Use caution and common sense if venturing onto the exposed path during a winter storm, as there is no shelter from potentially furious winds and vigorous downpours.

Access and parking: To reach the Coronado ferry complex from Interstate 5 in San Diego, take the California 75 exit, and go west, over the lovely bridge, to Coronado. Follow the highway, which becomes Fourth Street, to Orange Avenue, and turn right (east). Follow Orange Avenue to First Street, which is on the waterfront. The ferry complex is in the shopping center to the right (south) of the intersection of Orange Avenue and First Street. There is ample parking available along the street.

To reach the Imperial Beach end point from Interstate 5 in Chula Vista, take California 75/Palm Avenue east to 13th Street. Turn right (north) on 13th Street to the trailhead, which is at the end of the road. Parking is available at the trailhead.

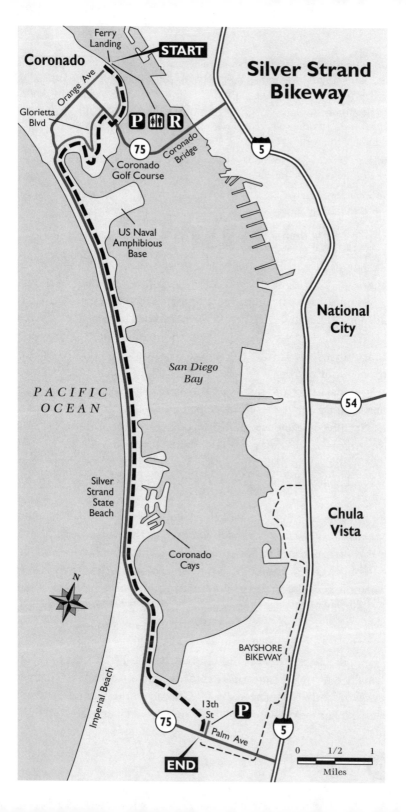

Transportation: The Metropolitan Transit System provides a variety of transportation services, as well as links to other transportation authorities and services throughout San Diego County. The MTS can be reached by dialing (800) 266–6883 (north county) or (619) 233–3004 (south county). You also can get information about San Diego transportation services via the Internet by visiting www.sandag.cog.ca.us/sdmts.

Rentals: Bicycles are available at Bikes and Beyond in the Coronado ferry complex. The phone number is (619) 435–7180.

Contact: Joel Rizzo, Bike Coordinator, City of San Diego, 1010 Second Avenue, Suite 800 MS609, San Diego, CA 92101; (619) 533–3110.

• •

A more lovely stretch of seaside trail would be difficult to find anywhere in Southern California. Miles and miles of the Silver Strand Bikeway lie on the narrow spit of land that connects Coronado with Imperial Beach, bordered on the west by the Pacific Ocean, and on the east by San Diego Bay, which separates you from the continent proper. When you travel on this path, you travel on the very edge of America.

The tidal areas and dunes on the San Diego Bay side of the spit, along with the fragile environments and species that they support, are partially protected within the confines of the California Least Tern Preserve. On the ocean side, the Silver Strand State Beach offers duneland perches from which you can watch the sun set into the Pacific, staining sky, sea, and sand vivid shades of orange and pink.

The culture and history of the area are rich and multifaceted. There is the military: Coronado is home to the North Island Naval Air Station and the U.S. Naval Amphibious Base, and the beach just south of the city is littered with the shells of military aircraft. There is the cultural: Coronado is alive with restaurants, theaters, shopping, and art galleries. There is the natural beauty: the stunning views of the San Diego skyline, the state beach, the least tern preserve, and San Diego Bay.

And, of course, there is the railroad: The rail-trail runs on a line originally built by the Coronado Railroad Company, which was merged into several other San Diego–based railroad companies before finally being incorporated into the Southern Pacific rail empire. The right-

THE BAY SHORE BIKEWAY

The Silver Strand Bikeway is but one link in an ever growing system of rail-trails being built in the San Diego area. As signs along the trail note, the Silver Strand is part of the Bay Shore Bikeway, a work in progress that will be a wonderful addition to California's rail-trail system when finished.

The Bay Shore Bikeway, which will run at least in part on abandoned railroad right-of-way, will continue from Imperial Beach north through Chula Vista and National City to the ferry landing in downtown San Diego. Completely funded and in the process of being designed when this guide went to press, the route is expected to be completed within two years. The entire trail will be about 22 miles long.

The City of San Diego, along with other entities in the San Diego area, is also working on a Coastal Rail-Trail, which will be about 44 miles long when completed. Although this project was only partially funded in early 2000, plans call for the trail to run from the Santa Fe Depot in downtown San Diego north to Del Mar, then up the coast through Solana Beach, Encinitas, Carlsbad, and Oceanside. The rail-trail would include the Rose Canyon Bicycle Path, described later in this guide.

of-way was abandoned by Southern Pacific in 1977 and is now the bed of the rail-trail.

The trail begins along the eastern shoreline of the island at the ferry terminal and shopping mall. It meanders south past the storefronts, leaving the bustle behind after less than a quarter mile.

At 0.5 mile, you will cruise through Tidelands Park, which offers picnic tables, a tot lot, rest rooms, and large expanses of lawn upon which you can lie back and enjoy the scenery. Continuing south, a switchback arcs under the Coronado Bridge, then the trail parallels a fence that screens it from the Coronado Golf Course.

At 1.2 miles, the trail turns left (west) and runs alongside Glorietta Boulevard. Cross Glorietta at Fifth Street and continue westward, circling around the golf course and tennis courts to Pomona Avenue. Use the crosswalk to get across the street; the trail continues 100 yards west of the intersection. A sign indicates the rail-trail is also part of the Bay Shore Bikeway.

The route skirts the Glorietta Marina and by the 2-mile mark is on the strand, with California 75 a near neighbor. Large hotels screen the views to the west, but they are almost as fun to look at as the ocean. Almost.

Pass the U.S. Naval Amphibious Base at about 2.5 miles. Both trail and highway are now bordered by dunes and water. On the left (east) is the bay, on the right (west) is the beach, which serves here as a graveyard for naval equipment and is posted off-limits. At 2.8 miles, you will pass a Silver Strand sign and overlook; pause to take in the views, then continue south on the trail.

You may feel constrained by the signs warning you to stay off the beach on the Pacific side and the fence that guards the bay side. The restrictions serve their purposes. While it is apparent the graveyard is private property, the fence's purpose is less obvious; it was erect-

The Silver Strand Bikeway offers views of the Pacific Ocean and the Coronado Bridge.

ed to protect the habitat of the California least tern. Another over-look is at the 3.5-mile mark, and a dirt path now parallels the paved route.

At 4 miles, you will pass the Fiddlers Cove Marina and the Silver Strand residential community. The path continues southward, wedged between the dunes and the now fence-free bay shore, to the Silver Strand State Beach at 5.2 miles. Here, you will find rest rooms, pic-nic sites, and camping opportunities, as well as unrestricted access to the beach and views of an endless horizon.

From the rail-trail, however, the ocean and the islands that sit off-shore flicker in and out of view between the dunes. Looking across the bay, the mountains rising east of San Diego sculpt a striking sky-line, especially when they glow with the fading light of a setting sun.

The trail continues south to pass the Coronado Cays at 6.2 miles. About a mile beyond the Cays, you will lose sight of the ocean and the islands as the rail-trail slowly bends eastward around the south end of the bay. Salt marsh sweeps in from the bay toward the trail.

At about 8 miles, the trail borders the parking area for the South Bay Marine Biology Study Area. A half mile beyond, the route pulls away from the highway as it arcs ever eastward, and some of the rails that used to carry trains appear alongside the trail. The path weaves around residences and businesses that border the bay as it enters the city of Imperial Beach. The trail leaves the railroad grade behind at an abandoned trestle that lunges east into the wetland. It ends in the cul-de-sac at the end of 13th Street. If you've arranged for a shuttle, this is the end of the line. Otherwise, return as you came.

(L) Duarte Bike Trail

Running along the base of the San Gabriel Mountains, the Duarte Bike Trail ties the east end of this small city to the west end, and offers access to a local park and elementary school.

Activities: 🚶 🚲 🏃 🛼 🎣

Location: City of Duarte, Los Angeles County

Length: 1.6 miles one-way

Surface: Asphalt and concrete

Wheelchair access: The trail is wheelchair accessible for its entire length.

Difficulty: Easy

Food: There are no outlets for food along the trail, but you will find a smorgasbord of choices within surrounding communities.

Rest rooms: There are rest rooms at Royal Oaks Park, but none along the rest of the trail.

Seasons: The trail can be used year-round.

Access and parking: To reach the eastern end point at Royal Oaks Park, take Interstate 210 to the interchange with Interstate 605. Go north on I–605 until it ends on Mount Olive Drive. Follow Mount Olive Drive north for 0.3 mile, crossing Huntington Drive, to Royal Oaks Drive. Go right (east) on Royal Oaks Drive for 0.4 mile to Royal Oaks Park. The small but adequate parking area is located just beyond (east of) Vineyard Avenue.

There is limited on-street parking at the trail's western end point at Buena Vista Street. To reach this end point, follow the directions above, but turn left (west) on Royal Oaks Drive, and follow it to Buena Vista Street.

Transportation: Duarte Mini Transit offers public transportation along the route. Call (626) 357–7931 for more information.

Rentals: There are no rentals available in the area of the trail.

Contact: Donna Georgino, Duarte Parks and Recreation Department, 1600 East Huntington Drive, Duarte, CA 91010; (626) 357–6118, ext. 201.

• • • • • • • • • • • • • • • • •

The Duarte Bike Trail exemplifies how a former railroad grade can be turned into a lovely suburban trail. The path spans nearly the entirety of the northern border of this small city, which is tucked against the arid San Gabriel Mountains on the northern edge of the Los Angeles basin. The rail-trail provides safe, off-street access to the playground, tennis and basketball courts, and greens of Royal Oaks Park, as well as to the Royal Oaks Elementary School.

The path, like so many within the Los Angeles area, runs along an abandoned stretch of the former Pacific Electric Railway's Red Car passenger line. The trail was installed in 1980; there are no plans to extend the route.

Beginning at Royal Oaks Park, the trail heads west along the shady greenbelt that borders Royal Oaks Drive. The lacy greenery of the trees shades the trail, and the folded walls of the San Gabriel range rises to the north. At 0.1 mile, pass the access road to the Royal Oaks Elementary School.

After crossing Mount Olive Drive at about the 0.3-mile mark, the trail is wedged between a canal and Royal Oaks Drive. About a half mile farther you will pass a sign for the city of Bradbury. The canal dives under Royal Oaks Drive, and landscaped knolls rise on

Two women and a child stroll the suburban Duarte Bike Trail.

either side of the path. Pass beneath a rustic bridge.

Beyond the bridge a dirt walkway runs parallel to the paved track, separated by a row of upright railroad ties. Climb a final, gentle rise, cross Royal Oaks Drive North, and meander to the trail's end at Buena Vista Street.

Return as you came.

Culver City Median Bikeway

The nicely landscaped median park that holds the Culver City rail-trail is mostly frequented by local residents, but also is long enough to give runners or walkers a good workout.

Activities:

Location: Culver City, Los Angeles County

Length: 2 miles one-way

Surface: Asphalt

Wheelchair access: The trail is entirely wheelchair accessible.

Difficulty: Easy

Food: There are small markets and restaurants on Culver Boulevard near the trail, as well as in other areas of Culver City.

Rest rooms: There are no rest rooms along the trail.

Seasons: The trail can be used year-round.

Access and parking: To reach the Culver City Median Bike Path from Interstate 405 in Culver City, exit at Sawtelle Boulevard or Sepulveda Boulevard. You can follow either Sawtelle Boulevard or Sepulveda Boulevard south to Culver Boulevard. The trail runs down the center of Culver Boulevard, so it can't be missed. The best parking is at the western end point of the trail at Panama Street and McConnell Avenue. This trailhead can be reached by driving right (southwest) along Culver Boulevard to McConnell Avenue, then turning left (southwest) onto Panama Street, which parallels the rail-trail. There is abundant on-street parking along Panama Street.

There is limited on-street parking at the eastern end point of the trail, which is at Elenda Street.

Transportation: Transit services in Los Angeles County may be obtained by calling (800) COMMUTE in the Los Angeles calling area. The Los Angeles Metropolitan Transportation Authority Web site is www.met.net.

Rentals: Wheel World Cycles is located less than a mile northwest of the trail at the intersection of Sepulveda Boulevard and Washington Boulevard. Contact Wheel World Cycles at 4051 Sepulveda Boulevard, Culver City, CA 90230; (310) 473–3417.

Contact: Michelle Mowery, Bicycle Coordinator for the City of Los Angeles, can be reached by calling (213) 580–1199. Her e-mail address is mowery con@aol.com.

• •

The Culver City Median Bike Path does a surprisingly good job of sprucing up an otherwise predictable urban environment. Wedged between the opposing lanes of traffic on Culver Boulevard, the rail-trail is a vibrant strip of greenery in the midst of the grays and tans of area businesses and residences. Although not blatantly recreational, the trail is frequented by locals walking to work, residents walking their dogs, and families with kids wobbly on bicycles or skates, or strapped safely into strollers.

The lovely landscaping contributes much to this trail's charm. The broad umbrellas of mature palm trees create pools of shade on patches of grass or hover over park benches. The flower beds are meticulously maintained, adding splashes of color to the background of green and brown.

The trail runs along the old bed of the Red Car Line that ran through this area. Like much of the rest of the Pacific Electric Railroad, it moved people from one area of the Los Angeles basin to the other for more than fifty years.

The trail runs through a predominantly residential neighborhood at its west end. The trees aren't as mature here as they are farther east, but the flowers are just as vibrant as they are elsewhere on the trail.

The winding asphalt path is shadowed by a dirt walkway, which serves nicely to separate walkers from cyclists and in-line skaters. Strategically placed benches and trash cans round out the list of amenities.

The route intersects a number of cross streets as it runs north and east: Take care at all these intersections, using signal lights to assist in safe passage. At about the 1.4-mile mark, the trail passes under Interstate 405. Here the trees are expansive, and the meandering path wanders through an area boasting more small businesses

The Culver City Median Bikeway divides opposing lanes of traffic.

than private residences. But by the time you reach the trail's eastern end at Elenda Street, you are back among the houses again.

Although the median path ends here, you can continue north along the sidewalk to Veteran's Memorial Park and beyond.

(N) Watts Towers Crescent Greenway

This is an extremely short rail-trail that parallels an existing rail line in the vicinity of the Watts Towers Art Center, home of the striking and unique sculptures known as the Watts Towers.

Activities: 🚶 🚲 🛼

Location: The Watts section of Los Angeles, Los Angeles County

Length: 0.2 mile one-way

Surface: Concrete

Wheelchair access: The trail is wheelchair accessible for its entire length.

Difficulty: Easy

Food: There are no restaurants or food markets along the route, but these can be found elsewhere in Watts and adjacent neighborhoods.

Rest rooms: There are no rest rooms along the trail.

Seasons: The trail can be used year-round.

Access and parking: To reach the Watts Towers Crescent Greenway from the intersection of Interstates 110 and 105 in Lost Angeles, go east on I–105 for 2.2 miles to Wilmington Avenue. Go left (north) on Wilmington Avenue for 1.0 mile to 108th Avenue. Turn left (west) on 108th Avenue for 0.2 mile to Willowbrook. Go right (north) on Willowbrook for 0.1 mile to the trailhead. There is no formal parking area, but there is on-street parking available.

Transportation: Transit information for Watts can be obtained by calling (800) COMMUTE in the Los Angeles calling area. The Los Angeles Metropolitan Transportation Authority Web site is www.met.net.

Rentals: There are no rentals available along the route.

Contact: Metropolitan Transportation Authority, P.O. Box 194, Los Angeles, CA 90053-0194; (213) 244–6456.

• •

The shortest rail-trail in this guidebook, what the Watts Towers Crescent Greenway lacks in recreational values it more than makes up for as a utilitarian path for locals. The paved route serves as the perfect training ground for neighborhood youngsters learning to skateboard or ride their bikes, and as a pleasant walkway from nearby residences to businesses located along 103rd Avenue. However, you should be aware that nearby homes are protected by 8-foot fences with spikes on top, which might make you justifiably concerned about your safety.

That said, the rail-trail lies within walking distance of the Watts Towers, two unique and beautiful structures—and an integral part of the Watts Towers Arts Center—that rise above what is otherwise a rather unremarkable neighborhood. They resemble a twin set of Eiffel Towers, fragile and colorful in the midst of an ordinary setting.

The palm-lined rail-trail is a winding pathway wedged between Willowbrook and the active Metro Blue Line tracks. You can see from one end to the other: The only major landmark is an overpass that arcs over the route at the intersection of 108th Avenue and Graham. It's a brief walk which can be covered in a matter of minutes.

⊙ Hoover Street Trail

Three transportation corridors run along Hoover Street between Bolsa Avenue and the Garden Grove Freeway: the four-lane street itself, the tracks of an active railroad, and a paved rail-trail.

Activities:

Location: Westminster, Orange County

Length: 1.3 miles of the 2-mile trail is on the railroad grade.

Surface: Asphalt

Wheelchair access: The trail is wheelchair accessible.

Difficulty: Easy

Food: There are no restaurants located along the route, but a neighborhood grocery store is on the corner of Trask Avenue and Hoover Street. Restaurants and supermarkets can be found elsewhere in Westminster.

Rest rooms: There are no rest rooms at either trailhead, nor are there any along the trail.

Seasons: The trail can be used year-round.

Access and parking: To reach the Bolsa Avenue trailhead from Interstate 405 in Westminster, take the Bolsa Avenue exit. Head east on Bolsa Avenue for 0.4 mile to Hoover Street. The trail is obvious, running between the street and the active Union Pacific Railroad line. The second end point, at Garden Grove Boulevard, is most easily reached by following Hoover Street north to the trail's end. There are no formal parking areas at either end of the trail, and only limited parking along the street.

Transportation: For transit information, call the Orange County Transportation Authority (OCTA) at (714) 636–RIDE (7433), or write OCTA, 550 South Main Street, P.O. Box 14184, Orange, CA 92868-1584.

Rentals: No rentals are available along the route.

Contact: Dennis Koenig, Engineering Technician, City of Westminster, 8200 Westminster Boulevard, Westminster, CA 92683-3395; (714) 898–3311.

· ·

The Hoover Street Trail, a paved rail-trail that lies between busy, four-lane Hoover Street on the east and the Union Pacific Railroad line on the west, is used primarily by local residents and commuters.

The trail begins at the intersection of Bolsa Avenue and Hoover Street and runs north to the Garden Grove Freeway. The first mile

The Hoover Street Trail is a perfect example of an urban rail-trail.

is very exposed, running alongside the railroad tracks and under a massive power line. The second mile is screened by a tall hedge that serves as a buffer between the rail line and the trail, which is at this point a wide sidewalk on the west side of Hoover Street. At about the 2-mile mark, the trail passes under the Garden Grove Freeway (California 22), then ends at Garden Grove Boulevard.

Ⓟ Pacific Electric Bicycle Trail

A neighborhood trail of the first order, the Pacific Electric Bicycle Trail links well-kept middle-class neighborhoods on either side of tree-lined Maple Street.

Activities:

Location: City of Santa Ana, Orange County
Length: 2.1 miles one-way
Surface: Asphalt
Wheelchair access: The trail is wheelchair accessible for its entire length.
Difficulty: Easy

Food: There are no restaurants or grocery stores along the trail, but such amenities are available elsewhere in Santa Ana. Verdant strips of grass and occasional benches offer trail users the chance to picnic.

Rest rooms: There are no rest rooms at either end point or along the trail.

Seasons: The trail can be used year-round.

Access and parking: To reach the northern end point from Interstate 5, take the Fourth Street exit in Santa Ana. Follow Fourth Street west to Grand Avenue and go left (south) on Grand Avenue to East First Street. Turn right (west) on East First Street, and follow it to Maple Street, which is on the left (south) side of the road. Go south on Maple to East Chestnut Avenue; the rail-trail starts at this intersection.

To reach the southern end point on East Adams Street, you can either follow Maple and then Rousselle Street south along the route to the southern end point, or go left one block to Orange Avenue, which also goes south all the way to East Adams Street.

There is parking along the streets at both end points.

Transportation: For transit information, call the Orange County Transportation Authority (OCTA) at (714) 636–RIDE (7433), or write OCTA, 550 South Main Street, P.O. Box 14184, Orange, CA 92868-1584. Transportation

The Pacific Electric Bicycle Trail runs through a pleasant Santa Ana neighborhood.

service information can also be obtained by calling (800) COMMUTE from the Los Angeles calling area.

Rentals: There are no rental shops along the route.

Contact: Ron Ono, Design Manager, Recreation and Community Services for the City of Santa Ana, P.O. Box 1988, Santa Ana, CA 92702-1988; phone: (714) 571–4200.

• •

This well-used route follows an abandoned right-of-way of the Pacific Electric Railway Company, which ran an extensive electric rail line throughout the Los Angeles area that served the transportation needs of local residents. Today the route still serves the locals: Mothers and children chat with friends they've met on the route, young men and women walk hand-in-hand under the sycamores, boys and girls ride bicycles on the smooth asphalt, and older folks use the route for evening strolls.

This well-maintained asphalt path, which meanders along a greenway through a clean, quaint residential community, is described here from north to south. It begins by paralleling South Maple Street, sketching a sinuous route among manicured lawn and shade trees. At about 0.6 mile, it crosses East McFadden Avenue and is wedged behind homes lining Maple Street on the west and Oak Street on the east for about 0.2 mile.

After crossing Edinger Avenue, the path traces Maple Street again for about 0.2 mile, then abandons Maple to parallel Rousselle Street. Rousselle Street ends in a cul-de-sac at Warner Avenue; to continue on the rail-trail, you must carefully cross Warner Avenue. On the south side of this street, the trail snakes alongside a school, then ends in a tiny grassy park at East Adams Street.

The City of Santa Ana plans to link this trail with the Alton Avenue Bike Trail, but for now you must travel a series of city streets to reach the Flower Street end point of the Alton trail. A good street map of the area will show you how to link the two trails; the link is also described as part of the next trail, the Alton Avenue Bike Trail.

Ⓠ Alton Avenue Bike Trail

Running alongside an active railroad line, this trail primarily serves the recreational needs of local residents and commuters.

Activities: 🚶 🏃 🚲 ⛸

Location: City of Santa Ana, Orange County

Length: 1.8 miles one-way

Surface: Asphalt

Wheelchair access: The entire length of the trail is wheelchair accessible.

Difficulty: Easy

Food: There are no restaurants, grocery stores, or picnic sites along the trail. There are, however, abundant gastronomic outlets in other areas of Santa Ana and neighboring cities.

Rest rooms: There are no rest rooms located at either trailhead or along the trail.

Seasons: The trail can be used year-round.

Access and parking: To access the trail from Interstate 405 in Santa Ana, take the South Bristol Street exit. Head north for 1.1 mile on South Bristol to Alton Avenue. You can turn right (east) on Alton Avenue and park along the street, or continue west along Alton Avenue to the Susan Street end point and start there.

Parking for this trail is limited. None is available at the Flower Street end point. There is limited parking along the street at the Susan Street end point and at points along the trail.

Transportation: For transit information, call the Orange County Transportation Authority (OCTA) at (714) 636–RIDE (7433), or write OCTA, 550 South Main Street, P.O. Box 14184, Orange, CA 92868-1584.

Rentals: There are no rentals available along the trail.

Contact: Paul Johnson, Senior Park Supervisor, City of Santa Ana, Recreation and Community Services, P.O. Box 1988-M-23, Santa Ana, CA 92702-1988; (714) 571–4211.

• •

The Alton Avenue Bike Trail is clearly not a recreational trail in the scenic sense of the term. It follows the route of an active railroad, is overhung by the towers of a power line, and passes through industrial and residential areas protected by stone and concrete walls. Still, it serves an important purpose, providing local residents with an opportunity to stretch their limbs, and an alternative to traveling by automobile through this section of Santa Ana.

The route follows the right-of-way of the existing Southern Pacific Railroad. The rail-trail is an easy-to-follow paved path wedged between Alton Avenue and the railroad tracks; it runs west to east for 1.8 miles from Susan Street to Bristol Street. The best parking opportunities, and thus the best trailhead, are at Susan Street.

Pick up the paved route on the north side of Alton Avenue and head east. The trail crosses several residential roads as it cuts a nearly perfectly straight path along the open street, which is bordered by alternating fences and the large, blank facades of warehouses.

Once you pass Bristol Street, the trail, along with the train tracks, ducks behind homes for a quarter mile or so, before the rail-trail ends at South Flower Street.

There are plans to link this trail with the nearby Pacific Electric Bicycle Trail. As of the spring of 2000, the City of Santa Ana was working to get this connection in place; contact the city to learn the status of the improvements.

Until the connecting trail is built, linking the Alton Avenue and Pacific Electric bike trails involves some interesting maneuvering along both busy and quiet area roadways. To connect the two paths from the South Flower Street trailhead, go left (north) on South Flower to Dyer Road. Go right (east) on Dyer to Main Street. Go left (north) on Main Street to East Central Avenue, then go right (east) on East Central to Cypress Street. Turn right (south) on Cypress Street, following it to East Adams; go left (east) on East Adams and follow it for a block to the southern end point of the Pacific Electric Bicycle Trail.

Ⓡ Tustin Branch Trail

The Tustin Branch Trail is a work in progress. Each link of this disjointed rail-trail has a unique feel and serves a different population; when the connections are completed, it will be one of the most diverse trails in the system.

Activities:

Location: Tustin and Villa Park, Orange County

Length: 2.5 miles total, broken into three disconnected sections. The Newport Avenue section is 1 mile long, the Esplanade Avenue section is 1 mile long, and the Wanda Road section is 0.5 mile long.

Surface: Asphalt and crushed stone

Wheelchair access: The Newport Avenue and Wanda Road sections of the trail are paved and easily accessible to those using wheelchairs. The Esplanade Avenue section is nicely surfaced with crushed stone and may be passable for hardy wheelchair users.

Difficulty: Easy

Food: There is a variety of food outlets located along the Newport Avenue section of the trail. Both the Esplanade Avenue and Wanda Road sections are in residential areas and offer no trailside eateries, but the surrounding towns of Tustin and Villa Park host restaurants and grocery stores.

Rest rooms: There are no public rest rooms located along any of the sections of the trail.

Seasons: The trail can be used year-round.

Access and parking: To reach the Newport Avenue section of the trail from Interstate 5 in Tustin, take the Newport Avenue exit and head northeast on Newport Avenue. The trail runs along the northwest side of the road between El Camino Real and Irvine Boulevard.

To reach the Esplanade Avenue section of the trail, continue north on Newport Avenue to 17th Street, which is about 2.3 miles from Interstate 5. Turn left (west) on 17th Street and go 0.6 mile to the Esplanade section of the rail-trail, which parallels Esplanade Avenue on its east side.

To reach Wanda Road from Interstate 5 in Tustin, take California 55 (the Costa Mesa Freeway) north through the city of Orange to the Katella Avenue exit. Go right (east) on East Katella Avenue to Wanda Road, and turn left (south). The trail begins at Lincoln Street and goes south to East Collins Avenue.

There are no formal parking areas for any sections of the trail. However, there are parking lots for shopping centers along the Newport Avenue section of the trail. Limited on-street parking is available along Esplanade Avenue. There is no parking along Wanda Road.

Transportation: For transit information, call the Orange County Transportation Authority (OCTA) at (714) 636–RIDE (7433), or write OCTA, 550 South Main Street, P.O. Box 14184, Orange, CA 92868-1584.

Rentals: There are no rentals available along this rail-trail.

Contact: Sherri Miller, Trails Planner, Harbors, Beaches, and Parks, Public Facilities and Resources Department, County of Orange, P.O. Box 4048, Santa Ana, CA 92702-4048; (714) 834–3137.

• •

Rail-trails come in all descriptions, as evidenced by the variety in this guidebook, but the sections of the Tustin Branch Trail display the many guises an urban rail-trail can take.

Like the Tustin Branch of the Pacific Electric Railway upon whose abandoned bed it lies, the Tustin Branch Trail exists primarily to provide the people living in this area of Orange County an alternative to driving a car from locale to locale. But where once you heard the clack-clack-clack of passing trains, you are now more likely to hear the clacking of in-line skates as they skim over sections of sidewalk, or the thump of a runner's shoe on crushed stone.

This urban and suburban utility extends to other existing and proposed trails in Orange County, including the Venta Spur Line Trail in Irvine, which runs along a portion of the railroad that once served the Irvine Ranch.

The section of trail that runs alongside Newport Avenue is basically a glorified sidewalk. A scattering of railroad ties along the route hints at its origin. The trail parallels the road for about 1 mile, offering pleasant pedestrian access to the multitude of businesses along the way.

The Esplanade Avenue section of the Tustin Branch Trail is bordered by a high fence overgrown with bougainvillea.

The Esplanade Avenue section of the trail is more suburban in nature—a quiet, unpaved path in a quiet residential area. The unpaved track is bordered on one side by a fence overgrown with bougainvillea and eucalyptus, and features benches and a water fountain. You will cross Dodge Avenue and a canal before the trail ends at the 1-mile mark at Fairhaven Avenue. You can see the abandoned grade that proceeds northward from here. If the County of Orange has its way, this grade will one day be a continuation of the trail.

The Wanda Road section is a bit farther afield, in the city of Villa Park. This half-mile-long piece of the rail-trail also leads through a residential neighborhood, but it borders a much busier four-lane road than does the Esplanade section. The paved path is buffered by rolling mounds of grass and runs from East Collins Avenue on the south to Lincoln Street on the north.

Ⓢ Bud Turner Trail

The Bud Turner Trail is hitched to the Juanita Cooke Greenbelt at pretty Laguna Lake Park, circling the northern edge of the lake and a riding ring for equestrians before narrowing into a streetside walkway.

Activities:

Location: City of Fullerton, Orange County

Length: 1.7 miles one-way

Surface: Dirt

Wheelchair access: There is limited access for wheelchairs around the north and east shores of Laguna Lake.

Difficulty: Easy

Food: There are no restaurants or grocery stores along the trail, but if you pack a lunch you can picnic by the lakeshore. Restaurants and grocery stores are abundant in Fullerton.

Rest rooms: There are rest rooms available near the dam at Laguna Lake Park.

Seasons: The trail can be used year-round, but it may be muddy during and immediately after rain.

Access and parking: To reach the Laguna Lake Park end point from California 91 (the Riverside Freeway) in Fullerton, take the Euclid Street exit, and head north on Euclid Street for about 4 miles to Lakeview Road. Turn right (east) on Lakeview Road and go 0.5 mile to Hermosa Drive. Turn right (east) on Hermosa Drive and go 0.1 mile to Lakeside Drive; the northwest entrance to Laguna Lake Park is at this intersection. There is parking along the street. There is no parking or easy trail access at the Euclid and Bastanchury intersection.

Transportation: For transit information, call the Orange County Transportation Authority (OCTA) at (714) 636–RIDE (7433), or write OCTA, 550 South Main Street, P.O. Box 14184, Orange, CA 92868-1584.

Rentals: There are no rental shops located along the route.

Contact: Community Services Department, City of Fullerton, 303 West Commonwealth Avenue, Fullerton, CA 92832-1710; (714) 738–6575, www.ci.fullerton.ca.us.

• •

The Bud Turner Trail begins with great scenic and recreational promise. Its first half mile or so, as it circles Laguna Lake, makes a nice extension to the Juanita Cooke Greenbelt Trail (see Trail 31). But after less than a mile, the trail leaves the former railroad grade—this, like the Juanita Cooke Greenbelt, was once part of the Pacific Electric Red Car line—and becomes little more than a narrow strip of dirt alongside a busy city street.

The Bud Turner Trail begins at the sign on the north shore of Laguna Lake. Head counterclockwise around the lake's northwestern shoreline, passing picnic areas, a small fishing pier, and some rest rooms before reaching the dam at the southwestern end of the lake. Stairs and dirt ramps lead down from the dam to Clarion Drive; cross both the street and the adjacent parking lot, then climb a narrow footpath onto the railroad grade.

At about 0.7 mile, the trail skirts an equestrian riding ring, then grows quite broad before splitting into two narrower tracks. Stay on the left (eastern) track, which ends on Laguna Street about 50 yards from busy Euclid Street.

From here on out, the trail becomes utilitarian in nature. Cross Laguna Street onto Yuma Way, and follow the paved residential street south until it ends at a gate. This is also the end of the former railroad grade. The dirt trail veers right (west) toward Euclid Street, circling a small urban farm. When the path reaches the side of the street, it veers left (south) and becomes a narrow dirt walkway with only a white fence serving as barrier between trail and thoroughfare. Follow the dirt footpath south to its end at Bastanchury Road at 1.7 miles.

Atchison, Topeka & Santa Fe Trail

The AT&SF Trail has surprising appeal for a route that runs adjacent to active railroad tracks. It primarily serves local residents, offering a nice stretch of open space upon which to ride a bike, walk, or run. Two small parks bordering the rail-trail allow neighbors to stretch out on the grass and let their children run free.

Activities:

Location: Irvine, Orange County

Length: 3 miles one-way

Surface: Asphalt

Wheelchair access: The trail is wheelchair accessible.

Difficulty: Easy

Food: There are no restaurants or grocery stores located along the route, but if you pack a lunch or snack, you can picnic in Flagstone Park or Hoepner Park. You can find restaurants and grocery stores at other locations in the city of Irvine.

Rest rooms: There are no rest rooms along the trail.

Seasons: The trail can be used year-round.

Access and parking: To reach the Sand Canyon Avenue trailhead from Interstate 5, take the Sand Canyon Avenue exit. Go west on Sand Canyon Avenue for 0.5 mile, across the Orange County Transportation Authority (OCTA) Metrolink Railroad tracks, to the rail-trail, which is on the right (west) and is signed Walnut Trail. There is no parking at the Sand Canyon Avenue end point, but you might find on-street parking along Oak Canyon Road, which is about 100 yards west of the trail.

To reach the Harvard Avenue end point from Interstate 5, take the Culver Drive exit. Take Culver Drive west for 0.5 mile to Walnut Avenue. Turn right (north) on Walnut and go 0.5 mile to Harvard Avenue. Go left (west) on Harvard for 0.5 mile, crossing the OCTA Metrolink tracks, to the trail, which is also signed Walnut Trail at this end point. There is limited on street parking here and on nearby neighborhood streets.

Transportation: For transit information, call the Orange County Transportation Authority (OCTA) at (714) 636–RIDE (7433), or write OCTA, 550 South Main Street, P.O. Box 14184, Orange, CA 92868-1584.

Rentals: There are no rentals available along the trail.

Contact: Sherri Miller, Trails Planner, Harbors, Beaches, and Parks, Public Facilities and Resources Department, County of Orange, P.O. Box 4048, Santa Ana, CA 92702-4048; (714) 834–3137. The City of Irvine maintains the bikeway.

• • • • • • • • • • • • • • • • • • •

The Atchison, Topeka & Santa Fe Trail, which parallels an active railroad corridor and runs beneath massive power lines, adds a whole new dimension to the concept of "utility corridor." The pairing of recreational and industrial facilities, becoming ever more common on the urban landscape, is a clean concept with a big future in a world where open spaces are becoming harder and harder to find and preserve.

The AT&SF rail line and the trail that meanders along it are surprisingly scenic. The snaking asphalt path passes two small parks framed by broad, well-manicured lawns, and even skirts a small orange grove. It is nicely landscaped in sections and is crossed by relatively few streets. Also known as the Walnut Trail, the trail primarily serves local resi-

The AT&SF Trail winds along a greenbelt in Orange County.

dents, who access the route via short spur trails that lead west into neighboring housing subdivisions. Children living in area homes use the path, with its broad dirt margins, to practice dirt biking skills, as well as skateboarding and in-line skating.

As the name implies, the trail runs parallel to the existing Atchison, Topeka & Santa Fe rail line. The tracks also are used by the Orange County Transportation Authority Metrolink, which offers passenger service between metropolitan Los Angeles and San Diego.

The trail is described here beginning from the Harvard Avenue end point, from which the rail-trail heads southeast along the railroad tracks. After about a quarter mile, it passes the lawns of Flagstone Park; a tenth of a mile beyond the park, it crosses a bridge that arcs over Culver Drive.

At 1.3 miles, the path reaches Yale Avenue and forks; stay on the railroad grade, which dives under the elevated roadway. At 2 miles the rail-trail cruises past Hoepner Park, which offers a tot lot, tennis courts, benches, manicured lawns, and local access. The two parks are little oases along the trail, which is otherwise sparsely landscaped.

At 2.2 miles the trail crosses Jeffrey Road. On the south side of the roadway, a little orange grove sits to the west of the trail, and on the right (east) side, a line of eucalyptus provides a barrier between the trail and the railroad tracks.

Pass through an industrial area to the trail's end, at 3 miles, on Sand Canyon Avenue. Orange County officials would like to extend the trail for 2 miles south along the tracks to the Irvine Transportation Center, where it will hook up with the Peters Canyon Bikeway. Contact the county for information on the status of this "wish list" extension.

Ⓤ Rose Canyon Bicycle Path

Tucked in scenic Rose Canyon, and wedged between Interstate 5 and an active railroad line, the Rose Canyon Bike Path is a brief but exhilarating rail-trail.

Activities:

Location: San Diego

Length: 1.3 miles one-way

Surface: Asphalt

Wheelchair access: The trail is wheelchair accessible. Those using wheelchairs should use the southern access point at the end of Santa Fe Street.

Difficulty: Moderate

Food: There are no food outlets along the trail.

Rest rooms: No rest rooms are available along the trail.

Seasons: The trail can be used year-round.

Access and parking: To reach the southern end point on Santa Fe Street from northbound Interstate 5 in San Diego, take the Balboa Avenue/Garnet Avenue exit. Head left (west) on Garnet Avenue to Mission Bay Drive, and turn right (north). Follow Mission Bay Drive to Damon Avenue and turn right (east) on Damon. Follow Damon Avenue for 0.3 mile to Santa Fe Street and turn left (north). Follow Santa Fe Street north to its end in a cul-de-sac.

To reach the Santa Fe end point from southbound Interstate 5, take the Balboa Avenue/Garnet Avenue exit. This puts you right on Mission Bay Drive. Turn left (east) onto Damon Avenue, then follow the directions above to reach the trailhead.

To reach the northern end point from either northbound or southbound I-5, take the La Jolla Colony exit. Go west on Gilman Drive for about 0.1 mile to a left-hand turn into the Park-and-Ride lot, which is on the left (south) side of Gilman Drive.

There is ample parking at both end points.

Transportation: The Metropolitan Transit System provides a variety of transportation services, as well as links to other transportation authorities and services throughout San Diego County. The MTS can be reached by dialing (800) 266–6883 (north county) or (619) 233–3004 (south county). You also can get information about San Diego transportation services via the Internet by visiting www.sandag.cog.ca.us/sdmts.

Rentals: There are no rentals available near the trail.

Contact: Joel Rizzo, Bike Coordinator, City of San Diego, 1010 Second Avenue, Suite 800 MS609, San Diego, CA 92101; (619) 533–3110.

. . . .

Snuggled into a shallow canyon thick with shade trees and rustling grasses, the Rose Canyon Bicycle Path borders both an existing railroad and busy Interstate 5. Most modes of wheeled transportation are captured in this narrow swath: You can ride the rails, ride the

The Rose Canyon Bicycle Path parallels an active train track.

trail, or sit tight behind the wheel of your automobile. In a pinch, I suppose, you could also go for a swim in the shallow stream.

The popular Coaster, which offers folks living in outlying areas of San Diego access to the downtown area, frequently runs on the tracks that are adjacent to the trail, so there is a good chance you'll see a train as you use the path. You'll also pass the Elvira switching station, which is directly under the towering interchange of I–5 and California Highway 52.

Beginning at the southern end point on Santa Fe Street, the trail climbs gently north along the western side of the canyon, with the railroad tracks on the east side. At 0.2 mile, the rail-trail dives under the freeway interchange and passes the Elvira station, which, along with the tracks, is protected by high fences. Sycamores line the stream that spills out of San Clemente Canyon to the east.

Continuing up Rose Canyon, the trail swings over a culvert at about the 0.6-mile mark. Here, dense brush guards the freeway side of the trail, but the tracks on the east side of the rail-trail are open to view, as are the surrounding scrub-covered canyon walls.

At 1.1 mile, you will start to climb steeply off the grade and up to the trail's intersection with the interstate and Gilman and La Jolla Colony roads. Return as you came.

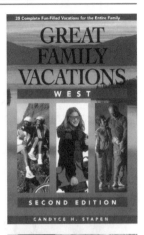

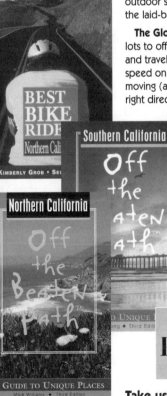

FREE T!*

*with a $50 contribution or more

100% cotton T-shirt with Rails-to-Trails Conservancy logo printed on the front; and a circle of trail users printed in royal blue on back.

JOIN RAILS-TO-TRAILS CONSERVANCY NOW, get a FREE T-SHIRT and connect yourself with the largest national trail-building organization. As a member of Rails-to-Trails Conservancy, you will receive the following benefits:

- *Rails to Trails*, a colorful magazine dedicated to celebrating trails and greenways, published four times a year
- A free copy of *Sampler of America's Rail-Trails*
- Discounts on publications, merchandise and conferences
- A free t-shirt with your contribution of $50 or more
- Additional membership benefits for Trailblazer Society members, including invitation to the annual rail-trail excursions

Most importantly, you will have the satisfaction that comes from helping to build a nationwide network of beautiful trails for all of us to enjoy for years and generations to come.

PLEASE JOIN TODAY by calling toll-free: 1-800-888-7747, ext. 11(credit card orders only), or mail your membership contribution with the form on the following page, or see our web site, **www.railtrails.org**.

RAILS-TO-TRAILS CONSERVANCY • *Connecting People and Communities*

Yes! I want to join Rails-to-Trails Conservancy!

Send me my member packet, including my *Sampler of America's Rail-Trails,* one year (four issues) of *Rails to Trails,* the colorful magazine that celebrates trails and greenways and my FREE T-SHIRT with my contribution of $50 or more. I will also receive discounts on publications, merchandise and conferences. Here is my membership gift of:

❑ $18 – Individual   ❑ $100 – Benefactor
❑ $25 – Supporting   ❑ $500 – Advocate
❑ $50 – Patron *(Free t-shirt* **T-shirt size XL only**   ❑ $1,000 – Trailblazer Society
at this giving level or higher!)   ❑ Other $_____

❑ Monthly Giving, *please see box below*

PAYMENT METHOD: ❑ VISA   ❑ MasterCard   ❑ American Express
Card # _____ Exp. Date _____
Signature _____
Member Name _____
Street _____
City _____ State _____ Zip _____
Telephone _____ email_____

Rails-to-Trails Conservancy is a non-profit charitable 501(c)(3) organization. Contributions are tax-deductible.

I want to support Rails-to-Trails Conservancy in the smartest, easiest and best way possible by donating monthly. Enclosed is my first monthly gift of:
❑ $5   ❑ $10   ❑ $15   ❑ Other $_____ *($5 minimum monthly contribution, please)*

Charge my future monthly gifts to my :
❑ Checking Account — Please transfer the amount indicated from my bank account each month
❑ Credit Card — Please charge the amount indicated to my credit card each month: ❑ VISA   ❑ MasterCard   ❑ American Express

Card Number: _____ Exp. Date: _____
Signature: _____ Date: _____

PAPERLESS PLEDGE AUTHORIZATION: I authorize Rails-to-Trails Conservancy to transfer my monthly contribution from my bank account or to charge my credit card (whichever I have indicated). I understand I may cancel or change my monthly pledge at any time by notifying Rails-to-Trails Conservancy. A record of each payment will appear on my monthly bank or credit card statement and will serve as my receipt.

Signature: _____ Date Signed: _____

EFT

Rails-to-Trails Conservancy
1100 17th St. NW • Washington, DC 20036
1-800-888-7747, ext. 11 (credit card orders only) • www.railtrails.org

To contact our membership department, please call (202) 974-5105 or email rtchelen@transact.org

RAILS to TRAILS CONSERVANCY